Poppa Won

By

Michael Anthony

This book is a work of non-fiction. Names and places have been changed to protect the privacy of all individuals. The events and situations are true.

Michael Anthony Publishing

In partnership with:
Parchment Global Publishing
1500 Market Street, 12th Floor, East Tower
Philadelphia, Pennsylvania, 19102
www.parchmentglobalpublishing.com

ISBN: 978-1-952302-35-0 (e-book)
ISBN: 978-1-952302-42-8 (Paperback)

Library of Congress Control Number: 2020921992

This book is printed on acid free paper.

1stBooks - rev. 01/28/03

This book is dedicated to my daughter,
the one for whom this war was waged.
Your Poppa loves you baby girl

Table of Contents

Foreword

This book was written for several reasons. It is not intended to offend anyone nor is it a parenting manual. Awareness of the tribulations some non-custodial parents suffer and the severe trials for everyone involved in a custody battle; and it exposes some of the tactics that an embittered parent will use to remain in control, even if it means hurting the kids. When a person judges another, this action usually originates from a matter of opinion. Discernment is made from the obvious enabling the person to know what is right and what is wrong. It is my hope that the readers may see something in this writing that will cause some to take a look at themselves and make changes that are necessary to avoid hurting their innocent youngsters.

It's very difficult to live our lives the way we're supposed to in today's world. Things are very different from when I grew up as a kid. Society has grown to welcome absurd acts and unusual behaviors as being normal. With ease, plenty of people get drawn into trends that can change what they think, how they appear and their lifestyle. There are many ways a person can be lured into being part of this crowd. Unknowingly, he or she chooses to become the follower instead of a leader. The most vulnerable victims are our children who will often react to what they see and hear. When left unguided, our youngsters may feed on the trash given by their peers, seen on the screen or heard over the airwaves. Just take a close look at some of the present-day teenagers and young adults. When their parents are gone, on loose footing will these generations be left to survive in a world that's becoming more predatory everyday? Wouldn't now be a good time to warn our kids about the trickery that is used to seduce and destroy our youth? Here is the decision every Dad and Mom needs to make.

Do you ever wonder why kids, teenagers and young adults act and behave the way they do? Television, radios, newspapers and magazines are great sources of information. They let us see and hear the right and wrong, the good and the bad. The news they deliver can sometimes be pleasant or disturbing. Who ever thought that so much of their propaganda would become the number one enemy for many parents of today? In our ears we hear and with our eyes we see misleading information that is processed by our minds. From here it trickles into our heart and finds a vacancy is waiting. Are we so numb that we didn't feel the media infiltrate us with these seeds of dishonesty, violence, lewdness, addiction and corruption? When this garbage is allowed to remain inside us, it can become the motive that persuades our thoughts and changes our emotions. Could it be that we have been conditioned to believe that this is acceptable?

When anyone or anything systematically finds a way to continually destroy the unity in the families of a country, they'll successfully force the moral foundation of that nation to crumble. The promotion of secularism helps to speed up this process. It is here that faithless people can develop instructional weapons to further the damage psychologically. All this happens while we look the other way and say everything's okay. Meanwhile, our children are deceived.

Down here in the south when I grew up education wasn't taken too seriously. Members in my family were encouraged to do well in school but rewards for our progress were never seen. We all heard about college but had no incentive to attend because we weren't taught about how useful it would be in our adult years. In addition to this, tuition expenses were something my parents couldn't afford. Nowadays, even people with degrees have trouble finding a job that pays enough to support their families. I'm a product of the faulty public school system so I wrote this book in southern style, making it easy to understand.

Introduction

Here is the story of a man's desperate struggle to remain in the life of his child and keep the right to be her father. It started out as a division from his spouse and evolved into a full-scale war filled with false allegations. Instantly he became the victim. Many attempts were made to sway the child's love and affection away from him. On several occasions he found himself repairing and rebuilding his relationship with the child. If not handled correctly, he knew this high conflict separation of Dad and Mom would confuse and hurt his little girl.

He was accused of being a threat to his child, a stalker, a drug and alcohol abuser, and an endangerment to the mother. These declarations automatically made him guilty and he was now the centerpiece of this situation. Simple observations and investigations, a large paper trail, extensive research and refusing to give up on his daughter became the key components in developing a plan that would prove his innocence. As evidence accumulated he became aware of what needed to be done in order to build a strong defense and achieve victory.

When a couple unites to become one and a baby is born to them, great changes occur for the benefit of their infant. Whether they remain together or not, this little one will have that father and mother for the rest of their life. It's very important for every child to know that they have two parents. The ability to bond with both should never be interfered with or the end results will be damaging. Everyone has a Dad and a Mom. It's not fair or good to take from a child what naturally belongs to them. For the sake of the children, these grown ups should act civil towards each other and remain friendly regardless of what they prefer to do. Animosity must cease to exist between the parents at all times while their youngsters are present. Like a tape recorder, they will remember what is said about the other parent.

If a man and a woman separate, the kids should never be denied the love of their folks. This action of neglect does not refer to a specific gender. It points to the one who consciously or unconsciously creates harm by obstructing the connection between the child and the other parent. Sometimes the children are used as high-powered weapons to devastate the one who departs from the arrangement. After the split, the non-custodial half wants involvement with the child but their efforts are deterred or hindered. Without justification, to disrupt the union of a child and the other parent is an injustice to both.

The absence of a healthy relationship between the child and both parents can reap havoc. This missing link can lead to spiritual, emotional, or psychological damage that will linger on forever. Protecting the children from this kind of mental abuse must become top priority.

It helps to know what kind of life the character in this story lived. From his childhood to the present, the mistakes he made and lessons learned, his family and what he was taught to believe became the structure of his being. Later in life he would discover methods that assisted in salvaging what he considered to be his personal disaster. A spiritual awakening helped him stop this destructiveness. This part of his existence resembled an earthquake in which few victims survive. Many in this country still suffer from this self-inflicted abuse.

Hopefully the experience of this man can help prevent the readers from having to go through the pain, misery, and fear of being erased from the lives of their children. It's a real heartache to go from a full time parent to a visiting one, with most of your activities under scrutiny. Within these pages you will read from his documentation what this man did, how he fought and won so he could keep his privilege to be Poppa.

Chapter One

BORN TO X-RAY

Born here at a hospital near New Orleans in 1962, I am second the youngest in a family of eight. With five sisters and two brothers, we had a fairly large group compared to the families of today. My sister before me died when I was almost a year old. Her name was Amanda and I was too young to know her. We were raised in the Catholic religion and lived a traditional southern life in the city that never sleeps. With family outings and school events, my childhood was about the same as all my relatives. It was my sisters that helped momma in getting us ready for school and looking after us. Having a large family with lots of cousins, we had plenty of friends. Family gatherings with all the relatives became an annual event at different holidays with lots of drinking and plenty of food to eat. Our celebrated holidays being New Years, Mardi Gras, Easter, Independence Day, Thanksgiving and Christmas, most everything was associated with alcohol in one way or another. In those days, that's how it was. Pictures of my uncles, aunts and cousins would confirm the good time we had.

My dad was an only child and I had five aunts and two uncles from my mom's side of the family. Each family had similarities in the way we were raised. High regard and good morals were a family tradition. First of all, we were taught to respect our elders. We did what we were told and did not talk back. If you had nothing nice to say about someone, then you didn't say anything at all. Learning the consequences of not telling the truth became a lesson well learned. We knew how important it was to get a good education and were all encouraged to finish school. If we had homework, it was done when you got home or you didn't play outside. When it was time to eat, you ate what was on your plate or you went hungry. Allowances were given if you did the chores that were assigned to you. To remember that blood is thicker than water helps keep the family together. This taught us to look after each other and care for one another. This is how I was brought up.

We loved and honored our father and mother. If you misbehaved, you got a spanking. In those days it wasn't uncommon to be disciplined and different families had their own methods. I now believe it helped me to do what was in my best interest and this was dad's way of showing his love for us. If you had something taken away from you, or you had to sit in the corner, or you had to write something on the chalk board a hundred times, that didn't bother you too much. You may not have liked it but you did it anyway. But let them say "I'm gonna tell your dad", and you'd experience the fear of his wrath depending on the seriousness of the incident. As we became of age, all of us had different opinions or thoughts about the way our parents corrected and disciplined us. Our feelings about this varied yet without it, I don't believe we'd be the way we are today.

As I grew older I became smarter and the knowledge of right from wrong wasn't hard to figure out. If something was wrong, there were consequences. If it was right, there were privileges. Simple things like going to a show or the circus, playing in a football or baseball game or going to a dance were just some of the privileges for behaving and doing what was right. Playing with matches, getting caught on the roof of a house that was being built, skipping Sunday school, lying or fibbing deserved consequences, which usually involved a spanking. Had we not been disciplined or corrected, a house fire, a broken leg and no education may have resulted. If dad didn't love us, nothing would have happened and we would have grown up like wild weeds in a burnt up house. I now appreciate the way I was raised and hold no grudges against my parents for the corrections, although there were many. Without emendation, how will you learn? I wasn't a real bad kid or a saint either.

I now realize the importance of reform and discipline where as before, I resented it. Unlike most kids today I'm thankful for it. There is a right way and a wrong way to chastise children when they are young. The wrong way can lead to serious problems in the future.

My dad was a welder and my mother, a homemaker. That's how he was able to support a large family like ours. Welders make good money and there's always been a need for this craft. While I was young, dad was always there at home when he wasn't working. He kept us all in line and fixed most problems as they arose. We all remained close to mom because although he was at home, at times dad seemed distant from us. In my older years I was told how they both had bouts with alcohol. I didn't recognize this when I was young and didn't know what a drinking problem was. We all sat at the same table, at the same time everyday to eat dinner. My mother was a real good cook. My younger brother Jack and me wanted to hang out with our friends all the time. If we were good and did what we were told, ate all our dinner and do some of the chores, we got to play outside. We went to a Catholic church on Sunday, school during the week and played in our neighborhood every chance we had. Until we moved out of our home, that's what my world was about as a child.

There were times when momma and her sisters would talk about their folks, our grandparents. My grandpa whom they called Poppa sometimes became a topic of their discussion. By the way they talked, he seemed to be stern with the way he brought them up. All my aunts and uncles from moms side of the family were straightforward with high moral values and they tried to rear us the same way. Without being told, I believe they were all thankful for the way their Poppa, my grandpa raised them. They loved grandpa and grandma equally and never mentioned any arguments they might have had. Grandpa passed away before I was born. As I grew up, there were many trips we made to grandma's house.

About the time I was eight, we began to experience apartment life. Dad sold our house and we started living in nearby complexes. Members of my family were soon departing because they graduated from high school and wanted their own space. Soon they were not living at home any longer. My older brother Mick was the first to go. He used to call me the ugly duckling of our family. His ridicule was not missed. For unknown reasons dad and mom would quarrel. Those of us left at home would witness the arguments they had.

It soon became evident of the drug and alcohol abuse in my parents. Dad was becoming disinterested in us. Mom was doing all she could to keep up the routine life we had been living. As always she would do the laundry and cook. Arguments between them became abusive. They ended up separating and dad went off to live by himself. My mother got an apartment above my sister and that's where we lived. Our home was now broken.

With dad being gone, my brother Jack and I became connected with an unruly group of kids. They also lived in a single parent home with a dad or mom that was never there. One day at home while mom was away, we smelled an odor like burning grass in the house. Our two sisters were home in their room with the door locked. Jack and I heard of marijuana (pot) from the kids we were hanging around with but never had access to it. There was a wide gap at the bottom of our sister's bedroom door and we peeked through it only to see them smoking the funny cigarette. They were caught and that's when we said "you either give us some or we're telling mom"! Their door opened up and they showed us what they were doing. To keep mom from finding out, we got what we asked for. Our friends in the neighborhood were also using drugs so our supply circle began to grow. This was my first experience with marijuana. I did not realize the consequences of making this mistake and never knew anything about the word addiction. In the years to come this turned out to be a huge downfall for me, affecting my life in every way.

As time went on, dad and mom never reconciled. We moved to another place without my two sisters. They wanted to do their own thing, which involved a lot of partying. They didn't like mom telling them what to do. With our sisters gone and mom abusing her medicine, we were not properly looked after and began to do most anything we wanted. She picked an apartment close to her sister, and we moved to Perrytown. Our cousins lived about five blocks away from us and they all had paper routes. One of my cousins was a little mischievous and smoked pot. Jack and I had the same kind of habit so we fit right in. Delivering newspapers became our daily activity. It helped pay for things we wanted to do. In addition to this, we played ball at the local gym. Our distinct talents had us assigned to different ball teams and we had other games to play. We all went to the same school, participated at the same recreation facility and learned the paper routes. Needless to say, we spent a lot of time together. Because I didn't have a good example to follow and didn't know any better, my drug usage began to increase. School became the place I had to go. My poor grades reflected the attitude I had towards it. Dropping out at this time was out of the question. This downward spiral of my life wasn't recognized by anyone.

In my teen years we moved to an apartment complex in Algears. This was the suburb where we all grew up in our younger years. My dad and mom were back together. There were many youngsters for Jack and me to hang out with. We made a bunch of friends that all had the same interests. The slogan, "a friend with weed is a friend indeed" became our motto. Truancy was common amongst the group of kids we associated with. We competed against each other to see who could cut the most classes without getting caught. There were no more ballgames and we rarely saw any of our relatives. One of our cousins gave us a paper route for the complex we lived in. The job was taken away from us because we were keeping the cash and buying pot with it. It didn't feel like we had a drug problem at the time. Education was no longer important and going to school became a bother.

Jack stole a car and ran away to central Louisiana. This is where my sister Mary lived. Her husband was selling pot at the time so my brother felt right at home. Jack never returned to us and went to school up there. I'd go visit them whenever I could. As the years went on I didn't see my younger. We were both in high school now and kept in touch by phone. The education system was flawed in the south. I failed every year since the sixth grade. Although my scores were unsatisfactory, I would still advance to the next level.

We moved to a town called Belle Cherre where my bad grades continued and I flunked tenth grade twice. No one ever suspected me of having a drug problem. Mom knew about it because of my glassy red eyes all the time. She tried to warn me but I wouldn't listen. My dad was awarded a settlement from an injury he sustained on a job. He bought him a new truck and when Christmas came, he bought me a new motorcycle. I used this cycle to go back and forth to school or for recreation. His favoritism didn't settle to well with members of my family. Months later, Jack came down for a visit. He had a motorcycle like mine up where he lived that belonged to Mary's husband. One evening we went to a friend we knew in Perrytown for a party he was having. Mixing drugs with rum put both of us in a blackout and I woke up in the hospital. I was told how we slammed into a vehicle that crossed our path. The impact almost caused me to lose one of my arms. "How's Jack", I asked. "He's okay, Mary took him back home", dad replied. My bike was damaged beyond repair and it was stored at my cousin's house. At the age of sixteen this was my first DUI and I was involved in a nearly fatal accident that almost killed both my younger brother and me.

As Easter approached, dad let me go visit Jack and Mary. An abscess forced me to travel home and visit my dentist on Easter Sunday. He gave me a root canal and sent me home. When I got to my parent's house, they were not there. I climbed in through the bathroom window and saw that our house was empty. The furniture in my room was all that was left. My sister Tabby lived next door. I went over to her place and called our aunt. She didn't know where my folks were. All of a sudden my dad calls and we talk. He wanted to know how I got in the house. A while later the police arrive wanting to arrest me for breaking in and entering. Tabby knew the officer and explained the situation. There was no arrest. In a state of shock, I packed all my belongings and moved to central Louisiana where Jack and Mary were living. One of the good things about this new location was the country like atmosphere. Returning to school, I started in the tenth grade again for the third time. I didn't want to attend and was nearing the legal age to be working. It was hard to get used to all the moving around. I was almost seventeen years old and in a new place again.

Eventually I got tired of school and dropped out. Needing money, I began looking for different job opportunities in various fields. I had no experience but was willing to learn. My academic years were finished. I wanted to work doing something and get paid for it.

At an early age I began working. I tried carpentry and earned enough money to get my motorcycle fixed. For a while it was used as my transportation until Jack and a friend of his came down from where he lived with my sister and stole it out my shed. I didn't know who would've done this to me. I figured it had to be someone I knew. When Mary's husband found out what my brother did, they drove down and returned it. I wanted to fight with Jack for doing this to me. From now on I would no longer trust my brother the thief.

My friends that had good jobs told me about the work offshore. I ventured out into the Gulf of Mexico and worked as a sandblaster's helper. This work was too strenuous because I was never a big person and the heavy lifting was something I couldn't do. Following my dad, I chose to do welding and started out as a helper. Soon I learned how to weld but wasn't good enough to pass x-ray so this job didn't suit me. I became interested in x-ray and applied to work doing that. This occupation was appealing for many reasons and paid good money. Performing these inspections became a challenge for me and I liked it.

Using a radioactive source and a piece of film I could make a x-ray of pipe welds to see if it was acceptable to the code used for that project. Because of radiation levels, the area had to be roped off and signs placed to prevent unauthorized people from coming in. This was perfect because most all the people involved in this line of work had some kind of habit or was addicted to something. We'd set up a barricade, get high and then go to work. Drug policies at that time weren't too strict. Some of the companies didn't even require a drug test. As long as you did good work and turned in acceptable film with the report, that was all they cared about. There was never an onsite drug-testing lab to catch anyone using drugs.

It was five years into this line of work before they required me to take the safety course. I rode my bicycle back and forth to a school nine miles away to get the 40-hour training. My skills and talent allowed me to work for the company of my choice. I became a radiography technician taking x-rays as a test method in the field of Non-Destructive Testing. (NDT) This line of work has you on 24-hour call and can summon you to work at anytime without notice. Since I started doing this occupation it has always been unexpected like that. NDT also stands for No Dinner Tonight. You can be having a barbecue with friends and get a call to be at the shop in an hour. This is not a 9 to 5 kind of job. Because some assignments can last all night and the strange hours, most people don't stay with this type of work. Welders will come in during the day and make the welds. When the day is over and they go home to their families, we come in and x-ray while no one's there. Our production is greater when the workers are gone. By having the facility to ourselves, we don't have to worry about people getting into our area. We can perform at an effective pace that enables us to complete the job. Unnecessary mistakes are avoided when we're not rushed to finish our work.

Inspection careers teach people how to assure quality. Refineries, chemical plants and papermills require some form of testing. If pipes welded together are being used to carry flammables and the welds haven't been tested, a fatal explosion may occur. It's necessary for welding to be inspected by an approved NDT method. Sometimes x-ray determines whether or not other people will keep their jobs. If there are too many bad welds, the welder gets fired. This occupation will interfere with your personal life to the point where you have none. When assignments are given, you have to cancel your arrangements. You can't make any plans without notifying your boss. Because of the strange hours and the separation of family, this work can ruin a relationship. If you have no family, no wife or girlfriend, x-ray could be the job for you. Not many people remain in this line of work.

Non Destructive Test methods reveal the internal nature of a part without destroying it. In Radiography, the results of a pipe weld are recorded on film in the form of a negative. This method involves carrying a 65-pound camera to the place where the x-ray needs to be taken. The weld can be on the ground, ten feet in the air, a hundred feet in the air and only accessible from a ladder. You can have 30, 60 to 90 welds to x-ray and the boss wants it all done on that day. This seasonal occupation can only be done when conditions permit it. Bad weather, poor lighting, extreme temperatures and inaccessibility can prevent you from being able to do this test. The client usually looks at the film so it has to be right. As always, this kind of work is in demand. Skilled and qualified personnel are hard to find. Top quality people in radiography don't always respect the company that employs them. They're loyal to the large amounts of money this kind of work can provide. I usually stay with a company that has plenty of projects and gives me a good pay rate. When I see a decrease in either of these, I move on. Most technicians who make a living doing this type of work will quickly relocate for a better offer. After some jobs are completed, you may not work for weeks.

My reputation grew to become known as highly skilled and talented. I had documents to prove my qualifications. The time it takes to make a phone call was all I needed to find a job. It was comforting to have an occupation that was in demand and would help keep me out of the unemployment line. This kind of work took me to see different places in the United States and the Virgin Islands. I inspected the piping in the facilities that produced gas for your car, oil for your lawnmower, cleaners for your house, fertilizers for your garden or made the paper you need to write on. Chemicals are needed for many reasons and I worked in the places where most of them are made. Demand for these items made my job secure.

In 1991 I answered a newspaper ad and took a job to work in Oregon. It was the chance that changed my life. They said I wouldn't be needed for a month. I stayed away from the drugs so I could pass the required drug test. From New Orleans to Portland I traveled. I had numerous mechanical problems with my car. My speedometer didn't work. The universal joint broke before leaving Louisiana. In Oklahoma my radiator fan broke causing my car to overheat. The power steering pump went out in Idaho. It was still an exciting road trip. Our country is a beautiful sight to behold. To see all the mountains, waterfalls and tall fir trees were real sites I had only seen on television. The air smelled crisp and clean. The cool temperatures added freshness not felt in the south. This is where I wanted to stay.

Arriving at the company, I filled out all the forms for my employment here. A week later I told them about their branch in New Orleans where I used to work. The secretary was happy to hear this because it eliminated a lot of paperwork. I didn't tell them the reason why they fired me, which was refusing to take a drug screen. I had already passed that test here. When they contacted their other office down south, I was terminated immediately. They didn't have to tell me why I was dismissed. This put me in a bad predicament. Almost three thousand miles away from home and I was unemployed. If I couldn't find a place to work, I'd have to return. The search for a job began so I wouldn't have to leave Portland.

The large house I lived in had many rooms and residents. I explained to the owner what happened at work and he let me stay there, doing small jobs for him. I fell into a deep depression and started drinking. I always managed to have money. About five days later I went to work for a competitor of the company that fired me. Shortly after getting hired I was arrested for driving under the influence of alcohol (DUI) and six days later arrested for the same offense. Now I had serious financial problems and needed a lawyer. Denying that I had a problem with alcohol, I switched my indulgence. It didn't take long to find someone at this company who was a smoker. Combining pot with the booze made me think that I didn't need as much alcohol. It was hard to see my situation was progressively getting worse.

Moving out the rooming house to another place put me closer to work. I was ordered to attend Alcoholics Anonymous meetings (AA) until my trial date. The court proceedings seemed to drag on forever. I would drink on the way to meetings and then buy more when I left. Beer wasn't doing it for me anymore so I started drinking gin. One night on my way home I hit a parked car and got my third DUI arrest. This was the second time that I hit a parked vehicle due to my drunkenness. Here I was in Portland Oregon, the state where Mothers Against Drunk Drivers (MADD) originated with three arrests for drunk driving within the first eight months of living here. Losing my car and going to prison were the consequences I was told about. It would do me no good to run from this issue with the law. Eventually they would catch me. All my life I was taught not to run from my problems and now was no time to start. If it was possible to get help with this problem, I needed it.

In my best interest, I felt it was necessary to inform my employer of these incidents and that this was my third. He told the vice president of the company and we all had a gathering. My boss remained silent throughout this entire meeting and the vice did all the talking. I was complimented on my work and they told me how much they liked my performance. He said that I fit the description of an alcoholic and asked if there was such a problem. How could I say no? With all the events that occurred involving alcohol, I couldn't deny that things had become unmanageable. Alcohol was ruining my life. I remember clearly how he stood up and admitted that he was a recovering alcoholic. They gave me a choice, to accept treatment and recover from alcoholism or be fired immediately. He told me to use my insurance with the company and find a facility. If I got help, my job would be waiting for me when I came back. He suggested I contact an acquaintance of his that was an attorney. This lawyer was also in recovery and would represent me in court. I really wanted to try and recover, and made a promise to do so. This was the turning point that changed my life forever.

Nationally, this was the tenth time I had been arrested for this driving under the influence offense, with 6 in Louisiana, 1 in the Virgin Islands and 3 here in Oregon. Down south, who you know and how much money you have will determine how easily a person can slip into and out of court. The right attorneys can get things erased from your driving record. It wasn't like that up here. A serious decision had to be made on my part as to whether or not I wanted to continue destroying myself with this kind of abuse. There had to be a way out, something that would help me leave this poison alone. At the time, I didn't know of any.

Arriving home, I began looking for a treatment facility that would accept my insurance. Ending up in a place called Providence, I remained an inpatient there for 35 days. We went to AA meetings and I was educated on the dangers of drug and alcohol abuse. When they released me, I rented an apartment nearby and remained close to the hospital. My outpatient schedule lasted for seven months. What was said about my job was true. It was waiting for me when I returned. I had never been clean and sober like this and was given a new start in life. My success was attributed to the program of AA and everything seemed to fit together like a puzzle. I only had to change one thing, and that was everything. My social life, the people I associated with and the places I went all had to change. If I didn't want to slip, I didn't go to slippery places. Most all my friends were people who were in recovery.

Much to my surprise was how the people there in AA were really concerned with me. I had two sponsors that would take me to meetings because I lost my car to the forfeiture law in Oregon. My driver's license was replaced with an ID card. It was the meetings and the recovery program of AA that put me on the spiritual level I needed to help stay away from both drugs and alcohol. I would have had no success with out it. One of my sponsors named Saul was a big help to me when I needed advice or a ride to a meeting.

The education I received in treatment made me aware of how dangerous drug and alcohol abuse is. It made me realize that the internal organs in our bodies don't consist of plastics, rubber or other synthetic materials. We're flesh and bones that aren't made to pour in toxins like alcohol or substances that affect our ability to function properly, correctly or morally. It taught me that alcoholism is like death on the installment plan and sooner or later it's bound to pay off. Most of the time the victims are innocent people, women and children. Alcohol can be one of the deadliest drugs because of the easy access and it's legal. The harmful effects aren't realized until it's too late. It's a great remover too. It can remove money from your wallet, bumpers from cars, remove parents from the lives of their children and destroy a family. When I remember my alcoholism, I'm thankful to know that it doesn't have to be that way anymore. Acceptance of life on life's terms became the key to my success. You can't change people, places or things. The only one I had control over was me. I had to accept this along with the proven fact that I was an alcoholic. This was something I couldn't forget.

With seven months of sobriety under my belt and my mother being very ill, I went home to be with her. At her dying bedside I gave assurance not to go back and use like some members of my family. They still abused drugs and alcohol. During my trip back to Portland momma passed away. I couldn't attend her wake because of the rumble with Mick. He was very drunk and slapped my sister Kim in her face while she sat in her wheel chair. He then started with me and I sent him to the hospital as the result of our fistfight. Had I gone to mom's funeral, the fighting may have resumed. The promise I made to myself was not to give up on recovery and lose my sobriety. With all these traumatic events going on I still remained sober.

Using the program of AA and the fellowship within, it helped me stay clean and remain focused on fulfilling my priorities. Life took on a whole new meaning. The court proceedings went along smooth and things finally leveled off. I had a large variety of friends. We all had common goals and were there to help each other when we could. Some still had addiction problems but that didn't sway me. I was there to carry a message. If someone wanted to know about my recovery, I could reveal to him or her what was so freely given to me. It didn't take long to recognize whether a person was serious or not about their willingness to participate. My sobriety was truly a gift and my gratitude was evident. Things were not the same.

Work had slowed down and I had to move on to another company. Not having a car or a driver's license began to affect my ability to be available for certain jobs. Several months later, this new employer sold out to a larger company that was located in another town away from Portland. It was hard to find a job making the money I needed and apply the skill that took me years to develop. Soon I began to realize that I'd have to return to my hometown.

Making a call to my friend back home, I found out that work was picking up in the south. There were two companies that needed qualified people. I made a phone call to one company and was hired immediately. They said that I'd be needed to start in a month.

My stay in Portland lasted 25 months. It's a learning experience I will never forget. I am very thankful for all the people I met and the lessons well learned. My friends advised me to stay in Portland. They felt that I'd be returning to the scene of the accident by going back home. They feared I would surely relapse and go back to using. Because of financial reasons, I had to go and figured I could remain sober for a long time. Going to meetings and staying busy at work would help deter me from the thoughts of returning to that kind of abusive lifestyle. My education in treatment taught me different methods to stay clean.

The decision was made to return to New Orleans. Many of my friends were in disbelief and with watery eyes, tried persuading me to stay. I had so many belongings that some were left behind and another trip back to would be needed. They encouraged me to use this time as a trial run and if things didn't work out, I could always come back. I admitted to being a little leery about relocating. A new job, being with my family and an opportunity to start over became my reasons to go forward. To prosper and take life more seriously was an interest I never had before. I had to remember my change made me different from the way I used to be. In defense I'd have to keep my guard up against situations that would tempt me.

Oregon is a beautiful state. I remember looking down the street I lived on and could see the snow capped Mount Hood off in the distance. It wasn't all flat like the southern part of Louisiana. There were hills and mountains everywhere. The neighborhood I lived in was built on Mount Tabor. The weather was pleasant. In the evenings after the sun went down you'd need a sweater because the temperature dropped. Some parts of the year there was that unique rain that came down in the form of a mist and it'd last all day. Other times there'd be clear blue sky with a cool breeze that blew constantly. I was thankful to be there when two feet of snow fell on Portland. Here I was in my thirties and finally got the chance to play like a kid, making a snowman and huge snowballs. It was easy to see that this was a state preserved by people who cared. I found out the hard way of the zero tolerance they have here for the people who drink and drive. It made a believer out of me. The stringent laws they have here may have saved my life. In my opinion, every state should have the car forfeiture law like Oregon does. It would save many lives. One good way to reach an alcoholic is through his wallet.

The last rooming house I lived in was close to the treatment facility. Helping the landlord with chores around her house became part of my recovery program. It was nice the way she had things set up. The three-story house had a basement that was converted into a retirement home for the elderly. When she bought the place, she rented out the five rooms in the bottom to people like me. She and her family lived in the upper two stories. Every time I returned from New Orleans I'd bring souvenirs back with me. My room started to resemble a museum with Mardi Gras posters, beads and other memorabilia on the walls. Of all the places I stayed in Portland, this one was the best. My landlord was very nice to me and she didn't like having to see me go. She understood when I told her that there was no other choice for me.

One night after an AA meeting I sat in my room and thought about what it was that helped me stop the chemical and substance abuse that plagued my life for almost twenty years. There are twelve steps in the program of Alcoholics Anonymous. I saw that alcohol is mentioned only once and God's name is mentioned seven times. When alcoholism and drug abuse is left untreated, it can develop into a spiritual illness. When thinking about this I became thoroughly convinced it was the spiritual awakening that unshackled these chains of misery from me. In treatment I remembered how the bible said we were created in His image. Is it possible that if we don't know Him, we may not know ourselves? By not knowing Him or His love for us, could this be the reason that allows the opportunity for people to continue in their sickness of drug and alcohol addiction, a condition that is successful in destroying the lives of many?

Employment had come to a halt. This gave me the opportunity to visit the places I wanted to remember and spend time with my friends. A trip to Mount Hood, the Grotto, the parks and the beautiful waterfalls I saw upon arriving here became places I wanted to see before I left Oregon. Going to AA meetings and announcing my departure was the most difficult thing I had to do. Many of my friends couldn't believe what they were hearing. Was I sure about this, a few of them had to ask? The response I gave revealed that not too many choices were left for me to select from. Assurance was given that all would be fine and told them of the plan I had to insure my wellbeing. The chance to live a clean and sober life in the place where all I did was party all the time became the challenge in my life that I needed to grasp. They were quick to remind me that when life becomes unmanageable, not to drink over it.

Saul told me to be very careful when I returned home. "If you have any problems, give me a call, any time of the day", he insisted. He said that there'd be some rough times and urged me to always remember that help was only a call away. While living here, one of my solutions for when I became tempted was to keep some change in my pocket in case I needed to make that phone call for help. In addition were numbers in my wallet to members of this self-help organization. All I had to do was provide the willingness to stop using. With the help of my friends here and the instructional program of Alcoholics Anonymous, I finally found a way to eliminate the self-inflicted disaster of alcohol and drug addiction. The best part about AA was that it was no big secret, available to everyone and it's free.

Chapter Two

RETURNING HOME

My sister Tabby had a spare room and I moved in with her. It was good to be back with family and the wounds from the time of momma's death had healed. The relationship with my siblings had changed and everything was different. It was imperative that I follow specific guidelines and develop a routine to maintain the kind of lifestyle that I lived in Portland. Not going to the same places, associating with the people I used to and doing the things that bought me calamity or trouble became ground rules. By adhering to these simple principles my problems would be few. Trying to be helpful any way I could became a method in taking me out of myself. When times got rough this was easy to do and worked perfectly.

One night while listening to a Christian radio station in Little Rock Arkansas I developed an appetite for the bible. It had become a practice to listen to this program. Because of work I wasn't attending many AA meetings. What I was hearing began to teach me ways to live. This would increase my belief in God and it became a refuge. My spirit was being fed and freed at the same time. I learned that many things in life are spiritual, including music. It brought to mind something momma used to say, "you can't live without God". Here was a path I wanted to be on. The thirst for more knowledge came quickly. Searching diligently, I miraculously found answers to most all of my questions. Soon I realized that this was a gift anyone could possess when they were spiritually drawn to Him. The Christian faith seemed different and taught me things I never knew as a Catholic. Before reading the word of God I'd pray to have the spirit of understanding and this helped me learn. A great interest was created in me.

The new job at X-ray Information House (XIH) was the same as all the other companies I worked for. My boss was an assistant pastor at his church and we'd converse about what I was learning and what he already knew. After reviewing my performance I quickly became a fixture there. Having him as my superior was a true asset. He also was a recovered alcoholic. It was a real relief for me to have someone I could go to when questions would arise. He began to hire employees of the Christian faith and we felt like a family at work. Here was a man that if you needed something fixed or additional equipment, he was always there to provide. There was promptness about him that everyone appreciated. This helped build incentive for the employees by having good material to work with. Most NDT companies didn't operate in this manner. He kept a tight ship and the boat always stayed afloat. Some liked his stern attitude and some didn't. Regardless of that, our employer was fair to all of us. For that he gained our utmost respect. There was plenty of work and everyone was busy. It was easy to recognize the ones who didn't fit in. Poor work habits, disobedience, drug and alcohol abuse, and theft were some of the problems the newer recruits caused.

The southern environment at this time of the year was the same as always. It was mid July, hot, humid and muggy. This is when my job becomes a real bother because of the exhausting heat. The extreme temperatures can make the pipe real hot. The areas most companies have for us to work at were usually out in the sun, away from any shade. At times, gloves were needed to operate or move our equipment. The darkroom where the film is developed has an air conditioner. It becomes a rescue shelter when symptoms of heat stroke began to appear. The company encourages personal safety but they also want you to finish. Taking too many breaks can result in disciplinary action or being removed from the job. Most companies don't want to hear about these hazards. They want you to earn their money so you can get paid. Drinking plenty of water and taking small breaks is the only way to survive the heat.

Working at night created little relief with the absence of the sun. Mosquitoes and other flying insects would make their presence known. Large amounts swarmed about where ever you went. There was no place to hide from them. Working in the dark made it worse because you couldn't see. With numerous bites and plenty of bumps to scratch, doing this job at night became miserable. Breathing would send them up your nose and if your mouth was open, they'd fly in. These bugs tasted terrible when they weren't cooked. Sometimes it seemed like the insect repellent only attracted them. There was no way possible to evade the Louisiana State bird, the mosquito. If projects were offshore on the oil platforms, that'd be too far for them to fly. It was the only time we'd be able to get away from this nuisance.

Our clientele started to accumulate and the work hours quickly added up. The time spent on these projects began to make everyone irritable. We began to miss jobs and lose money because there wasn't enough manpower to fill the schedule. With an increase in the work force, more employees had to be hired. My boss sometimes would consult with me about a new hire since I knew plenty of technicians from my years in the field.

Familiar faces began to appear from the past. Friends I hadn't seen in years came on board to help us out. One of these was Dom, a co-worker from my earlier years when I started out as a helper. My news to him was that I cleaned up my act and didn't drink or do drugs anymore. He accepted my adjustment and complimented me. We got along good as always and my change didn't become an obstacle in our friendship. Although he was still a drinker, that never bothered me. The way I lived years ago reminded me that at one time I was like that too.

The bowling alley became our recreational spot. A small group of us from work would go there to unwind and have fun. Dom was a good player and won most of the games. After too many six-packs of aiming fluid, I'd start to excel. This was a surprise to me because I wasn't the best of players. When they were drunk and I was tired of winning, we'd quit.

Our entertainment changed one night when Dom suggested we go to the Cablanka, a lounge in the heart of Gretta. A couple of pool tables were there and we could play a tournament. The thought of this made me hesitant but figured it'd be alright since I wasn't going to drink. What I was taught in Portland, "if you don't want to slip, don't go to slippery places", didn't even occur to me. This was the place where all the technicians from Okay X-ray would go when they weren't on jobs. It was also considered a drug store in my earlier days when I went there.

Dom, Johnny and I were the only ones to go shoot pool. They won most all the games while I sat at the bar and talked to the barmaid. Her name was Cassie and she was from up north. I told her of my recent move back here from Oregon. Spending my time talking with her, we drank instant coffee. She was a divorcee and had two sons. One was in the army somewhere in Asia and the other son, living at home. Talking for hours, it was as though we'd known each other for years. Our conversations took on a wide variety of subjects. Our families, how she loved it down here and what I thought about being back home were just some of the topics. Dom came to the bar and ordered another bloody mary. While Cassie made his drink he asked, "hitting on the barmaid huh, she looks good". I just smiled and nodded. He said we'd be leaving after he finished his drink. I agreed because it was getting late. Taking his drink back to the pool table, I remained at the bar with Cassie. She asked if I wanted more coffee. I said yes and we both had a cup. As we were holding hands I asked her, "if I had your phone number, would you want me to call you"? She looked into my eyes and replied, "yes". She had to go make a drink and Dom came over and said, "I'm ready to go". "Me too", Johnny says. I looked at Dom's glass and saw it was half full. "You're not finished your drink", I said. "There's too much alcohol in it", he replied. I never heard Dom say that before. "Okay, let me tell my friend good-bye and we'll go", I told him. Telling Cassie that I couldn't call her without a number, she got a napkin and wrote something on it. Not thinking she'd put her real telephone number on it, I gave her my business card. Exchanging smiles, we parted. She went to the other end of the bar and I left out the door. Dom and Johnny were already in the car with the engine running. "Did you get you a date", Dom asked. "I don't know, I think she gave me her phone number, I guess I'll find out", I responded.

We dropped Johnny off at the shop so he could get his car and then proceeded to my sister's house. Dom was almost drunk and his driving made me nervous. When we arrived I asked if he wanted to stay and sleep on couch. I told him Tabby wouldn't mind. He refused and insisted on going home. "Are you sure", I asked? "Yeah, I'm okay", he replied. I said to him jokingly, "try not to run over the mailbox". Shutting the door, I watched him drive off.

As I lay in bed, thoughts about what all happened filled my mind. We went to a lounge where there was plenty of alcohol, and I never had the urge or temptation to drink. What I was taught in the AA meetings and treatment seemed to work like a defense mechanism. A feeling of gratitude had come over me. After my friends had a few drinks I could see a transformation in the way they acted. Their personality changed. It had been a long time since I was around people who were under the influence of alcohol. Knowing that I didn't have to be like that anymore was a relief. On top of that I met Cassie, a nice lady whom I became interested in getting to know more about. I knew what time she went to work and was anxious to call her. I wondered whether or not she gave me the right phone number or was she playing a game. I didn't sense any dishonesty in her and the curiosity was killing me.

The next day before work I called Cassie. We were both happy to talk. Informing her of how strange my work schedule was, I wanted to get together for dinner when we could find the time. She liked the idea and told me where she lived. After I finished my job the next evening we'd meet at her apartment and go out to eat. The directions she gave me were precise. I found her place and knocked on the door. She answered wearing a beautiful black dress and greeted me with her pretty smile. I said hello and she invited me in. She kept making trips to the kitchen and coming back with a full glass of wine. "I don't drink that often but I'm a little nervous tonight, you understand, huh", she asked? And I said, "yeah, me too". A while later we became hungry and went to Copperheads, a fancy Cajun restaurant with a variety of entrees to choose from. We sat at a secluded table with the lights dimmed. This created a romantic atmosphere. Her eyes would glisten in the candlelight, as our conversations became more personal. We found delight in being together and this felt like an occasion that was long overdue. The joy we felt being with each other was like a missing link in our lives. It was obvious we made each other feel warm inside. Cassie continued to drink and loosen up as the night progressed. Not wanting our night to end, we took a ride over to the Cablanka lounge where she felt right at home. This time the barmaid waited on her and everything she wanted was there for the asking. Intimacy began to blossom as we danced. This was very satisfying to both of us. It was getting late and I had a job to go on the next day. We said good-bye to friends and made way to her apartment. When we walked in her son was there, asleep on the couch. She turned and said, "I had a real good time". "I did too", I responded. With a long embrace and a passionate kiss, our date had ended. "We need to do this again", I suggested. "Yeah okay", she replied.

Although we kept in touch by telephone, it was a week later before Cassie and I was back together again. At this time I wasn't working and called, asking to see her. She wanted to see me too so we got together at her apartment. Walking in, I saw a candle lit and it felt like the cozy atmosphere from our first date. We talked about anything and everything. Her job and mine, and the stuff we liked to do were some of our subjects. The conversations we had were comfortable ones. She kept going to the kitchen and coming back with a full glass of wine. "Nervous again, huh", I asked? "Yeah", she replied. Our talk drifted to sex. The things we started to reveal about ourselves began to arouse both of us. We soon hinted to each other how we'd like to be alone. She was expecting her son to be home soon so I suggested we take a ride. We drove around for a long while talking about the city until I stopped in front of a nice hotel. "Wanna go in", I asked? "Lets go", she said. I went to the desk and requested a room on the 10th floor. Being this high up, we'd get a good view of New Orleans. The shyness we had was replaced with anticipation. We were very aware of what was about to happen. Energy from the body heat fanned the flames of our passion for each other. It seemed that our personal satisfaction was all we were concerned about. We stayed almost three hours and then departed as quickly as we arrived. This rendezvous created the unity between us that would last for years. From this point on we were always together or on the phone. What had developed between us was lustfully intriguing.

Cassie would come pick me up from my sister's house after work. Even though I didn't have a car, this wouldn't interfere with us being with together. Tabby started to warn me of her drinking. She was worried that I'd go back to partying because of the company I kept. There were times when I'd use my sister's van to go see my girlfriend at her apartment when she got off work. She appeared to be drunk and this started to bother me. We had been together a good while and she was beginning to expose some of her secrets. I had to tell her that I was a recovering alcoholic and if she continued to drink, I couldn't hang around. She stopped drinking on February 14th, valentine's day. I assured her that she would not regret leaving the stuff alone. At this time I believe we were falling in love. For her to stay away from the alcohol to keep me around gave the message that I meant something to her. It was a bit hard for her at first. Telling her some of the things I learned in treatment made things easier. On the weekends when she wasn't working we were together. I would spend nights at her house and stay until there was a job for me to go on. All the spare time we had was spent with each other. When apart, the telephone became our communication line.

One morning Cassie came home from work to find me waiting for her. I hadn't been there long and we were both tired. We climbed into bed and were almost asleep when a noise came from the other room. Going to see what happened, we found her son Brad passed out on the floor in his room. She called to him several times to get in his bed and it didn't work. She came in her room, lit a cigarette and sat down by me. Now she couldn't sleep. "He's drunk", she said. Starting to reveal some things about her sons caught my attention and I sat up to listen. Brad is her problem child with a bad temper. "Where's his dad", I asked? "Their father was abusive to me so I took him and Donny away, they haven't seen him since", she told me. She remarried when she moved here. To know she was a victim of spousal abuse gained my sympathy. I hugged her and said it'll be okay. As we tried to lie back down she asked me to go check on him. When I looked, he wasn't in his room. I found him slumped in the bathroom hugging the toilet. He had to vomit and this is where he passed out again. After learning that his last name was Upchuck, this situation seemed to fit perfectly. He was too heavy to carry so I left him where he was. Cassie went in after him and cleaned up the mess he made in the bathroom. She was upset with him and embarrassed that I saw all this. Reluctantly, she had to tend to her son and told me to get some rest, that she'd be in later.

Lying in bed, I began to wonder if there was something I could do that would help this guy. His behavior was that of a kid. Here was this 20-year-old man with no job, living off his mom and going nowhere. I thought about confronting him with the proposition of doing x-ray work. There was a school I knew about where he could go and get his 40-hour safety course. He'd be able to do inspection jobs at the company where I was employed and I'd be the one training him to become a technician. Presenting this idea to Cassie, she encouraged him to enroll. She paid his tuition and he used her car to go to class. With good attendance and passing grades, he obtained the certificate needed to get a job. He put in an application XIH where I was working. Because he failed his drug screen, they couldn't hire him. He didn't appear to be a person who had a problem doing drugs. It was evident that he didn't want to work. I don't know if Cassie was aware that her son had this addiction. This was something that didn't concern me so I never got involved.

I had to make a trip back to Oregon to get the rest of my belongings. Cassie and Tabby brought me to the airport. This would be my final farewell to Portland. Planning to stay a week, I wanted to spend time and talk with friends. Needing to talk with my sponsor Saul about the situation I was in, we met at a local AA club. I told him about my girlfriend and her son. He asked me if I loved her and I told him yes. He said I'd have to accept her son for being the way he is, reminding me not to try and change people, that's not my job. They have to do that themselves. When suggestions are made to encourage someone of a needed change or adjustment, if they don't co-operate it can drive you crazy. This made sense to me, remembering that I was the only one I had control over. We went to many meetings and I enjoyed the scenery I wouldn't see for a long time. I missed Cassie and wanted to give her a call. We were happy to hear each other's voice. It felt like I was in love. The affection I had for her was strong. When I told her how I was feeling and what I thought about us, she reciprocated the same. After this conversation I wanted to get my stuff and go home.

My arrival home was stricken with excitement. Our relationship made me happy. I had to return to work but eventually we'd find the time to be together again. We settled back into the same routine. She worked at the lounge during the week and I went on jobs whenever they called me. We had been together a long time now and our relationship was pretty solid. My opinions were considered when she had concerns about her sons.

Her son Donny had come back to the states but was living in Nevada with a woman he met in the military. This upset Cassie because she wanted him to come home. Many phone conversations with him helped ease the grief she felt for his absence. Much time had passed, the heartache finally healed and she felt better. Several weeks later he called one night to say that he'd left his girlfriend and was coming back. It made Cassie happy that he was returning home. The way he departed from his mate was a bit disturbing and she told him about it. He agreed to do what was right and returned to get the woman he loved. They would all move here and live in the apartment. Donny arrived with his girlfriend Sue, and her daughter and all their belongings. It was crowded with six people in a place that had only two bedrooms.

All the bills had tripled. Donny was just like Brad, always wanting to party. Cassie and I were the only ones paying the expenses here and I started to complain. They spent most of their time at the lounge using Cassie's tip money to drink with. Hardly any attempts were made to find a job by either of these guys or the girlfriend. After enough complaints they started looking. When any of them found a job, it wasn't long before they lost it and became unemployed again. This situation was taking its toll on me. Finally I had enough and went back to Tabby's house. I felt bad about leaving my girlfriend and told her the actions of her sons were affecting us. Within a week we were back together and ground rules were set. Donny and Sue were upset with this and wouldn't hang around whenever I was there. This chaotic situation caused friction to develop between her sons and me.

With the training he received in the military, Donny landed a job as an electrician. His pay rate was good and he was beginning to save some money. Sue simply refused to work. She was happy staying at the apartment and watching soap operas. Cassie became angry because everyone except her was working and trying to contribute. With all the bills soaring she began to complain to Donny and he approached Sue about it. This created a squabble and they decided to move out. Sue left her daughter to live with us so she could attend the school nearby. Donny was not speaking to Cassie so he could avoid arguments with Sue.

Work for me was picking up and I had some money saved. I wanted to do something nice for Cassie. Her car was running bad so I suggested she get a new one. We drove around and looked for something she liked. A maroon hatchback is what she picked and we got it. She gave her other car to Brad so he'd have a ride to work. If he paid the insurance, he could have the car. This deal sounded fair and would help him develop some responsibility.

Brad lost his job immediately and wouldn't work. Cassie was now paying insurance on two vehicles. I suggested she sell the other car. She made him turn over the keys and Brad was very upset. Now he had nothing to ride around in and party with his friends. This put me in hot water with him. He did not hold up his end of the bargain, which was to pay the insurance. Cassie sold the car for $50.00 and cut her car insurance bill in half.

Through thick and thin, Cassie and I remained together. I tried to get back into my bible studies and hold on to our relationship. She tried to encourage Brad to join us but he refused. "This is the 90s, no one reads the bible anymore", he replied. I would find out later that Brad's statement spoke for his generation and younger; that no one reads the bible anymore. Cassie and I continued to read and discuss scripture. This didn't work especially when we got to the part about fornication. I didn't believe it was right and she thought because we loved each other, that it was okay. She had recently divorced and I wanted to be married. When I proposed to her we both agreed it was too soon and decided to wait.

Listening to a ministry on the radio, I began attending the bible studies they talked about. Most all the people there were married. I found myself to be one of a few single persons here. When I spoke of my situation, the subject of fornication came out. One lady told me that a situation like that wasn't worth losing my salvation. They suggested that we go to a marriage counselor in the church and eventually get married. After attending several of the gatherings, I decided to approach Cassie on how I felt about this part of us. She wouldn't go with me to the meetings and was angry with the fact that I discussed our relationship with strangers. The way she reacted showed that we were never getting married. Her uncompromising remarks upset me. I moved back to Tabby's house. This wasn't a good idea considering the way I felt about Cassie. We never talked too much on this issue and my reaction to leave was very premature. This really hurt my girlfriend. It was always uncomfortable for me to be apart from her. After I realized my mistake, it began to stress me out. When I was able to reach her, we talked about our love for each other. Our connection wasn't a one-night stand or a fling. We agreed to this, got back together and decided that one day we will be married.

We began to stay close to each other and I stopped going to the bible studies. If she were at work, I'd go visit her there. On the weekends we'd go to a nice restaurant or shops in the French Quarter. We ended up going to many places. She'd ask me, "you love me"? And I'd say, "yes I do, you know I do". We slipped away from the contact we had with God but held on to our belief. We didn't read the bible much any more. We had lots of love for each other and we thought this was good enough. I was really happy and it felt good to be in love. In an attempt to enhance our spiritual growth we went to a concert where a musical group "Point of Grace" was playing. They sang all Christian music. It was this group that helped me convert from the Catholic religion to the Christian faith I now believed. I thought we both enjoyed the show but found out later that Cassie didn't like it. "I only went there for you", she told me. Had I known she felt this way, I would have gone to the show by myself.

Overlooking the obstacles in our relationship began to worry me. I was in love with a woman that was a drinker when I met her. She was married and divorced three times. Donnie and Brad had no connection with their father and both had a drinking problem. Cassie remained generous to them so they'd stay around. She said that they didn't get to spend enough time together when her sons were younger because she worked all the time. It felt good to have them close by and she would do anything to make up for the time they lost. It was hard for me to understand why they were so irresponsible and dependent. I knew this was a subject that would easily offend Cassie and felt it was none of my business.

As weeks turned to months I never said much about anything that was bothering me. I just didn't want to lose Cassie and tried to give her anything she wanted. We spent much time in the sack and this had become a big part of our togetherness. Her sons had to know that I wasn't there just because she told good stories. Cassie would tell me I could leave my shoes under her bed anytime. This made me feel somewhat secure but for the wrong reason. In the beginning when we got together I told Cassie how I wanted to have a wife and kids someday. Apologizing, she told me that it wasn't possible for her to have kids and said that something was wrong with the position of her uterus. It was tilted and because of that she couldn't conceive. I wasn't upset about this but was starting to lose hope on the chance of having a family with her in the future. This thought and others were troublesome to me. Cassie was nine years older than I was. Already in my thirties, the time to have kids was now. If I wanted to hold on to this woman whom I was now in love with, it was best that I keep my mouth shut. No matter what I said, things weren't going to change anyway. I had accepted everything as being the way it was supposed to. Suppression had become my way of not letting her know how I felt. An argument may cause a disruption that would end our relationship. I found myself to be in a lustful affair. This was a situation that was starting to feel uncomfortable for me. Considering my feelings for her, to separate would only make me miserable. With patience I decided to wait and hoped that things would get better.

Chapter Three

A JOYFUL ARRIVAL

We had been together for almost two years. We settled in a way that was comfortable for us. The entire time we were together there wasn't any arguments, just disagreements. Most of the time things were easily resolved. The rough edges between her sons and me were finally smooth. Cassie didn't go to Tabby's house much. If we were to see each other, I went to her apartment. That was fine to me because it gave us the privacy we needed to do our favorite dance, the horizontal tango. For a long time it seemed like this is what our relationship mostly consisted of. When either of us weren't at work or out somewhere, we were dancing between her sheets. She didn't like me to use any protection. I wanted to see if she was telling the truth about not being able to conceive. If I tried hard enough, maybe the child I wanted would become a reality. It would be beautiful to have a little one running around. Cassie was like me and she loved kids. My hope was that she'd get pregnant and we could have a child to call our own. In my heart I knew this was the wrong way to go about starting a family. We were in love, somewhat living together and seemed to have a good connection. We had everything a married couple had, except a marriage certificate and kids.

I remember coming home from work one day and Cassie was full of smiles. She said, "I did it twice". "What are you talking about", I asked? She left and came back with a pregnancy test. She showed it to me and said, "it's positive, I'm pregnant". We were both extremely happy about this. At this stage in my life all I wanted was to have a wife and a child. I was finally going to be a dad. My priority was to make sure Cassie took care of her self. I asked both her sons to please refrain from any disagreements or arguments.

Her pregnancy didn't stop her from working. Cassie wanted to remain in the lounge until it was time to deliver. I didn't agree with this because the stress of the job and the loud music there. She remained employed because I couldn't persuade her to quit.

One evening I saw Mitch, the Cablanka's barback in a store. This is the man that stands guard at the lounge and prevents things from getting out of hand. I told him of Cassie's situation, that she'd soon be on maternity leave. His happiness about the news was evident as he congratulated me. He made the owner of the Cablanka aware of her condition. The following day she was fired from the lounge. Mitch's big mouth got her terminated.

Moving into her apartment, I assumed all the finances. My responsibility was to see that all the bills were paid. Her sons were now upset because the well dried up since Cassie wasn't at the lounge any longer. Being able to get money from her had stopped abruptly. I had more say in the decision making. The hostility with her sons and me began to grow. When I came to the apartment, her sons would leave. When a situation gets rough the most powerful weapon I had was to leave. It was better to do this than stay and argue. We had an argument over giving money to her son Brad and once again for the third time, I left.

Being away from Cassie made me feel guilty. I had remembered my sponsor when he said that I'd have to accept her son for the way he is. Three days later I was on the phone with her, apologizing for what I did. She asked me to be lenient with Brad cause he wasn't working but was trying to find a job. "I love him, he's my son", she said. I moved back in and did as she asked. After this I had no intention of ever leaving her again.

The way we used to talk all the time had ceased. I was working plenty, putting in lots of hours. My jobs were mostly at night. Cassie was awake while I would sleep and when she was sleeping, I was away at work. This began to trouble our relationship.

One evening as we were getting ready for bed Cassie made a premonition that scared me. "I want to have an abortion", she said. In shock I dropped to my knees and begged her not to do this. "Please don't kill our baby, why do you want to do that", I asked? "I don't want to raise another child by myself", she said. "I want you to see something", I told her. At Tabby's house a ministry sent me a video called "Hard Truth". It's about 10 minutes long and has explicit content on the subject of abortion. We watched it twice. After viewing the tape two times she switched from being pro-choice to pro-life. A while later she said that the statement she made was to get my attention and had no intention of having an abortion. I had a tough time believing this and would remember Cassie's threat forever.

An ultrasound exam revealed we were going to have a little girl. Cassie always wanted one but had boys instead. This changed her entire attitude about everything. There was a glowing of happiness about her. She started to take better care of herself and cut back on her smoking. Her doctor gave her prenatal vitamins to assist in the nourishment of our baby.

Five months into her pregnancy, Cassie had surgery to remove a large ovarian cyst. Going into labor, she had to be put on medication to prevent delivery. She insisted that we needed money and I was offshore at the time of her operation. I wanted to be with her but with my kind of job, it was hard to get away from work. Our relationship got stronger. Until the time for her delivery she stayed home and took it easy. She didn't need to do anything but take care of herself. With anticipation we waited the time for our child to arrive.

Arriving home from work one evening, Cassie informs me that her water busted and it was time to go to the hospital. I began to panic and tried to stay calm at the same time. I had a job offshore and was trying to get out of going. She had her friend Barbara and I had Tabby meet us at the hospital. From there I made several calls in an attempt to cancel my job. I told Cassie that I wasn't having any success. She urged me to go saying, "it's okay, Barbara's here and we need the money anyway". Calling the owner of BBX, (Blue Bayou X-ray), I informed him of my situation. He told me that there was no one else available and if I didn't go, to turn in my equipment, I'd be fired. Cassie encouraged me to go saying, "it's alright, Barbara's here".

It was impossible for me to function properly at work. I told the platform supervisor of my problem. He fired me from the job and put me a helicopter saying "no matter what son, don't you ever do this again"! When the chopper landed I ran to the truck and hurried home. Running red lights, stop signs and driving fast, I turned a four-hour trip into two. The danger of breaking these rules of the road didn't even occur to me. I raced to get to the hospital.

Arriving at 6pm, I went to the nurse's station and asked for directions. She sent me to a small room with a large glass enclosure for parents to see their baby. Approaching the window, I could see the infants exploring their new surroundings. When I saw the nametag Cassie Dixon, it told me I was too late. I missed her delivery. The nurse knew which of the newborns was mine and brought her closer. There I was looking face to face and eye to eye with my little girl, Amanda. I began to cry. The nurse smiled and turned to go do her work. With tears of joy and a feeling of happiness, I was thankful. Finally, I was a Daddy and we had a beautiful child to call our own. A baby to love and care for. Amanda was wide-eyed, kicking and moving about where she laid. Regaining my composure, I found out what room Cassie was in and went to see her. She was happy to see me when I walked in. "Did you see her", she asked? "Yes I did, she's beautiful" I said. I sat on the edge of her bed and told her, "I'm sorry I wasn't here, baby". "It's okay, you're here now", she replied. She asked what happened to the job and I let her know they fired me. "What are you going to do now", she asked? "Find another job", I said. We lay next to each other and talked about our little girl and going home. She wanted to leave right then but it was hospital policy to remain 24 hours for observation reasons. The attendant would come in periodically and make sure that she was doing well in her recovery. Just then the door opened and a nurse came in for a routine check. While she did this, I walked down the hall to go see Amanda again.

After getting a full night's rest we both awoke to breakfast being served by the hospital staff. A while later the nurse brought Amanda in. We both held her and she was showered with plenty of love and kisses. Cassie had all her things packed and was ready to leave. She put Amanda in my arms and said, "you carry the baby". "Where are we going", I asked. "We're leaving", she said. I wasn't too sure about this as we made our way down the hall to the elevator. When we got to the nurse's station the red light came on. "Where do you think yall are going", the nurse asked. "We're going home", Cassie responded. "No, I don't think so; you have to stay a full 24 hours and follow hospital procedure, there's paperwork you'll have to sign before you can leave and you'll have to be escorted in a wheel chair", the nurse said. I was very embarrassed. We both returned to the room and waited for the time to expire. I held on to Amanda while Cassie expressed her discontent with not being able to leave.

We were already prepared by the time we got home to the apartment. There were diapers, formula, a bassinet and plenty of baby clothes waiting for us. All we needed was Amanda. Many nights we'd sit by her side and watch her sleep. Anyone that held her had to wash his or her hands and I shaved my moustache off so I wouldn't scratch her. Plenty of pictures were taken to remember how small our little angel was. We both shared diaper duty and made sure she never missed a feeding. When I wasn't working, home with our baby is where I wanted to be. This joy of parenthood was a new experience to me. It was great being a father. The way Cassie nurtured Amanda was a beautiful sight to behold. Her motherly instinct was easily noticed. She was very happy with the little girl she wanted all her life.

Concerns began to arise about the neighboring environment where her apartment was. People were raising their voices all hours of the night in the walkway outside Cassie's door. It appeared that there were too many parties. Across the street you'd see cars drive up slow and then stop. Someone would then run up to the car and there'd be an exchange done through the window. We knew they weren't swapping phone numbers. With me working all the time and Cassie at the lounge, we were never home enough to notice this kind of activity going on so close to home. It became evident that we were residing in a drug-infested neighborhood. We both decided it'd be in our best interest to move. I had saved up some money and told Cassie she could start looking around for us a new place to live.

We checked out a few places and found a house in Old Gretta that appealed to us. Cassie really loved it because it had a fireplace, carport and a nice yard. It was back away, far from the road and the neighbors weren't too close. Packing up all our stuff, we moved there a month and a half after Amanda was born. Cassie informed me that Brad would be living with us because he had no place to go and she wasn't going to abandon him.

So we moved over to a house on Blaire Street and this was our new home. There was a pecan tree out front. We'd pick and peel the pecans and Cassie would make pies. In the springtime I planted a garden with plenty of vegetables for us to eat. We'd sit on the porch swing in the cool of the evening and enjoy the new place we found. Cassie bought a swing and a small pool for Amanda. It was a real joy to watch our little girl growing up.

We made adjustments on the house to suit our needs. Cassie changed and remodeled some of the inside. She had a special talent for this and always wanted to be an interior designer or decorator. This was a side of her I didn't know about and she was good. She'd finish some projects and others never got completed. The landlord Mr. Boudreaux would compensate us for the work and money I spent. After we were there a while it really felt like home.

Cassie's niece, Wendy and her friend came from Ohio to visit and see our baby. They were the same age as Brad and went out just about every night. Wendy was a large girl and expressed the need for having it cold in our house. The thermostat was at 68 degrees all the time because she couldn't take the heat. It was summer here, hot and muggy with 100% humidity always. Cassie told me to bite my tongue.

Doing as she requested I never said a word. They were only to be here a week and she didn't want to inconvenience them in any way. After Wendy broke the washing machine by over stuffing her clothes in it, I never uttered a sound. I just went out and bought a new one. After they left and went back home, the phone bill had a $40 charge on it for calling a psychic hotline. It wasn't any of us that made the call and we knew who did it. Cassie asked me not to say anything about it.

Searching for employment, I landed a job at SWX. (Southern Way X-ray) Dennis, the owner was someone I knew from my employment there years before. He was a technician from long ago and spent years doing this kind of work. All his equipment was in good shape. He had a major contract in a nearby plant but didn't have the people. He needed a good helper and asked if I knew of anyone. I told him about Cassie's son. He had the certificate for his safety training and was looking for a job. A drug test wasn't required at the time and this is just what Brad wanted to hear. They hired him and I helped with his training. We got along better now that we worked together. When he saw my seriousness toward taking care of his mom and my daughter, it seemed like I was beginning to gain a little respect from him.

Non Destructive Testing is the same as it always was. Like most jobs, you do what you're told. When my pager goes off and I contact the shop, we can be gone for an evening, two days, a week or a month. You never know where you're going or how long you'll be gone. That's the way it is. Our schedule was interfering with the tournaments Brad played in. He didn't like not being able to go shoot pool and drink beer all night in the lounge like he used to do.

Brad and I had been working together two months and one day we were caught violating plant procedure. We were working in a restricted area. The managers found that we had false badges and this only added to the problem. We were banned from the plant while they did further investigations. A company letter was written accepting fault and a drug test was now required. I took the test but Brad refused. "Forcing him to submit to a urine analysis is an invasion of his privacy", Cassie said in his defense. He was terminated immediately.

It was five months after Amanda was born that I decided to approach Cassie with my proposition. Our relationship was solid now. It was time to let her know how I felt, that we should be married. One night after we had a nice dinner I was preparing to present her with my proposal. We retreated to the living room where the candles were lit and settled back on the couch to watch television. We snuggled together and were feeling very relaxed. It was getting late and we moved to the bedroom. As Cassie sat on the edge of our bed I got close to her and we held hands. I looked in her eyes and told her, "I love you". With a smile she said, "I love you". Dropping to one knee, "will you marry me", I asked? "Yes", she replied. Now I felt everything was complete. Finally I was going to have a wife and a child. The family life I told her about having in the beginning of our relationship was going to become a reality. I was hoping to have more children but with Cassie being nine years older than me, her childbearing days were about over. I was content with what we had. Amanda was our little angel, the baby I wanted to have with the woman I love.

Three days after I proposed to Cassie, she came to me and asked if I'd write Brad a check for $25 so he could go shoot in a pool tournament at the Cablanka. I had to say no because the funds in our account were already low. Brad became angry and had words with Cassie. He was living here, didn't have a job, never contributed to any of the household expenses, he boldly asks for money and then gets mad when I refuse to give him any. After he left Cassie came to me and vented her anger. Raising her voice she accused me of being selfish, self-centered and jealous of Brad. Not returning her argument, I picked up Amanda and went to the living room to get away. Marriage was never discussed between us again.

The next day I called the bank to look into our account. It was over drawn and I had two bounced checks. If I wrote Brad a check like she asked me to, that would've made three. I got a list of all the withdrawals and went to see what Cassie had recorded in the checkbook. The bank said that $200 was taken out the Automatic Teller Machine and our records revealed that it was only $20. I confronted her about this and she denied it. This explained why I had non-sufficient funds. When we opened this account two ATM cards were mailed. She said we only received one and held on to it for emergencies. I had to wonder. If she didn't take the money out, then who did? Could Brad have the other card that was supposed to be mine? There was no way I could find out. After this incident I could not trust her financially. I had to close our account. A week later she and her son opened an account. Brad was working and provided the money they needed. The resentment from this event lingered on for a long time.

Our relationship ventured on to shaky ground. Not much was said between us and I asked if she wanted to attend marriage counseling. I was hoping to restore what we had. She refused because it was at my church where we'd have this meeting. She had a problem with ministries and would openly mock and criticize, calling them hypocrites. Making accusations of how they misused innocent people's money. She hated the Catholic Church. When I talked about giving money to any of the Christian organizations I belonged to, Cassie would quickly object.

One day while working I got a call from Cassie at the hospital. She had to bring Amanda there. She was busy doing something and our little girl skated along the kitchen floor in her walker and fell down the steps that led to the living room. Our little girl Crashed into the bookcase and suffered a cut on her forehead. Brad was leaving in her car to go by a friend's house when she waved him down so he could drive them to the emergency room. The doctor put a bandage on the laceration and gave us instructions on taking care of her wound. He then sent us home. Amanda was getting bigger and it was easier for her to get away. This incident caused both of us to realize that we'd have to start keeping a closer eye on her.

We had been living in the new house about 7 months when Cassie started to reveal some debts she had. I never knew anything about this and she needed money. I helped pay these bills to keep the collectors off her back. My cousin had a cleaning business and she went to work there with Tabby. Two weeks into her new job I received a page on my beeper from Brad. Cassie had been in a car accident on her way to work and was at the hospital. I rushed over there to find them releasing her. They said that because she was juggled around a bit, she'd be sore with aches and pain for a few days. The injuries progressively got worse and never went away. She went to an attorney who sent her to a specialist. Cassie had two ruptured discs in her back and a mild concussion. After several appointments with the neurologists she was told that major back surgery would be necessary if she was to live a normal life again. Now she had a lawsuit and would make future plans to sue the insurance companies. The attorney she hired promised her several thousand dollars from this suit. This was good news financially to Cassie but it didn't ease the pain she was experiencing.

While getting ready for work one morning I was in the kitchen and could hear something coming from Brad's room. He had a private entrance located in the front of the house. It was lots of moaning and the sound of furniture knocking. He had a girlfriend in there and the noise of their copulation would echo through out the house. Our little girl lives here and her son's bringing strange women home from the lounge. I wasn't comfortable with this. In the evening I told Cassie about it and she defended Brad saying this is his house too. Refusing to argue with her, I asked that she have a talk with him. Later I found out why she stood in his defense. He was giving her the money she needed to help pay off her credit card bills.

Cassie had a visit from her sister Micki and Wendy came with her. They drove from Ohio to see Amanda and the city. Her niece brought a different friend this time and they would go out with Brad almost every night. We all had a good time and they really loved our little girl. Micki was much bigger than Wendy was so I offered to wash their clothes. Nearing the end of the year, the weather cooled down a bit. It was pleasant to go tour the city of New Orleans. When I was working, Cassie would take them out and spend the day wherever they wanted to go. Micki acted like she was on a shopping spree and her wealth had no limit. When their stay ended, Cassie had a tearful good-bye. She hadn't seen this sister in many years and it hurt to see her leave. Micki assured her that she'd be back one day for another visit.

As Thanksgiving approached, Tabby told us she was getting married and we got a verbal invitation to their wedding. This was nice and I was happy for my sister. When it was time to attend the ceremony Cassie refused to go because we didn't get a formal invitation mailed to us. That wasn't a good enough reason for me so Amanda and I went. When Tabby saw us there without Cassie she became worried. I assured her that everything was good and there was nothing to be concerned about. It had been a long time since I saw my sister this happy.

It was the end of the year now and we were planning for Christmas. A small recliner chair was one of my gifts to Amanda. I brought it home and she would enjoy sitting in it. It was hard for her to make it recline. She didn't like her playpen anymore. Cassie had to put her in it when she was busy or cleaning house. The toys and stuffed animals for our little girl began to accumulate rapidly. She always had something to play with and we enjoyed teaching her all we could. We had a fun time for Amanda's first Christmas. Our little girl was very smart.

Working plenty of over time, money started to add up. Finally being able to save a little became a relief. In the event something happened to Amanda again, I'd have the money to handle the emergency. We both began to notice how much curiosity our tot had developed for her surroundings. If you didn't keep an eye on her, she'd get away. When I'd leave for work it became a habit of reminding Cassie to keep a close watch so she doesn't get hurt.

Amanda had her first birthday and was introduced to cake and ice cream. She managed to eat some of it and played in the rest. Not having a nap made her tired and she fell asleep. This gave me a chance to take snap shots of the annual event we'd always remember. The months passed by quickly and I always had to work. I didn't like being away from home all the time.

We became well adjusted to how peaceful it was to live in this house. Our place was far from the road so there wasn't too much noise with the cars passing by. Amanda had lots of fun in the yard and she never wandered off. I enjoyed taking her around the yard and showing her plants, bugs or something for us to look at. I'd explain whatever it was we'd find. It was that time of the year when it'd rain almost everyday. She was fascinated by the deluge but was afraid of the lightning and thunder. A flash of the light followed by thunder would frighten her. I'd pick her up and console her saying, "I gotcha, it's okay, Poppa's got ya". After this we wouldn't stay outside any longer. We'd go inside and play some game or watch television. She'd liked to sit in her little recliner while I sat close by on the couch.

An agency hired me to work at More Speed Space Agency (MSSA) near New Orleans. The job was nice except for the favoritism. If you had a father, mother, uncle, aunt or some kind of relative working here, your job was secure. The temperature-controlled environment here was a relief. There was no more working in the hot sun. They were very stringent on promptness, tardiness and attendance. If you were late or absent too many times, you were dismissed. Their procedures and techniques were different from what

I was used to. It took me a little while to adjust. The pay was good and I started to save more money. They had good instructors here. If you did what you were told and didn't complain, everything went along smooth. The length of time I was away from Amanda and Cassie began to bother me. Working 84 hours a week was too much. I started to dislike the job.

During dinner one evening Cassie told me she got a call from her sister. Her mother was terminally ill and this news was very upsetting. I knew that they were close to each other and how badly she missed her mother. It had been a long time since she made a trip to Ohio and was able to see her folks. It was important for her to go see them now and I suggested that she make reservations. She readily agreed and took Amanda to go stay for a week. It was the best thing she could've done and it eased her grief. We kept in touch by phone until she returned.

About a month had passed after Cassie returned and she came to me with another problem that was troubling her. A new collector sent her a letter demanding she pay the money owed or face severe consequences. This really had her scared. I took the money out my savings and paid off the account. She was very thankful and relieved, promising to repay me when she got her settlement. I trusted her verbal commitment and nothing more was said about it.

My vehicle seemed to be falling apart. Always fixing it became a weekly chore. I bought this car long ago and now it was having major mechanical breakdowns. It was nice but the parts for it were expensive. Repair bills for it were beginning to accumulate. Cassie didn't hesitate to complain about all the money that was spent to fix it and suggested I buy a new car. She failed to realize that this car was my ride to and from work.

Another financial crisis came crashing down on Cassie. This time it was some bank that called and said the amount she owed exceeded its limit too excessively. They were demanding collection. The bank warned that if she didn't comply, she'd face incarceration. This problem had her trembling and that worried me because I had never seen her this way. I wrote a check and paid off a large portion of the debt. Adding up what I spent on her bills took most all of my savings away. Once again she promised to repay me when she received her settlement. I relied on her verbal commitment to be enough. To ask for something in writing might give her the feeling like I didn't trust her and that would cause unnecessary problems between us.

Chapter Four

HER DOMAIN

When Cassie's attorney gave some figures from her lawsuit, the hunt for a new place began. I was never informed of this. One evening I came home from work and she greeted me on the carport. As she came closer her smile got bigger. "I got a partial settlement and bought a house I've been looking at, we can move in this week", she said. "Just like that", I asked? "Yeah, I'm moving, you can either come with us or stay here with Brad", she said. "You know I'm not gonna to stay here, I'm going with you and Amanda", I told her. There was a house she saw in Perrytown and liked it very much. She gave me the address on Bloomington Street and the next day I went to see the new place. It was nice but needed some work. I saw good potential here and always liked a challenge. The yard was a mess with lava rocks but it could be worked with. The neighbor Pam recognized me instantly. When I was a teenager, I dated her sister, Myra. It had been years since we saw each other. She told me a little about the house and afterwards I left. Upon returning home I found Cassie to have almost everything packed up and ready to move. She stopped to say the landlord was informed that Brad was going to stay there and they wanted to talk to him and me. It was my guess that ground rules were going to be set.

When Brad got home, he and I walked up to see the landlord. This couple was much older, like grand parents. The house we had been living in was about 40 feet behind theirs. They were close enough to know when anyone came by our place. We had come to an agreement. Because Brad was living there with us and they knew him, a new lease wasn't necessary. There was to be no loud music or parties and no excessive amount of cars in the driveway. He had to pay the rent on time, keep the grass cut and everything clean. Brad assured them he would do all this. He agreed to the terms they made and didn't have to sign anything. He sounded very sincere about his commitments. Everything was understood and we left. Brad had to take off because there was somewhere he needed to go. Cassie told me how happy he was to have his own place and she promised me that he'd handle all his responsibilities.

Using a truck Brad borrowed from his friend, he and I began moving to the new house. Cassie gave most all her furniture to him because he didn't have any. It seemed as though he was in a hurry to get our stuff out of the old place. He forced my double door refrigerator out the front door damaging it with scratches. I bought this appliance used and rebuilt it when we moved here. Until now it worked and looked like new. After he did this it became obvious that he had no respect for things that belonged to other people. Because of the way he was handling our belongings I wouldn't have asked for his help had we not needed it.

In two days we were all moved in. The rent here cost quite a bit more. This didn't bother me because one day it would be ours. This was the happiest I had ever seen Cassie. There was an elementary school that was nearby where Amanda could attend when she was old enough. We discussed what needed to be done and would collaborate on future renovations. I looked for things that needed to be fixed or improved and I'd tell her of my plans before starting.

New furniture arrived and Cassie arranged it to her liking. I looked at everything and complimented her on the selection. It looked nice but I was concerned with the steel-framed coffee table. Amanda wasn't too stable when she walked. She was still a bit wobbly and I was afraid if she fell on it, we'd have to get her stitched up. Cassie assured me this wouldn't happen, that she always keeps a close eye on her. I went to sit on the couch. "No, don't sit on it, I got it for looks, not to sit on", she said. This was the craziest thing I ever heard. I got up and took Amanda to her room to play. She was getting sleepy so I put her in the baby bed. I took a shower and decided to turn in myself while Cassie stayed up and watched television.

Complaints were coming from Brad at the old place where he was living. The rent had gone up considerably after we left and he couldn't afford the new amount. Since the checking account was in their name, he and Cassie cancelled the payment they issued for that month's rent. Wanting to help her son, she found an apartment and co-signed the lease for him. He and his girlfriend packed up their things in a hurry. Immediately they moved in.

It was time for my birthday and I turned 35. We had a barbecue and spent most of the day playing with Amanda in the backyard. There were two nice trees that shaded the yard and the back of the house. I'd chase her around them. It was fun to hear her giggle. We played hide and seek or anything I could think of. Flowers growing in the yard put a fresh springtime scent in the air. Amanda was talking good and would sometimes call me Poppa. I liked to hear her call me by that name. Instead of buying gifts for me, Cassie got more toys for

Amanda. This was a good idea she had and it made our little angel sparkle with excitement.

When the house was built they used galvanized pipe for the water lines and I discovered a severe corrosion problem. After noticing the inside of the pipe was filled with rust I had to install some kind of filtration system to prevent us from drinking these contaminants. I used an external device that attached to the spout. The filter was enclosed in a transparent case and the water could be seen passing through it. The built-in indicator was white when it was new. When it turned brown, that let us know the filter was full of rust and had to be changed. Clean water is a necessity. It's important to be health conscience, especially when you have a little one running around. The hot tea that Cassie liked to drink also tasted better.

In front the house those lava rocks lining the drive and walkway had to go. A flood had taken some away but there was still plenty left. I pulled them all up and put some sod in its place. Putting the extra mud and left over sod in other low-lying areas also became part of this task. I bought a self-propelled lawn mower and other gardening tools to trim and cut with. When the grass began to grow, the house took on a more pleasant appearance. After this job was complete, a month later you couldn't tell the previous condition of our front yard.

The privacy fence in the back was rotten and needed to be replaced. Both sides were bad so I picked the worse and started on it. The lumber company delivered the materials and set them in the front yard. Brad came over for a visit. He sat inside and watched me bring all the planks to the backyard. I wished he would've helped me but he didn't. After the fence was finished I sprayed sealant on the wood so it'd last longer and not get water damaged by the rain. When I could take off from work again and be able to afford it, I'd replace the other side.

There were several things wrong with the waterworks inside the house. There were leaks below the sink. The spouts were old, dripping and needed to be changed. I put in all new faucets and installed flex hose to replace the metal tubing that was underneath. The drain lines were repaired. These revisions were a good improvement. All the leaks and drips had stopped. The new chrome fixtures really enhanced the bathrooms and kitchen.

Between my job and doing all these different projects around the house, I still remained restless. The thrill of having our new home created an energy that always had me looking for something to do. Cassie told me of all these additions that she wanted to have done. I was only able to fix or replace the things my finances would allow me to, not buy a Gazebo.

A good while after moving in we discovered freon; the coolant was leaking out of the air conditioner. It was an old unit that needed to be replaced. I dipped into my savings and hired a company to come out and install one for us. They also re-insulated the attic. A new system, furnace and insulating the attic cost me a small fortune. This knocked a huge dent in my savings. When Cassie saw the bill she insisted on paying me back when she got the rest of her settlement. “It’s my house and I’ll pay you back”, she said. Later I found out she was right. My name wasn’t on any of the paperwork and it really was her house. It felt like she was my landlord instead of my girlfriend, my lover, or my wife to be and this made me feel out of place. From now on I became hesitant to put out money on a house that I’d never own.

Cassie had some habits that seemed a bit extreme to me. Two cartons of cigarettes, a case of diet cola and a 100 count box of tea bags had to be purchased every week. She drank hot tea and diet cola throughout the day. Her daily smoking habit had grown to three packs. I installed three fire alarms because she loved to burn candles and never did extinguish them at night. She’d let them burn out. This made me nervous so I relied on the alarms to protect us. “I’m a grown woman”, she told me. It did no good to explain how dangerous her action was.

Independence Day arrived and our new neighbors put on a spectacular display. This was our chance to get acquainted because the housework kept me busy all the time. I knew Pam since my teen years but didn’t get to meet her husband Nat. He was having fun lighting all the fireworks for their kids and making sure the other activities were supervised. We watched the little ones enjoy themselves and talked for a while. Nat and Pam had a daughter Diana. She was seventeen days younger than Amanda was. It was good for our little girl to have a friend living close by to play with. In the weeks to come the girls would play in our backyard or theirs. Pam expressed her gratitude to me for fixing the fence and gave compliments on it.

Going back inside I found Amanda to be frightened. She didn't like the noises fireworks were making outside. I could see that she was sensitive to loud noises. Comforting her, we went to her room and played with her toys. After having her bath she became sleepy. While lying on Cassie's lap she fell asleep. It was getting late and the party outside had quieted down. As we sat gazing at our baby girl sleep Cassie says, "as long as I have her, you won't be far behind". "What, why did you say that", I asked? "It's true, as long as I have her, you won't be far behind", she said. Her profound statement would stay with me always. She knew how much I loved our little girl. Amanda was the gift from God I always dreamed of having and I'll do whatever it takes to be with her. A few days earlier, "no matter what happens between us, I'll never keep you from seeing your daughter", Cassie told me. That comment and the one she just made had the wheels in my head spinning. I took Amanda with me and we went to bed.

Visiting our former landlord, I wanted to see how they were and if Brad caused them any trouble. They told me of all the parties he had. Some nights there were up to nine cars parked in the driveway and she had the plate numbers. He didn't cut the grass or keep the place clean. I couldn't blame her for serving him with eviction notices. Brad didn't fulfill his obligations.

During a trip to the super market I saw Jazzy, a friend from high school. We talked for a little bit. She told me of her marriage to another friend of mine whom I haven't seen in years. Her family of two boys and two girls always kept her busy with a full schedule. It was good to see her. She asked me to follow her home so I'd know where they lived. Upon arriving she was greeted by four young kids who were happy to see their mother. Her husband Kyle became a welder and attended the same schools I did when we were younger. I knew that someday I'd see him on a job and have to x-ray some of his welds. It was a nice visit and I looked forward to returning with Amanda so she could play with Jazzy's two daughters.

My car broke down for the last time. I never wanted to own another one like it or anything made by Misusedbitsy. After finding out the dealership across the river took advantage of me by excessive overcharges, no more money was going to be spent on it. The mechanic there and the man who assigns the jobs had taken me for several thousand dollars in unnecessary repairs. Not having any credit always prevented me from buying a new car. Taking a chance, I decided to go apply at the car lots by where we lived. The first car I bought was made in Japan. After driving it off the lot, I found some mechanical problems. It had too many miles for the price they were asking and the car was missing parts inside. The next day I took the car back. The manager tried to convince me that I had to keep it. I left him the keys and walked over to the next car lot. After I was here a while, a sales person came out and spoke to me about the car I was looking at. He was very informative. It was a blue 4-door sedan that had the options I wanted. This was a nice vehicle and appeared to have aerodynamic features. I was impressed with the consumer reports, the warranty and the way they ran this dealership. I was glad to know that this product was built in America. After getting the Neptune Essel II, my quest to find a good car was over. After the purchase they took a picture of me standing next to it. For the first time in my life, I had a new automobile that was mine to drive.

All the projects here at home began to slow down. On the weekends when I wasn't at work we'd have barbecues. Cassie's sons and their friends would come over to eat. They'd bring lots of beer and stock our refrigerator. They all knew I was a recovering alcoholic but that didn't stop them from having their fun. After a few beers I could see a big change in the way they were acting. I found their partying to be inconsiderate towards me. To avoid anyone getting upset, I didn't say anything. They were having a good time and I didn't want to spoil it. Many of my friends didn't drink so I wasn't going to invite them. I mostly stayed in the backyard watching the kids and tending to the food on the grill. When everyone left, the alcohol did too.

Working at MSSA was about the same. Although production had slowed down, we still had to be there. Rumors of lay-offs began to circulate and our department became nervous. This job wasn't that good anymore. It paid well but I didn't like being away from home all the time. Amanda was growing up fast and I was always gone. Some days when I'd get home Cassie would tell me of something new that she did and I missed it because I wasn't there.

Coming home from work one day Cassie presented a letter sent to me by the courthouse. It was from the Justice of the Peace requesting that I attend an upcoming hearing. Making a few phone calls I found out that our former landlord filed papers. They were suing me for damages and non-payment of rent. Because my name was on the lease, I was responsible. This was going to be settled by the court. I became upset with this news and confronted Cassie. I'll never forget how she laughed about it saying, "you can't win for trying". I began to ponder her feelings for me. She and her son cancelled the rent check, he damages the house, and I have to pay for it. I knew this would deplete my savings and it wasn't funny anymore. I couldn't believe this was happening. I went to court with nothing but my checkbook. Mr. Boudreaux told me he was sorry for this as he sat with his wife and their son. When we went before the judge they presented evidence, including pictures that I never knew they had. All I could do was to plead my case. They were asking $1700 for Brad's negligence. After trying to prove that I wasn't responsible for this, it dropped to $1160. The judge ruled in their favor and I had to pay. Every month I'd have to make a payment. When I told Cassie about this, "he's my son, I'll pay you back when I get my settlement", she told me. I felt cheated.

Money became real tight and I had to watch every penny that was spent. This seemed like a big joke to everyone else. Beginning to look for side jobs at companies that needed part time help didn't work out too well. At MSSA they didn't tolerate moonlighting. I was thankful to have an inexpensive and low maintenance car that didn't break down anymore. As time went on I hoped that my finances would began to level off and build back up.

Halloween arrived and Cassie wanted Amanda to go trick-a-treating. She bought her a Raggedy Ann costume. Although it was a bit too big, our little one was excited at all the colors it had. We both agreed that it'd be too much walking for her so we had candy at home and pretended like we were outside. I thought about a time in the future when I'd have to explain to my daughter about how people celebrated this event by dressing up as ghosts, witches or blood sucking vampires. Would she understand the blood and gore that sometimes becomes a part of this holiday? One day she may have questions to which I'll have to provide answers.

As Thanksgiving approached, Cassie saw an advertisement for a big battery operated toy jeep that she wanted for Amanda. I didn't feel our little girl was old enough for this and gave my opinion. As always when I disagree with her, she'll give me the silent treatment that can last for days until I give in. When there's no communication it's like living with a mute and the affection, if there is any, flies out the window. Going to the department store, I looked to see if they had one of these little toys. My brother-in law assembles them for a living and when he was through, I brought it home. I didn't say anything and put it in the backyard. Amanda came outside to play. She laughed and giggled as I put her in. She couldn't figure out how to operate it. Turning the steering wheel and pushing the gas pedal was too hard for her. It soon began to scare her and we had to stop. Knowing this wasn't going to work, I couldn't convince Cassie to change her mind. This was an expensive toy. We should've waited until Amanda was bigger. At this time she was 21 months old and still a baby.

My family would invite us over for holiday celebrations. I'd go and take Amanda with me. My nieces and nephew were delighted to see their cousin. Cassie would never attend any of these gatherings. I couldn't provide answers as to why she wouldn't come with me. I told them that she wasn't feeling well and had trouble with her back. Personally I didn't know why she preferred to stay at home. Maybe she didn't like my relatives and kept quiet about it so my feelings wouldn't get hurt. When I asked her about this she'd say, "I just didn't want to go". After we had been together a long while Cassie seemed like she didn't appreciate it when I'd visit Tabby, Mick, Mary or any other member of my family. I felt this wasn't too nice of her.

The decorations were all put up and Christmas was upon us. As always with this holiday, Cassie had to have a nice big tree, flocked, looking like it was covered in snow. She does all this herself. We decided not to get gifts for each other. It was more important to get gifts for our little girl and her sons. It bothered me that she'd use my money to buy these extravagant gifts for her grown up sons. Anytime I bought a gift for Cassie she'd return it to get the cash. This kind of hurt my feelings. This time I gave her plenty of cash and let her go do what she wanted. I figured this way she wouldn't have to go to the department store to get a refund for what I bought her.

What a joyful occasion it was to see Amanda celebrate her second Christmas. She had toys to help her talk and books to look at. There were stuffed animals, baby dolls to play with and a stocking full of candy that filled her with curiosity and excitement. She had fun opening all her presents and liked playing in the wrapping paper. Her room was stocked with plenty of toys now. She'd take my hand and ask me to join her by saying, "come on Daddy, let's go play"?

Amanda's room became cluttered with toys. There had to be a way I could make room for these items. Looking in her closet I came up with the idea of lowering her shelves to a height of 36 inches. This way she could reach anything she wanted in her closet. Everything could be seen because they were at her eye level. My hope was that she'd develop some independence by being able to get things herself. It also helped to keep her room straight and in order.

Some workers at MSSA would tamper with my job and I got even in a costly way. With the work slowing down, I was the first to go. This job had turned sour anyway. They had too much favoritism. During my employment here Dom came onboard earlier in the year. He was having some problems with his ex-wife and she had him over a barrel. When I told him what my relationship with Cassie was like he warned me to be careful and try to keep a record of everything. I was already keeping an eye on things, holding on to receipts and documenting certain occasions.

A new year had started and the oil field was booming. Most all the inspection companies were hiring and the choice was mine to choose which one I wanted to work for. I went back to work over at XIH. They had plenty of jobs. The only hang up with this company was that most of the assignments were either out of town or in the Gulf of Mexico. Taking whatever they had, I stayed busy. Not being home too often added more friction in my relationship with Cassie. As long as I was able to provide money for anything we needed, not much was said.

We had a communication problem with not speaking to each other about what was on our minds. When it looked like something was bothering Cassie I'd ask her if everything was ok? "Everything's fine, couldn't be better", she'd reply. The sarcasm was noticed but never questioned. We never had any arguments and to ask about what was troubling her was like being too inquisitive. All relationships should hold on to the friendship or you'll have nothing to build on. The separate directions we took made it difficult to tell if we were still friends.

Since I returned home from Oregon, attending AA meetings became part of my program to stay sober. It was quite a change from what I was accustomed to in Portland. There wasn't much unity until you got to know the people who attended. The gathering usually lasts a little over an hour. Afterwards we'd hang around and fellowship with one another. This was always a method of support and I got to know many people. We'd exchange phone numbers and if times got rough, help was only a phone call away. It was better to call someone than to drink over a temporary problem. When I'd come home from a meeting Cassie would ask why I was so late. She didn't like it when I remained at the club to socialize with my friends. This gave me the feeling of not being trusted so I stopped going to the meetings.

It was Mardi Gras and the city was in a frenzy anticipating this annual holiday. Parades would pass a block away from the house and Amanda could hear the noise from all the people who were celebrating. Cassie was having severe problems with her injuries from that car accident. We didn't participate in the parades by her place but did go to the one that passed by Brad's house on Fat Tuesday. It was Cassie's 45th birthday. After a few drinks and some medicine, you couldn't tell she was hurting. The doctor had prescribed some pain pills and they assisted in giving her some relief. I kept a close eye on Amanda and never let her out of arms reach. The crowd was enormous and she could easily get lost if I didn't watch her. At the end of the day Cassie had a little too much of everything and we had to leave. Amanda was also exhausted from all the excitement and fell asleep before we got home.

After our little one was in bed, Cassie and I got to spend some time alone. Looking back on the previous months, it was as though we had no sexual relationship between us. With Cassie being very loose at the ends, all that changed. Our lost desire for each other was rekindled in the act that was long overdue. We had not loved each other like this for a very long time. It brought us closer together and for a while we were able to open up to each other more often. Sex was a big part of our relationship. After we had it, everything seemed copesetic. This is what it took for us to get along as friends. The sad part was there wasn't enough of it.

After a bad thunderstorm one day Cassie heard a loud pop and went out in the backyard to look at the trees. She discovered the trunk of one had a split going up the back and the other was full of mud. We called to have an arbor specialist come out. He looked at both trees and told us that they needed to be cut down. He warned us if they fell on the house that we'd have unaffordable repairs. The prices to remove the trees were very high. It was cheaper for me to do it myself. I bought a chainsaw with a 14-inch blade for $99. Cassie's sons would leave when it was time for the work to be done. I asked Nat to help me with one of the trees. My other neighbor, Charles helped with the tree on his side of our yard. I paid to have most all of the brush hauled away and the rest went out for the trash. Amanda had fun climbing up on the stumps that were left. It was like having another toy for her to play with.

It was time for Cassie to have the first of her two major back surgeries. I was at work and made arrangements to take time off. She wanted Barbara to be at the hospital with her. Brad's girlfriend Tina was taking care of Amanda. The next day she was operated on and I called to see if she was up to a visit. "I miss my little angel, bring her to see me", she asked? When I expressed my concern that this might scare Amanda, she assured me that it'd be okay. We arrived at the hospital and went to her room. With all the tubes and monitors, our little girl was frightened because she didn't understand. She wanted to be close and climbed in bed to hug her mommy. Cassie was in a lot of pain after this surgery so we didn't stay long.

Cassie didn't like hospitals and couldn't wait to get home. I encouraged her to take it easy. The doctors gave her pain pills, sleeping pills and nerve pills to help with her healing. When she'd combine these medicines, pain was one thing she didn't have. While recovering from the surgery, she decided to remodel the inside of her house. Amanda and I would go to bed and Cassie would stay up working on the kitchen and the living room. We'd wake up in the morning and the wallpaper was removed from the kitchen. She had the walls ready to be painted. When I'd return home from work there'd be a new addition. She had a skill for fixing up the interior of a house but never wanted any help. All I ended up doing was getting in the way. It was amazing how she was able to do so much in her condition. It had to be all that medication from those doctors that enabled her make all these revisions. The kitchen and the living room were transformed into show rooms. This increased the value of her house.

Cassie's older brother Wendell came down from Ohio to help take care of Amanda. We didn't really need him and the truth was he needed a place to stay. He worked with plaster and did finishing work on houses. This was a good paying craft and jobs here was easy to find. He never met our little girl and now was his time to get acquainted. He was a serious drinker and brought this habit with him.

Our refrigerator was always stocked with large cans of beer and when he wasn't working, he'd sit at the table and drink most of the day. I rarely saw him eat anything. "Does his drinking bother you", Cassie asked? To prevent a disruption in her home, "no", I replied. Part of my recovery program is to stay away from alcoholics and now we had one living in the house. Why would her brother's alcoholism cause a problem for me?

Chapter Five

A SUDDEN RELAPSE

April showers arrived but this didn't deter Amanda from playing in the backyard. She loved the rain. Cassie and I decided that she needed a swing set. I found one on sale and the store delivered it. Brad and a friend of his came over and I asked for their help. They put their beer in the refrigerator and came out back. A funny thought occurred to me. I'd been sober all this time and figured it'd be okay if I had a beer. Just one wouldn't hurt me. While drinking my second one, Mary arrived and walked out in the backyard. "What are you doing drinking", she asked? Our conversation got rough and I urged her to leave. Brad and his friend also left quickly. I got Amanda to come out and play on her new toy. She would laugh as I pushed her on the swing. "Hold on", I'd tell her. When we went inside I could see Cassie was upset. She admitted to calling my sister. "Everyone else can drink but I can't", I asked? "No, you can't, you're an alcoholic", she responded. If I didn't want to slip and start drinking again I'd have to stay away from slippery places, such as lounges, is what I was taught. Cassie's house was not a lounge but she allowed Wendell and others to bring alcohol there. Without realizing it, her house had become a slippery place for me. My six years of sobriety was gone.

The house was being prepared for some renovations Cassie wanted. She was doing all the work herself. It was too hard for her to do this and watch Amanda. She suggested that our little girl go to a daycare. After I wrote the first voucher for Fantasyland Daycare, Cassie said that I could leave them blank from now on because they had a rubber stamp to address the check with. At the end of the month, the teacher informed me that my daughter hadn't been attending. When I confronted Cassie about this "Amanda don't want to go sometimes so I let her stay home", she told me. When my checks came back from the bank, I saw that Cassie was signing them and depositing this tuition money in the account she had with her son Brad. Our youngster wasn't going to the daycare and her mother had not been telling the truth.

As time went on, the work Cassie did inside her house began to look real nice. I couldn't understand how she was able to do all this after having major back surgery. It soon became evident of her method to gain the ability. She'd get a 30-day supply of her pain medicine at the first of each month. After taking a bunch of these pills she'd be pain free enough to do most anything. In about 10 days, all her medicine would be gone. I could see an addiction problem starting to develop and knowing this became an uncomfortable situation. I'd wake up to get ready for work and she'd still be working on her project. Shortly after I left she'd have to go to bed and get the rest she needed after being up all night. When Amanda woke up, Cassie stayed in bed. No one was there to watch our little girl. She remedied this problem by having a house alarm installed. If Amanda tried to get out, the alarm would sound and that'd wake her up. I did not like this idea at all. Amanda could still get hurt wandering around the house playing or messing with something she shouldn't be, like poisons. It was useless trying to convince Cassie how dangerous this was. She had to finish her house.

Summer was approaching and a storm dumped a large amount of rain on us. The backyard overflowed and water almost got in the house. Cassie was worried about this. If we had some kind of drainage system installed, this part of the yard wouldn't flood anymore. After the rain stopped I looked outside to see what could be done. The solution I came up with was to place a drainage line on the north side of the house. All the water would drain out to the front yard and onto the street. It took two weeks to dig the trench and put 70 feet of 3"pipe down below the ground. When I was finished, the backyard never flooded again. Cassie had lost the fear about getting water in her house from all the torrential rains that come this time of year.

Donny landed another good paying job as an electrician. The training he got in the military was starting to pay off. His girlfriend and Cassie were starting to be friendlier with each other. This helped remove the uneasiness between all of them and that made everyone happier. His work took him to Brownsville Texas and this project kept him there for a while. He became homesick and would call in the evening to talk with Sue and his mom. The phone bill became a topic of discussion between Cassie and me. I didn't agree with her 27-year-old son calling home most every night when it was at my expense. The phone calls stopped briefly and ended altogether with one last call. Donny called to say he used up all his per diem money and had no place to stay. Cassie came to me asking for money to send him. She was prepared to sell off the large collection of stuffed animals called Beanie Babies we were saving for Amanda. After this she would go wire the money down to Brownsville. I couldn't believe she'd give up these toys, some of which I paid for, to send money to Donny. Amanda loved these stuffed animals. I'd rather put up the money than to see our little girl be unhappy because she lost her toys. Off to the bank and over to Western Union I went. Donny got the $300 he needed the next day. Two nights later he called to say he couldn't get a bus ticket to come home on. The next morning his girlfriend left for Brownsville to pick him up. Cassie promised to repay me the money I sent when she got her settlement and we never discussed this incident again. It seemed to me that Donny either wasted or drank away all the money I sent him a couple days earlier. Here was another situation I didn't want to question.

It was summertime and as always, the weather was making my job miserable. Hot, humid and we don't have the privilege to work in the shade. In x-ray they just want you to get the job done and don't like to hear any complaints. At XIH there were plenty of new faces and lots of hours. The time added up quickly and I befriended a guy there named Marco. He really had an interest for inspection and I often didn't have to tell him what to do. This was an advantage to me because when we'd arrive on a job, he already knew what had to be done. He was a good learner and I taught him plenty. This allowed us to work at a fast efficient pace so we could finish quicker. Most of the time we didn't stop for lunch and worked from morning until evening. Marco became my best friend. I asked the boss to keep him working with me. By operating this way we were able to handle two or three jobs a day. I was making good money but getting burnt out in the process. The daytime was too hot and the heat drained me of all my energy. In the evenings, I was exhausted and worn out. I would hurry to get home before dark so Amanda would still be awake or in case Cassie needed something.

Donny and Sue split up and he sent her back to Nevada. It wasn't known until after she was gone that he had been talking to his ex wife Candy. They were planning to get back together again. Cassie was extremely happy with this. She'd always liked Candy and paid most of the expenses when they first got married. I didn't think their relationship was going to last. Donny would drink too much and come over to Cassie's house to discuss the distrust he had for Candy from events of the past. He'd lie on the couch I wasn't allowed to sit on, sleep off the alcohol and in the morning go back to her. This was confusing to me.

A pipeline came up and my boss put me on it. Marco went to work with another technician and I had to train a new helper. While on this job, the crane operator told me of all the work that was in Alaska. He said the pay rates were real good and they needed x-ray technicians. I made a phone call to APG. (Alaskan Pipeline Group) Finding out that I could make my annual salary in 6 months, this job became very tempting. The inspection companies there paid over twice the amount I was making here. I told Cassie about it. "If I worked half a year and had the rest off, that'd give me more time to be at home with you and help raise Amanda", I said. She didn't like me taking all this time off and believed that I'd lose money. "I like it better when you're away here locally, at least I know where you're working", she responded. Her comment took me by surprise. Not much was said about the work up north after this.

Donny's former mate received a loan for the house she had been looking at. They were going to get married again. I never knew if they were divorced or not. Cassie was upset at Candy's mother because she refused to attend the wedding. I never knew the reason for this and didn't ask. They all went before the same judge that performed the first ceremony. Later was the reception, celebrated the same way most everything is down here with plenty of food and lots of alcohol. It was their night to remember. I was thankful that Cassie didn't drink because she had taken Amanda with her. Afterwards the two lovebirds settled in their cozy little nest and everyone was happy. The newly weds didn't come around much after this.

As mid summer approached work began to slow down. That was unusual for this part of the country. With all the chemical plants and the gulf nearby, work is almost year round. I tried to discuss the job in Alaska with Cassie again. If I were to take this job, now would be the best time of the year because I wouldn't have to worry about the snow. This could be a trial run with this new company that would only last a month. If things didn't work out or I ran into problems, I'd terminate my employment with them. When I told her about the money I could make, she reconsidered. When I'm at work here, I always have my pager with me. If she needs to get in touch with me, I'm a phone call away. It wouldn't be like that in Alaska. If an emergency occurred, it'd take a while for me to get home. Arrangements were made with the airlines to change my flight schedule in the event something happened or there was a crisis. We decided to give this a try and my departure date was set for July 4th.

Off to Alaska I went. APG had a company representative meet me at the airport. It was late in the evening so they put me in a motel. The next day I'd take the written tests to qualify for the position. The examinations will assure the company of my qualifications to do the job I'm applying for. They told me that I'd be sent to the slope, in the northernmost parts of Alaska. Here is where most all their work was. I ended up staying in Anchorage for a long time and paying my own motel expenses. I complained because this began to drain my bank account.

In a survival class we took, I met this guy who was house sitting for the district attorney. He watched the place while the owner was on vacation. He offered to help me out by letting me stay there. Accepting his offer, I didn't have to pay anymore motel expenses. My venture here was beginning to take a turn for the worse. There was no work in Anchorage so they moved me south to a town called Kenai. I stayed here until a position became available. Finally I went to work on the northern slope. It was very cold with hills of snow. The NDT methods they used for x-ray were different from what I was used to. I lived in a big fancy camp that looked like a ritzy hotel. It was nice but my stay here was short. Nine days later I returned to Anchorage.

By phone I kept in contact with Cassie. "How ya doing, how's Amanda doing, is she okay", I asked? "Oh, I'm doing fine, I have your little duplicate running around here, she told me. I began to tell her that this job wasn't working out too good and I was ready to come home. Our talks were always brief and there were many. When I'd mention about returning she'd say, "you don't have to, we're fine, everything's okay". Her remark made me suspicious.

After looking at the hours on my check I found out that this company did not do what they promised. They were not generous with the hours and took from their employees. The workers told me many stories of how this employer swindled money from them. This company was a group of thieves and mistreated the people who worked here. Instantly I became dissatisfied.

APG painted a bright picture that quickly turned fuzzy when I got here. There wasn't too much work for me on the slope like they said. Having to pay my own motel and all my food expenses told me I wasn't needed here. Doing some calculations revealed that this job cost me more money than I earned. Not long after arriving here, I had a feeling this job wasn't going to be any good. They were liars. At the end of July, I quit. Cassie's second surgery was coming up and I had planned to be home for her and Amanda. My stay in Alaska was 25 days.

During the drive from the airport Cassie informed me of how Donny and Candy moved in. The new house she bought wasn't livable and Wendell was working on it. We now had seven people living in Cassie's home. When I walked in it looked like her place had been hit by a hurricane. Donny, Candy and her son took over Amanda's room. He was in there sleeping and had no job and Candy was at work. Wendell was away working on their place and he stayed in the spare room. I came back to a house full of people and a stack of bills. One of these was a $400 phone bill for making calls from Alaska. It didn't take long to figure out why she didn't want me to come back home. Cassie never smoked in the back part of her house but allowed Donny to do so. This had the place smelling like an ashtray. My refrigerator was always stocked with beer and I didn't drink. Her house had become more slippery to me.

Donny and Candy would shower together and this occupied the bathroom for long lengths of time. It was obvious that they were doing more than cleaning themselves with the sounds they made and the towel rack almost being pulled off the wall. I didn't appreciate this behavior with our little girl running around. I told Cassie about this and they had a talk. After the chat about this incident they began to stay locked up in Amanda's room whenever I was around.

Cassie was soon in the hospital for her second back surgery. It made me feel bad that she had to get cut on again. Leaving for the hospital, she called and asked me to bring Amanda. I was against this idea because of the last experience. All that equipment frightened her the last time and she didn't like seeing her mommy like that. She insisted and I took Amanda with me. This didn't go over too well. She wanted to climb in bed with Cassie. Our little girl was upset and didn't understand what was going on. Our stay here was short. Cassie said the doctor would release her tomorrow and she would call me when it was time to come get her. The next day when I picked her up she seemed stiff from the painful operation. The doctors prescribed to her new pain medicines and she appeared to be coping well. She needed some diet coke, tea bags and cigarettes from the store. When I was about to leave and go to the market she said, "I'm okay, I'll go get it, I need to get up and move around". After much persistence I let her go. She returned later and I unloaded the car. It took a lot of pills to make her feel better. While on her medication she was fine. Excessive amounts were the only way to ease her pain. It worried me that she may never be the same. She assured me that everything was fine.

In mid August I made one phone call and was back at work. NXC (Noble X-ray Company) was looking for people and I hired on there. They had a different way of doing things and it took a while to catch on. They asked me if I knew of any helpers. Brad was working doing x-ray at XIH. Cassie found some herbs he could take to hide the marijuana in his system so he'd pass their drug screen. He wasn't happy there and I offered to train him if he'd come to work with me. He said that he couldn't pass the drug test so I provided a specimen for him. After we passed his urine analysis he started work immediately. We were soon put on a pipeline in a town about 50 miles away. Adding the per diem to our weekly check, the money added up quickly. I was able to pay off all the bills that accumulated while I was away in Alaska.

One evening I arrived home to an empty house. Cassie and Donny soon arrived with Amanda. It looked like they had been shopping. She makes a statement to me, "you always ask what Donny does with his money, go look in the driveway". I looked out the door and saw a candy apple red, 95 Dodge Stealth. "Wow, whose that belong to", I exclaimed? "It's mine", Donny said. When they left and went to the store, Candy walked in. I began to inquire how was he able to afford that new car since he wasn't working. Candy said she co-signed a loan for him. "He'll get a job or I'll get the car", she said. Sounded like she was telling the truth.

The next day Brad and Tina came over. "Did you see my new car", he asked? "No, where is it", I responded? "In the driveway", he said. I looked out the door and saw a black, 95 Firebird. "Wow, that's nice", I said. Cassie and Donny soon arrived and they took a ride in Brad's new car. When they left I asked Tina how was Brad able to get that car? "My mom co-signed a loan for him", she said. He was working with me so I knew he'd be able to pay the notes on this new car. I didn't understand why her mother would go out on a limb and risk her credit for him. The only jobs Brad can take are ones that don't require a drug test. This became real suspicious and I didn't want to ask anymore questions. I was afraid of the answers.

Cassie was pleased with the inside of her house and decided it was time to fix the outside. She hired contractors to put up some vinyl siding. This cost a lot of money. I asked her if she received a settlement from her lawsuit. "No, my sister loaned me the money, she knows I'm going to be compensated soon and can pay her back", she replied. Brad and his cousin Terry, claiming to be siding specialists would hassle the workers about the way they did this job. With all the changes they insisted the workers make it took four weeks to complete this renovation. After the job was done, the house looked new and it cost Cassie an estimated $14,000.

The other side of the fence needed to be put up and Cassie had me go get the wood to do it. She paid for everything. The lumber company delivered the wood and set it in the front yard. Donny and Terry came over and watched me bring the supplies to the backyard. As I was setting up the planks, Terry came out to help. It took some persuasion to get Donny's help but his cousin offered. Donny had been drinking too much and all he could do was tell me when the boards were aligned so I could nail them. I shouldn't have trusted him because the fence had to be torn down and redone the next day. The tops were all uneven and Cassie didn't like that. This was a mistake that I'd have to fix by myself. I should have known better than to rely on help from a drunk. It made my wonder if Donny did this on purpose.

Contacting Ned, a Christian friend who worked with me, I told him of all the things that were going on at Cassie's house. These events sounded very familiar to him. His ex wife had him in the same situation. He found out she was possessed with the "Spirit of Jezebel", a spirit of malice and seduction. The ex spouse had taken Ned for lots of money, lied and hurt him. He gave some information to read that would help me understand this spiritual curse that mainly affects women. He said if Cassie found this material that she'd throw it away and I better make two copies, so I did. Everything I read was really interesting. This spirit has the "upper hand" and the last word in most all matters. It's very dishonest and can cause the person to scheme for their advantage. Eventually the woman will grow to become a self-centered person and will consistently use other people to achieve her own wants and desires. Relationships don't work and many of them fail. When I tried to talk with Cassie about this she blew a fuse, went to the back part of the house and refused to come out until I put the stuff away. We had a serious problem here. We never talked about this evil spirit again. My extra copies were well hidden.

Brad and I had been working together about a month. He began smoking pot on the job and I warned him not to get caught. In the evening at the office, our co-workers would drink a few beers to wind down. Brad and I eventually joined in. If I controlled the amount I drank, things wouldn't get out of hand was my thought. This was a big mistake. Brad was dealing pot and always had a supply when he came to work. He would encourage me to smoke with him. "You'll be alright, as long as mom doesn't find out, I'm not going to tell her", he said. Trying to remain strong, I kept refusing. I had left the stuff alone for so long and didn't need it in my life anymore. Then one day, I gave in. From time to time Brad and I would get high. I didn't realize the dangers of smoking this stuff again. All the times I watched Brad come to work with hangovers helped me keep the alcohol I drank limited to a small quantity. He'd come in sick and vomit next to the truck. One time he had to be replaced. When I called the office our boss asked, "is Upchuck sick again"? "Yeah and he wants to go home", I replied. Soon they had someone there to take his place. Brad's true colors were starting to shine bright.

One afternoon I came home to an empty house with no note and the phone ringing. When I answered, I found it to be Provider Financial. It sounded like they were offering me a credit card. After talking to them for a while, they told me that I already had a one in my name. I didn't know anything about this and ended the rude conversation abruptly. When Cassie came home I approached her about what happened. She didn't know anything about it. "The only one who can open up a credit card in your name is you", she told me. "Well someone opened up a credit card account in my name", I said. "Only you can open up a credit card in your name", Cassie said again. I began to focus my attention on her son Donny as the culprit.

With Thanksgiving a couple weeks away Cassie continued to add to her house. She got new carpet and appliances for her kitchen. A new Maytag stove and dishwasher was bought to replace the ones that weren't broke. When I asked why she did this, "I want all my appliances to be the same color", she replied. My refrigerator was white and I asked what about it. "I'll get a new one soon", she said. This sounded absurd to me and I couldn't help but wonder where all the money was coming from to pay for this. I asked her again if she got her settlement. "No, I didn't, why do you keep asking me that", she replied? "Because of all these new things you're getting", I answered. She insisted that her sister loaned her the money and I believed her.

One afternoon I came home from work to an empty house again. There was no note and I didn't know where Cassie and Amanda were. On the kitchen table was the title to a car. The envelope was opened so I looked in. The document was for the black Firebird. As I read further it was registered to Cassie Dixon. This revealed to me that the car actually belonged to her. When she came home, I told her of this. "I don't want to talk about it", she said. I didn't push the issue any further. It occurred to me that she was continuously being dishonest with me.

The weekend parties increased. Barbara, her husband Mark and their son would come over and we'd have a barbecue. Later on Brad and Tina along with Donny, Candy and her son would join us. Barbara and Cassie would drink Margaritas and all the others drank beer. The music and their conversations would get loud. Cassie had welcomed alcohol into her home without any consideration of what this was doing to me. Our refrigerator was always stocked with beer for her brother Wendell and an ice chest was outside to hold the rest. At first their drinking didn't bother me. After seeing several weekends of this I became upset. They had to know that my problems with alcohol made this a bit tempting to me. I hadn't been going to any AA meetings and that's what helps keep me strong in situations like this. When their behavior became inappropriate, I encouraged the kids to come outside. I had the grill ready, did all the cooking and kept an eye on the youngsters. Cassie knew these gatherings were annoying to me. She didn't care and wanted to party with her friends and family regardless of how I felt.

Opening up a post office box, I began to receive bills for two cell phone accounts I knew nothing about and that credit card. Cassie and Brad both had mobile phones. I didn't know they were registered in my name with the bill over $800. The credit card was over its limit. I told a friend at work about this and he gave me an idea to find out who did this to me. "Go home and act real happy, when they ask why you're so excited tell them that the FBI is involved, that they have pictures and are going to arrest the person that opened up that credit card account within three days", he said. When I did this, Cassie and

Donny were shocked and looked like they saw a ghost. The plan worked well. The next day she gave me the credit card. "I'm sorry, I was just trying to help you build up your credit", Cassie told me. In all the years we were together, this was the first time she ever apologized to me and I accepted it. I closed the account and had the mobile phones turned off. I kept the post office box to protect myself because she had a lock on her mailbox in front the house and I wasn't able to check the mail.

With Thanksgiving behind us, we were getting ready for Christmas. Once again we decided not to buy gifts for ourselves, that our daughter and her sons were more important. We didn't do what we agreed and I asked her sons what should I get their mom. Brad, Donny and Candy told me she wanted a vacuum cleaner. I didn't feel comfortable with this but they assured me that's what she wanted. Cassie complained of being out of money so I gave her $300 to buy gifts with. Amanda received a new variety of toys. Donny and Brad got new clothes and nice things for their home. Cassie gave me a new television with a built in VCR. I bought Donny and Brad some steel toed boots to "work in", hoping they'd take the hint. It was a great holiday celebration but I remained curious about all these new additions. The money I gave her wasn't enough to buy all these expensive items. She had a house that looked new inside and out, her two sons had new cars and all the extravagant gifts must have cost a small fortune. It did no good to ask questions because that may start an argument and I wouldn't get the truth anyhow. It felt like I was exploited and wondered what was my role in this family.

New Years approached quickly. It was the last year before the millennium was to start. Our neighbors next door put on a dazzling fireworks display as usual. The next day I helped Nat clean up the mess and he complimented me on how nice our house looked. "It's not mine", I told him. "You don't own any part of it", he asked? "Nope, it all belongs to Cassie, I just pay the rent and the bills here", I replied. "That's not right, you put a lot of money into that house", he said. In my heart I knew he was right but was in no position to put my foot down or she could kick my out. After our conversation it felt like I was just a tenant, here to pay the bills.

Making the decision to stop smoking pot with Brad caused turmoil. I didn't want it anymore and found myself returning to the dark and gloomy lifestyle that I had gotten away from. He didn't like it when I quit. I told him no more getting high on the job and he didn't want to work with me after this. We have an occupation where you're on call 24 hours a day. He went to the boss and refused to work past 7:30 at night. He was swiftly terminated for insubordination and they knew about his drug use. The truth was this; our job was interfering with the pool league he belonged to. If you were on a team and played in the tournaments, you got to drink beer all night for free. Due to our work schedule, Brad couldn't participate in most of the games.

When the list for random drug screens came out from the company, my name was on it. I had left the stuff alone for a little while and waited a bit longer before submitting to the test. Brad was gone and I was training a new helper. Things finally leveled off now that he wasn't working with me any longer. I didn't have to hear all the complaining he used to do when we arrived on a job. After taking the test, the results came back positive. Noble didn't fire me and I offered to resubmit. They told me that this wouldn't be necessary and said to clean up, that I'd have to retest again in the future. After this incident, my work time slowed down, the hours disappeared and I wasn't getting much money. I'd soon have to seek employment elsewhere.

One night Donny and Candy came to Cassie's house with three baskets of laundry. There were many times that they used my machines before. He was excited about the tournament being played tonight, hoping to win the cash prize. When they left I asked who is going to wash their clothes? "I am", Cassie replied. "You gonna wash all these, it'll take all night", I said. "I'll do anything for him, he's my son", she responded. When I got up for work the next morning all the clothes were folded nice and neat in the baskets they came in.

One evening I was out with a co-worker having a drink in a lounge and Cassie paged me. Returning her call, I told her where and what I was doing. She got very upset and told me not to come home. Her snap upset me. Doing as she requested, I went back to the shop and slept there. The next day I went to work and returned home afterwards. At first we didn't talk. When a conversation started between us, I was accused of having an affair. Cassie said two times that this wasn't going to work. When I asked her what's not going to work, "living together", she responded. We talked of separating. She asked if I could move back in with my sister. For her to ask me this sounded crazy and I refused to impose on John and Tabby. I had no place to go. Apologizing to Cassie for what happened, I promised not to do it again. After this incident, I quit drinking and went back to the AA meetings. I needed this kind of help to assist me in leaving the booze alone. My life was becoming unmanageable and I needed to clean it up.

Our conversations began to get crazy. Cassie began telling me things to hurt my feelings. She told me I wasn't needed. "I don't need a man to raise my daughter, I raised two boys on my own and they're fine", she said. Her two boys were actually grown men with drug and alcohol problems. They never knew their dad and if she had her way, Amanda would grow up not to know hers either. "And if you leave, I'm going to get $600 a month in child support, you don't want to mess with me, I'm a bitch", she growled. This sounded like a threat to me. I began to wonder if it'd be in my best interest to leave rather than stay and put up with this.

It started to look like she was pushing me out. The friction between us increased. A couple of nights later in the kitchen while Wendell was there, Cassie made a comment to me about leaving. "You can leave anytime you want, as long as you pay all the bills, there's the door", she said, pointing to the side door that led outside to the carport. When she left and went to the back of the house I told her brother that if I moved out, I wasn't paying all her bills. "I don't blame ya, I wouldn't either", he responded. It was a surprise that he sided with me.

With this controversy going on it became hard to keep my mind on the job. Soon I became plagued with numerous mistakes. It was hard to keep up with these younger workers doing the operations in Noble style. Something had to give. I gave up the pot and the booze and for a short time it seemed like things were getting back to normal. It was my fault for going back to using but considering the circumstances at home, that influence gave me a helping hand. I must have gotten weak and thought if they can do it, so can I. The consequences never even entered my mind until it was too late. Getting a vivid look at the self-destructive path I used to be on became the main key to unlock the grip drugs and alcohol can have. Once my decision was made, with His help I gave it up and never looked back. This was my spiritual maintenance.

The company truck I was using enabled me to leave my new car at home for Cassie to use. This way if there was an emergency she'd have reliable transportation. Noble was the most generous company I had ever worked for thus far. One evening I came home to find her way out in left field with glassy eyes and a bit incoherent. Amanda was just being herself and was playing with a little car. As she rolled it on the new Maytag Stove I heard a loud slap followed immediately with crying. Quickly I looked and saw Cassie had slapped her for moving the toy car across the oven door. "She's going to scratch it", she said in defense of her action. "You didn't have to do that", I snapped. Picking up Amanda, I consoled her. Cassie, looking up at the ceiling, says, "come on Brad, I need a Valium". "What did you say", I asked. She admitted to getting pills from her son when she ran out, to help with her pain. This told me what she was doing with the cash I gave her. When Brad got his first DUI, he told me how his mom gave him some of her pain pills. After mixing these with alcohol he became involved in a crash. A short while later the son came over and stayed about two minutes. He made his delivery and left. This transaction shed some light on something I knew nothing about. With the way she moved around, it didn't look like she was in any pain. Now I knew why. The need for all this medicine proved that Cassie was developing an addiction problem.

With carnival season approaching, Mardi Gras was in full swing and I had to take different routes home to avoid all the traffic. On top of this, it was dark and the crowds were enormous. It was important to be careful because lots of people drink at these celebrations. When I got home I found Cassie out in left field again, this time without a glove. She needed something from the store and I insisted on making the errand. Rather than driving the company truck I used my car instead. Opening the door I quickly noticed cigarette burns on the drivers seat. I had asked her to refrain from smoking in my car because I didn't want it to smell like an ashtray. As I looked further there were numerous burns in this area of the car. I went back inside to inquire about all this damage. "I don't recall doing that", she responded when I asked. She wouldn't even come outside to see what I was talking about. She accused me of doing this during one of my drinking binges. When I reminded her that I've been using the truck and rarely used my car, she continued to deny knowing anything about all these burns.

The next day I took my car over to a friend's house and we carefully looked at all the damaged areas. The sun visor, the head rest, four spots on the drivers seat and two spots on the carpet where it was burned all the way through to the floor. A burn on the seat matched the cigarette lighter perfectly. My friend said that by looking at all the locations, it appeared to him that this was done intentionally. I was not happy with his comment. A couple days later I stopped using the company truck and took my keys away from Cassie. She became extremely upset at my decision to do this. Now she had to get one of her cars back from one of her sons to have transportation. Now this made them all angry with me. I was determined not to give in.

It was the day before Fat Tuesday and as usual, I had to work. Being very tired, I came home to find Amanda asleep and Cassie watching television as always. I took a shower and went to bed. Not much was said between us. I could tell she was still perturbed. When I awoke the next day it was close to noon and the house was empty. I figured they went to the Mardi Gras because the parade passes by Brad's house. In the evening I called Brad to see how Cassie and Amanda were doing. He answered and said Cassie was next door with Mitch. (the barback from the Cablanka) "Where's Amanda", I asked? "I got her, she's here with me", he answered. This was another one of the few times Cassie goes over to Brad's place and leaves Amanda there while she goes next door to Mitch's house. Previously when I asked her why she was doing this, why don't she bring Amanda with her, she admitted to having an affair with him. I didn't take her response too seriously then but it was a bit different this time.

The love between us, if there was any, had diminished. Our affection for each other had ceased long ago. Cassie had a drug and alcohol problem. Her habit thrived openly in the home where we lived with our daughter. Her sons helped to propel the way that she acted. It would do neither of us any good to play the "whose at fault" game. This chaotic situation and the environment made it impossible for me to be a good father to my daughter. To maintain my program of recovery, I had to move aside from all these drinkers. In my best interest I decided to get away from her. Packing up the things that belonged to me, it was time for me to relocate.

When they came home, Cassie was drunk. She went directly to bed and passed out. Behind her followed Candy with Amanda asleep on her shoulder. She laid our daughter on the bed next to her mother. Later she called to check up, admitting that Cassie had too much to drink. This explained why she smelled like beer and appeared so inebriated. I was glad Candy called.

The next morning I needed to tell Cassie of my intentions. I was watching television with Amanda while we waited for her to wake up. Butterflies filled my stomach as I tried to think of the right way to say what was on my mind. Making a call to the boss, I informed him of my problem. He was already familiar with what I was going through. Telling him that I didn't have any place to go, he suggested moving into the shop temporarily. I thanked him for allowing me to do this. After checking on Amanda I went to the bedroom to see if Cassie was awake. My going in the room woke her up. She didn't have much of a hangover and slowly got out of bed.

Thoughts filled my mind of what I was about to do. It was simply intolerable for me to live in her house any longer. Although there wasn't much arguing, the dishonesty, her threats, her inconsiderate comments and actions affected me. It felt like I was being excluded from many occasions and events. I knew she loved her sons but to do "anything and everything" for them promotes irresponsibility. I'm certain that Donny and Brad talked about me behind my back and their opinions may have provoked Cassie to feel dissatisfied with our being together.

The statement I made to her long ago was my description of our relationship. "It feels like we're business partners and that business happens to be in the form of our daughter, Amanda", I told her. In many situations, whatever I said didn't matter and it seemed like I was the silent partner here. With Cassie being the type of woman she was, saying the things she did, it felt more like I wasn't wanted or needed. Her insidious actions could have a lasting effect on me when it comes to trusting other women. Although I was moving out, I had no intention of abandoning my daughter. To evade my responsibility for her in any way was not part of the plan. I am forever obligated to support my child. This was something I didn't have to be told.

Sitting at the kitchen table I watched her come in. She began to fix her a cup of tea. "Your not working today", she asked. "Not yet", I replied. Suddenly I blurted out my intention, "I'm moving out, I can't stay here with you, with all this going on, the drinking and stuff". "Okay", she said. With this, I started to pack my car. When it was full I went the shop. I returned with the company truck two more times. Packing everything for the last trip, I told her of not having a place to go and would be living at the shop. She wanted her house keys. I informed her that I'd have to return and get the rest of my things. "Okay", she responded as she stared out into the back yard. She made no attempt to try and stop me or talk about my decision to do this.

As I drove to the shop, a strong feeling of insecurity came over me. Uncertain of my future, I didn't know what was going to happen. My hours at work had decreased and I didn't have too much money saved. It was important for me to find a place to live as soon as possible. With Cassie's being the way she was and considering her condition, I wanted to be in the same neighborhood for Amanda's sake. I'm her father and my hope was that Cassie wouldn't deny me the right to see her. It was tough to be patient about this new situation of mine.

When all my things were unpacked at the shop, I sat on the bed and thought about what had happened. It was very hard to do this but Cassie didn't leave me a choice. Things between us were progressively getting worse. It was evident that she didn't love me anymore. I couldn't think of a way to make our relationship work and I became hesitant to even try. It didn't even feel like we were friends. She never even tried to reconcile and seemed content with my departure. All I could do was try to figure out the best way of handling this dilemma.

A couple days later I returned to find the rest of my belongings on the carport. Cassie put out the things she wanted me to have. She was not there. I was hoping to see her so we might be able to talk. My valuables were out back in her shed. Opening her gate, I went to the back and got my tools, weights, lawnmower and other stuff. If we ever became friends again, I was hoping to be the one she'd call to come over and cut the grass. This way I could see my little girl and make sure that the lawn was done right. When I was finished packing the truck I turned around and with tears in my eyes said good-bye to the house where Amanda lived.

Arriving at the shop, I put everything away. When she felt better, I hoped to get a call from Cassie. That never happened so I called over there. Wendell answered and she wasn't home. I asked him to tell her that she could keep all my appliances. They needed to be in the house where our daughter lived. He'd try to have her call me but she never did. When I was able to talk with her, we argued. She wanted to know if I was going to pay her house note. It sounded like her financial stability was all she was concerned about. A few days later she got her phone number changed to a non-published number. My connection with them was severed.

So much happened between Cassie and me that it's difficult to provide one or two causes for our split. There were many. Of all the reasons, no communication had to be the main one. Talking is the best therapy for most all problems. How else will you know what the other person is thinking. My occupation also played a damaging role in our relationship. The strange schedule of NDT forced me to be away from home too much and took from me the time I should've been with my family. I never considered this because of the need for a substantial amount of money. Putting in lots of overtime so I could pay all the bills, buy what we needed and make sure that nothing would get turned off became my duty. In my heart it felt like I was doing the right thing because I was providing for my household.

Not being able to call Cassie made me think that I was soon going to be erased from the life of my daughter. No matter what, I was not giving up on my little girl. Like unwanted friends, the feelings of helplessness and hopelessness had now moved in to live with me.

Chapter Six

THE BATTLE BEGINS

Like seasons of the year, everything changed for me. Getting off of the toxic chemicals was the best move I could have made and one of the solutions to fixing my accumulating problems. Work at Noble had miraculously picked up. The expertise I developed for my trade had returned. For a short time my employer appreciated this. The gift I had of being able to save money couldn't have come at a better time. My priorities were established and I began moving quickly to accomplish them. The goal was to have enough saved for a child support check and an apartment. The need for me to have a place to live would soon become a reality.

Spending lots of time alone at the shop, the nights began to haunt me. It was discouraging when I'd remember some of the things that Cassie said to me and the incidents at her house. Anger had set in and I reacted. She had three VCRs and one of them was mine. I knew she'd be returning the vacuum cleaner so I went with the police to her house. As the door opened I saw Amanda behind Cassie. "My daddy", she exclaimed as she darted towards me. Out of nowhere Candy quickly stepped in, picked her up and went to the back of the house. "I want my daddy, I want my daddy", Amanda screamed. With receipts in hand, I wanted these two articles. The officer explained our intentions and Cassie gathered my things. With a bang, the door slammed shut. I put the items in the truck and the policeman left. From the street I could hear our little girl crying loudly. The way I saw Candy snatch her up was engraved in my mind and this made me mad. That action told me it wouldn't be Cassie by herself I'd have to deal with from now on. I gave the cleaner to my neighbor Charles and took the VCR back to the shop with me. She kept the remote to it so I could only use the device as a player. It wasn't a good idea to go there and do this because it upset my daughter. Now I was really miserable.

Because my communication with Cassie stopped long ago I tried talking with her sister Cathleen in Ohio, hoping she could reach her. When I explained the reasons for my leaving and informed her of the way I was being treated, she offered to talk to Cassie. Not knowing if Amanda was okay began to affect my performance at work. I wasn't the bad guy here and talked of making a video to prove my innocence. Cathleen really liked my idea and asked me to send her a copy of the tape when it was complete. Her request was like the green light to go forward with this, especially when she gave me her address. From our conversation I became encouraged to take on this task. She always wanted to know what it was like down here where we lived. My desperation to see Amanda and the bewilderment I felt became the reasons to make the video. This was a shot in the dark and it seemed like I was running out of options.

My job is hard and the x-ray camera is heavy. This is where the video started, at work. From there I went over to the Cablanka where I first met Cassie. Going inside I found the barmaid dressed like she supposed to, wearing apparel that exposes lots of skin. Her skimpy dress revealed well shaped legs that ended at her hips and she was quick to show me. The owner had them wear outfits like this to attract many men who'd quickly open their wallets and freely squander money on alcohol or whatever drugs are sold there. I then moved over to the apartment where we lived when Amanda was born and showed the reason we had to move. The home we moved into on Blaire was next. It was empty and no one was living there. From here I went over to Cassie's house where it looked almost new from all the work she had done. It wouldn't be complete without seeing the backyard so I got permission from the neighbor to have a look. As I looked over the fence Amanda saw me. "Daddy", she called out. When she got closer, with her arms reaching for me, "hold me, Daddy hold me", she said. "I can't right now, I can't, Poppa loves you baby girl, Poppa loves you", I told her. I was so happy to see her but couldn't stay too long. Tears filled my eyes and the camcorder was hard to operate. It wasn't long before Cassie came out. "Here comes Jezebel", I said to myself. Grabbing Amanda by the arms, she picked her up and headed towards the house. "Barbara, dial 911, dial 911", she said. This was my clue to leave and I did. Showing how I was living at the shop, talking about my current situation and discussing some issues is how this project ended. The unfolding dialogue of my scenario filled this film. It was then all packaged up and sent to her sister as she requested. This was a big mistake because it exposed a side of Cassie that her family didn't need to know about. Cathleen mailed the video down south here for her sister to view. There were some things on the tape that was impossible for Cassie to deny.

By the first of the month I was able to mail a support check and get me a new apartment. Not having too much money or things to move in with, it remained empty for a long time. I didn't mind sleeping on the floor and would buy a bed when it was affordable. Dining out was a necessity because I had no utensils or cookware.

When it was time to shower, I had no wash cloths or towels so I used socks and a pillowcase. At first it was hard to live like this. I knew things would smooth out as time went on. Everything had to get better because this was the worse it could get. All I would think about was Amanda. Looking at her pictures became a tearful experience. Going to AA meetings several times a week helped to ease the pain I was experiencing. My place was in the same neighborhood as Cassie's house, almost three blocks away. If something was to happen, running, I could be there in less than a minute.

It was Cassie's birthday when I went over to Nat and Pam's house to ask if they had seen my daughter lately. As I went in Brad pulled up at his mother's house. "You're not supposed to be here", he said. While talking to my former neighbors about my little girl I could see out their window that the police arrived. Ending my visit quickly, I felt that it was time to leave. The officers stopped me before I could get to my car and made me wait. They were talking to Cassie, Donny and Candy, Brad and Tina. Candy and Tina began to giggle and Brad urged them to go inside. Cassie was putting on the act she used to do at the bar, which was very noticeable shaking or trembling, that displayed a pretended state of fear. The officers played right into her game and were very displeased when they got to me. "Are you going to arrest him", she asked? "No" replied the officer. They came over and forewarned me not to step foot on her property. "I never did that", I said. "Shut up", he yelled. I heeded their consequential threats and was allowed to leave. This event told me Cassie wasn't going to stop and would do all she could to have me arrested. I went home and wrote a 7-page letter revealing what I knew, some things I assumed about her, my desire to see Amanda and mailed it to her.

Bills from Provider Financial and Cell-U-Phone came to my post office box. Although I paid off the credit card Cassie forged, they issued me another one. I fell behind on my payments and requested that they send me a copy of the original application. I promised to pay on time and eventually close the account. The way in which my connection with this lender started wasn't appreciated. The two mobile phones combined for a debt over $800. I pleaded my innocence with them. Faxing them an affidavit with the names and numbers of the people who had the devices, they assured me that an investigation would pursue. They said a letter would be mailed to me explaining the results of their findings.

Funds began to add up and I was able to buy me a bed. There'd be no more sleeping on the floor. This was the first piece of furniture purchased for my apartment. At least I had one room that wasn't completely empty. As time went on I'd get more furnishings when it was affordable. It was imperative to have a place with two bedrooms because Amanda would need her own space. I focused my attention on fixing up my little girl's room next.

The bottom dropped out at Noble. Jobs that came in were not being assigned to me. The personal problems I had began to interfere with my ability to be reliable and dependable. My finances were diminishing. The boss told me someone with the police had been by the shop looking for me. He had some papers to serve. I had no idea why he'd be looking for me and was curious on what kind of documents he had. Needing some answers, I had to investigate.

Knowing my AA sponsor in Portland was once in a similar situation like mine, I gave Saul a call to find out what kind of papers this man could've had. "She filed suit and she's taking you to court", he said. He told me to go to the courthouse and if this were true, I'd find all this paperwork in the public records. I did what he told me and found out that he was correct.

Cassie was taking me to court before Judge Daniels, the domestic mediator. She also filed an Application for Pauper Status, claiming to be very poor and not getting any support. She didn't claim the two sports cars she bought for her sons and Wendell signed as a witness. This application was denied. Further review of this paperwork revealed she alleged that I subjected myself to chemical abuse, including alcohol. She claimed I threatened her and my daughter on several occasions. This allowed her to obtain a temporary restraining order to prevent us from harassing, threatening, and abusing each other, or the minor child. She was seeking to gain sole care custody, which would eliminate me from the life of our daughter. The papers continued to request supervised visitation for the benefit of the defendant, me. She claimed there was no child support and requested for me to show cause why I shouldn't have to pay. The documents ended stating that this was all being done in the best interest of the minor child. Other papers showed that she had $300 on hand. This may have been my support check and I wondered if she used it to pay for these proceedings. Our court date was set for April Fools Day.

A battle had now erupted. It felt as though a bomb exploded in my face. Refusing to give up on Amanda, I began to build a strategy. For days I scrambled to gather evidence for my defense. When enough documentation was put together, I looked for an attorney. Going to an old family friend, he referred me to his best child custody colleague, Jim. There was no way I could go into court without counsel. Paying for him to represent me nearly emptied my bank account. In our first meeting I presented information on what Cassie did to me along with a copy of the support check voluntarily sent to her. I left him a copy of the video I made and he requested to see my payroll check stubs. After doing some calculations he said I'd have to pay more support. At this time money didn't matter, I wanted to see my daughter.

To help occupy my time I volunteered to coach a 6 & 7 year old baseball team. It felt good to show these kids how to play. They'd get excited catching the ball but didn't know what to do with it. "Throw it to first, throw it to first", I'd tell them. We played two games a week and practiced in between. Some of the dads became assistant coaches and would take over for me when I couldn't attend. They were informed of my difficulty with Cassie. Rick, one of the dads, had this same problem with his ex-wife. He owned his own company and offered to help any way he could. Teaching these kids to play ball became a good escape from my personal quandary. It helped ease the misery I was experiencing with the absence of Amanda.

As the fourth week of the month came I had worked only 10 hours. Financially, that was not good. If I remained at Noble, it'd be impossible to get the funds I needed to afford the upcoming hearing. Without saying anything to my boss, I hired on at XIH and worked part time. This still wasn't enough. I made a call to Top Lab and found out my old buddy was the dispatcher there. They hired me also. Taking the pre-employment drug screens, I now had copies of two urine analyses with negative results and put them in my file. Noble was the only employer that paid every week. The other two paid twice a month. I figured that by working for three companies, this would help me pay my bills and the lawyer. Finally I met up with the guy who was seeking to serve me with those papers. After reading them again I realized that Cassie's false allegations might hold up in court. If all her requests were granted I may never get to see Amanda. From a distance I'd have to watch my little girl grow up amongst her mother's two dysfunctional sons. It wasn't easy to work all these jobs and have this hearing on my mind.

Going to work one morning I noticed the little red sports car that belonged to Candy abandoned in a parking lot. Previously my associates told me how Cassie had been driving it instead of getting her car back from Brad. It made me wonder if the car was here, where was she and who was watching Amanda. I got terribly upset and stopped behind the vehicle. Getting a dry-erase marker out of my trunk, I wanted to leave her a message. Whatever I wrote could easily be removed because of this type of marker. On the driver's side window and the windshield I wrote, "Y R U doing this to me". After writing it twice and asking myself this question, the answer quickly came to me. I remembered in the conversation we had when she demanded $600 a month in child support how she ended it with, "I'm a bitch". On her back windshield is where I put the answer. Friends told me how she took pictures of my graffiti when she came home. Candy called the police and attempted to press charges. She was very persistent with the officers. Claiming to be a victim, she wouldn't stop until they issued a warrant. Because the marker I used didn't create any permanent damage, the police couldn't think of anything to charge me with. Asking their sergeant, he came up with a misdemeanor, criminal mischief. Candy successfully intimidated the officer. Admitting to what I did and why, I turned myself into the police. The lawman apologized about this when I spoke to him. "I didn't even want to write the dumb report", he said. Now I had another date to be in court.

Trying to go about my everyday life, I hoped that things would return to normal. It helped to go to AA meetings. Simple chores and the baseball games helped to occupy my time. The washer woman at the laundry mat would sometimes wash my clothes for me when I could afford it. One afternoon I went there and she couldn't find my laundry. The line of people was long so I decided to come back later when she had time to look for them. I walked to a parlor that was close by to get me an ice cream. Almost to my destination I heard a recognizable voice say, "I should've killed you a long time ago". Turning around I saw it was Brad. Answering his statement with a chuckle, I turned to walk away. Suddenly I heard him spit and felt it land on my back. Turning to face him, he got closer and spit in my face. After wiping his saliva off me, with his cigarette he flicked ashes in my eye. This burned and I backed away quickly to a nearby payphone. He told me to dial 911 and I did. Officers arrived and questioned us separately. I could hear Brad telling them that I was stalking and harassing his mother. Officer Ruffwood collected our driver's licenses to run our records through. He came back to us and asked me if I knew how many times I've been arrested. I told him no because I wasn't certain of all the occasions. "You're a code 6, which means you've had multiple arrests, if I take anyone to jail it'll be both of you and you'll stay there longer, do you want to go to jail", he asked? "No", I responded. He suggested I find a different place to do my laundry, returned our licenses and everyone went their separate ways. It felt like the glimmer of hope I had to ever see Amanda again was now gone due to my past problems with the police.

It was a few days before our court date and I had an appointment with my attorney. When I told him of the incident with Brad, he wanted to know how I reacted. "You didn't get in a fight did you", he asked? "No I didn't" I replied. "Good, because if you did, it'll prove you to be of a violent nature and you'll never get to see your daughter", he said. The information I gave him about what Cassie did to me couldn't be used. It felt like all my work was in vain. The reason we were going to court was to establish custody, visitation and child support. He did say that she got her settlement and if her attorney didn't give us the papers, we'd subpoena them. We went over some things he'd try to discuss with the judge, I paid him some more money and our meeting was over. Jim was four years younger than I was, seemed a bit inexperienced and was starting to give me the impression of not taking my case seriously.

Our date had arrived, April Fools Day and this was no joking matter. I went with only ten dollars in my pocket. Being employed with three companies still couldn't provide the money I needed. No one had enough jobs for all their employees. We arrived to find a large crowd of people waiting to see the judge. A hive of butterflies filled my stomach and I was worried. Cassie had Tony with her, the personal injury lawyer she hired when she had the car accident. Looking across the room I could see our attorneys conversing with big smiles. I'd watch them as they laughed. It seemed like they were old golfing buddies. This made me wonder whose side was my counsel on. The time came when our pettifoggers went in to see Judge Daniels. Cassie and I avoided eye contact at all times and had to wait outside. A while later Jim came out to discuss the agreement they reached. “This is what we have; she’s agreed to supervised visitation every other weekend, eight hours on Saturday and eight hours on Sunday, and three hours every Wednesday, $500 a month child support to be divided into two payments, the 1st and 15th of every month, a restraining order to stop any kind of harassment, there’s to be no contact by mail or phone, and we’ll need an evaluation to be done over at the Children’s Custody Center”, he told me. I was traumatized with this information. “Is that it, that’s the best you can do”, I asked? “Yeah, You’re a code 6”, he said. He blamed the video; some postcards I mailed to Amanda at Cassie’s house in an attempt to resume communication and that I earned too much money as being reasons for the judge’s decision. “Tony said you have two sisters that she’ll allow to supervise for you, otherwise you’ll have to get a court appointed supervisor”, Jim told me. “Alright, I need to give my sisters a call”, I said.

It felt like this decision they made was unreasonable. I had no choice but to contact my sisters and get their commitment to being my supervisors. Using the pay phone, in a three-way conversation they promised to be there and help me when it was time to see Amanda. Without Tabby and Mary, I wouldn’t have been able to see my daughter. This was a relief because I had no money to afford someone appointed by the court. Cassie must have thought that their health problems would prevent them from being able to fulfill these obligations. Tabby has arthritis of the hip and can’t stand for long lengths of time or do a lot of walking. Mary’s had six major back surgeries and is on medication all the time to relieve the pain that never goes away. We all know that blood is thicker than water and Amanda is part of us. After promising to let them know what the final outcome of this hearing would be, I returned to court.

As I walked in Jim was there waiting at the counter. Telling him of my sisters consent to be used as the supervisors, he went over to Tony and relayed the message. After this he came back and continued writing notes. I began pondering a way to change this decision they made and went over to ask, “why does the visitation have to be supervised and why so much support”? “You want to see your daughter, don’t you”, he asked? “That goes without saying”, I replied. “Alright then”, he said as he continued writing. In the past I heard about couples that had intense arguments and verbal abuse but the father still got to see his kids. I never did anything like that and their agreement sounded unfair to me. A little time passed and I wanted to approach Jim again. "Isn't there something you can do, maybe talk to the judge", I asked? He slammed his pen on the tablet and looked at me. "Look, I thought you wanted to see your daughter", he snapped. Raising my hands up to my chest as a gesture of surrendering, "never mind", I said. We went before the judge and our statements were put on record. Everything was just as Jim said. In two days I'd have a supervised visit with Amanda for eight hours.

It had been 45 days since I saw my little girl and this visit was the day before Easter. We arrived shortly before 10am and I waited outside in my car. When Tabby knocked on the door, Cassie answered. I saw Amanda come to the door and run back in to the house. My sister went inside and I continued to wait. It was almost a half-hour when they all came out on the carport. I saw Cassie coerce my little girl to go. "I hired a private eye to watch you and if anything happens to her, you're responsible, I hate to put you in the middle like this", Cassie warned Tabby. My little girl was resisting my sister so I got out of the car. "Amanda", I called. She looked over and quickly ran to me, leaping into my arms. I hugged her tightly. "Poppa missed you baby girl", I said. There was a foul smell about her. With dirty fingernails and knotted hair, I could see that she never had a bath. Good personal hygiene is important for kids. We got in my car and went to my sister's house. I was so happy to see my daughter and we had a good time. It was disturbing to see the noticeable confusion in my child. Her mother called four times and talked to my sister, asking what we were doing. Later in the evening, Tabby told me of the threats Cassie made and how Amanda wasn't ready or prepared for this visit. There was nothing we could do. If I wanted to see my child, we had to submit.

Initiating our visits with the evaluator, I went to my first appointment. It was necessary to pawn my handgun to pay for my cost of living and help afford this evaluation. They gave me less than half of what it was worth. In my opinion, our meeting went well. Telling the truth and not hiding anything, I answered all her questions. My momma always said that honesty is the best policy. I'd return three more times to see this lady. The third visit would be with Amanda and the forth with Cassie. Upon completion of our sessions, a written report would be mailed to our attorneys and us. It was my intention to adhere to the courts ruling.

Work at Noble had become erratic. The first scheduled weekend to be with my little girl was coming up and they gave me a job to do. Intentional lack of communication on my behalf caused me to miss this assignment. The action of purposely avoiding work created problems and upset my boss. My reputation with the company was that of one who is unreliable. They didn't know I was working at XIH and Top Lab. If I lost my position here, I still had a job. It was hard to make myself available for work if it meant losing the chance to see my daughter. Not having a supervisor caused me to miss this first visit with Amanda.

After careful consideration, I was dissatisfied with the performance of my attorney. I called him and asked if he received the settlement papers from Cassie's lawyer. He said they came in recently and his receptionist would have a copy for me. I picked up the paperwork and went to my car. Looking at this information made me angry. Five months before I left she received $56,000. This explained how she was able to buy two new sports cars for her sons, completely remodel her house, buy new appliances and all that other stuff. And she had the audacity to apply for pauper status. Instantly I remembered what the bible said. (Ecclesiastes 7:26)

It was time for my Wednesday visit and I was filled with anticipation. We arrived at the scheduled time. Cassie continued with her verbal threats, "you make sure she's back here for 8pm", she demanded of Tabby. I was thankful for the three hours we were together. To hear her giggle was music to my heart. We played and had a wonderful time. To stay on good terms and avoid future problems with the mother, we brought Amanda back early.

The next day I went to see a man for a substance abuse assessment as ordered by the evaluator. He questioned me about the drug and alcohol usage in my life. It was hard for me not to talk about my situations with Cassie, both past and present. He told me that because these feelings were just under the surface, it was normal to talk about them. We discussed my participation in AA and the program of recovery. I provided to him two negative drug screens and the meeting ended. Cassie would also have to make an appointment to see this man.

Finding out about a parenting class, I decided to enroll and attend. Curious to know what this was about, it was my hope to learn something. This course involved three meetings. When it was my turn to speak I expressed the importance of relating to a child on their level. While they may look up to us as parents, they may not like looking up at us and to lower oneself to the child's level. I told the class about lowering the shelves in their closet to a height where the child can reach all the toys. We all agreed that instructional guidance and correction is better than discipline. When the course was over, the instructor mailed me a letter of appreciation stating that I was an eager participant and contributed much to the class.

Talking with a friend about my situation, he informed me that I was misrepresented. He said that I didn't have to agree to the terms my lawyer made for me. Unless there was solid evidence proving that I was an unfit father, supervision shouldn't be required. When I told him of the video, the postcards and the letter, he said that couldn't be used until the judge reviewed it. He urged me to fire Jim and hire a specialist, preferably a woman because of the false allegations made by Cassie. I took his advice and began looking for new counsel.

My second scheduled weekend visit came up and Tabby couldn't make it. Mary stepped in and we called early so everyone would be prepared. We were to be there at 10am and called at 9:45. Amanda answered because her mom was still asleep. "Get ready, we're coming to get you", I told her. With happiness, she hung up the phone. When we arrived, I waited in the van and Mary knocked on both doors repeatedly. It took almost 30 minutes for the angry mother to answer. "I can't believe I have to get up this early in the morning for this", Cassie snarled at Mary. She quickly got Amanda ready, shoved her out and slammed the door. This made our little girl very sad and she didn't say too much as we drove to my sister's house, three blocks away. Once inside, my child would cheer up. My niece Hannah was there and we all noticed how dirty Amanda was. Her hair was full of knots, she had dirty fingernails and she smelled awful. When Hannah helped her go to the bathroom, she smelled like urine. She was given a bath, cleaned and her nails painted. We washed her clothes. Afterwards she ate a waffle and a grilled cheese sandwich, the most I've ever seen her eat. It was upsetting to see my youngster being mistreated this way. It was obvious that she wasn't being looked after properly. How could a mother who claimed to love her daughter so much, let her live like this? Cassie was doing this to irritate me but our little girl was the one suffering. When it was time to return, Amanda didn't want to go. This made me suspicious. I wanted to know if there was any kind abuse at her mother's house. I wouldn't question my daughter and her mother wasn't talking to me. The next day, Sunday, I didn't have a supervisor and would have to lose another visit. Something had to be done about this and it'd start with a new counsel of record. All this time I was keeping notes on missed visits, the reasons and any incidents that happened.

Tabby received a phone call and was informed that Amanda had an accident. Her tooth was pulled out while blowing up a beach ball. I found this incident hard to believe. It was strange for one of her teeth to come out this easily at three years old. Was it possible that our daughter might have a nutrition problem? When we were still together, I wasn't comfortable with all the sweets the mother let her eat. "As long as she's eating something", Cassie claimed the doctor told her. I tried imparting to her the importance of vitamins and minerals for Amanda's sake. My opinion didn't matter at the time. It worried me that my little girl might have weakened teeth and bones. Here was another situation I couldn't do anything about.

It was time to go hunting and I selected the courthouse as the place to find my new lawyer. I met a prestigious lady there. "Are you a child custody lawyer", I asked. "No, I cant, it's too heartbreaking for me", she replied. Explaining to her that I preferred to be represented by a woman, I asked for help. She wrote two names on a piece of paper and as she looked upward, said, "let me think of someone who will fight for you". With that, she wrote a third name at the bottom. "Good luck", she said, handing me the paper. I picked the last one she wrote on her list and made arrangements to meet her. A strong feeling of confidence came over me.

Her name was Charlene, a well-adjusted and mature woman who gained my respect the moment I walked into her office. As she familiarized herself with the paperwork in my case, I could see it disturbed her. Looking at my evidence, she wanted to know why Jim wasn't doing anything. I couldn't answer. She said that by agreeing to supervised visitation, he made me look crazy to the court and automatically guilty of something, which calls for an evaluation. She asked if I had a criminal record and I said no. It was suggested to me that I get better counsel. If I didn't pick her, she urged me to select someone else. She told me how much it would cost for her to represent me. Jim is a traitor. He caused problems for me and backed down to Cassie's attorney. Charlene was just the opposite, a fighter. Now I needed money.

The mayflower month was upon us. It began with a Wednesday visit that went along smoothly with no incidents. Not having a supervisor started to reduce some of my parenting time. Tabby's condition was better and said that we'd try to do more visits this month. I was prepared to do that and missed work to be with my daughter. My third weekend came and we went over for the pick up. Cassie wasn't home and her brother answered the door. Amanda was running around in a sleeveless shirt and panties. This upset Tabby. She saw me outside and ran towards my car. Wendell caught her and made her go back inside. "My daddy, my daddy", I heard her yell. He wouldn't release her to us, saying that the mother was at the supermarket and would return in a half-hour. We drove over to Mary's house and waited. Calling repeatedly, Cassie would not answer her phone or return our calls. We didn't know what happened to her. I was denied visitation with Amanda. This upset all of us and I brought Tabby back to her house. Later that day I decided to go back to Mary's house. On the way there I noticed Brad following me in the black Firebird. When I was almost to my sister's, I rolled up my window and pulled over thinking he'd just pass me by. He stopped along side my car, rolled down his window and spit on the side of my vehicle where I was. He followed this action with obscenities. Because there was traffic behind him, he had to move on. When my sister saw this she became upset and called the police. There was nothing they could do. The next day was mother's day. I wanted our daughter to be with Cassie on this holiday.

The fun of my baseball team helped ease the grief I felt. We were undefeated and in first place. All I really imposed on them was to have fun. We had a perfect line up with Rick's son being the clean up hitter. He could hit homeruns. The practices got better and the games were great. Telling all my players how proud I was had them trying harder. "Good job", I'd always say. They understood that we all make mistakes and that no one's perfect. When they had questions, I answered. We were having fun, winning, the parents were happy and the kids told me I was a good coach. "I wish you were my dad", one little boy would tell me. We had some rain outs which seemed to prolong the season due to the games being rescheduled.

The stress from my situation with Cassie and her associates became too much for me. They all knew I was down and out, but still kept kicking. Something had to be done and I needed Charlene to represent me. I sold my lawnmower, borrowed some money and took the rest out of my savings to hire her. She liked a challenge and appeared to be happy when she took my case. My evidence accumulated and we now had proof that Cassie was a dishonest woman. Charlene told me to get caught up on my child support and document everything. She wrote a letter for me to deliver to Jim, telling him that he was fired. His office was in the building her brother owned. I'm sure she had something to do with the reason why I never got another bill from Jim. I had confidence in my new attorney and saw that she was a real contender.

We went to get my little girl for a Wednesday visit. After I buckled Amanda in and proceeded to leave, Brad quickly pulls into Cassie's driveway. He gets out and trots towards my car shouting obscenities and using offensive gestures. This frightened Tabby, "drive away, drive away", she screamed. We watched him chase my car. He was trying to scare us all. We went to Mary's house and called for an officer. They came out and suggested we use an escort to protect ourselves from Brad's dangerous behavior. It disturbed me that my child had to see her brother acting violent like that. These exchanges were getting crazy. During the visit Amanda revealed to us how mommy was hitting her in the face and making her cry. She was too young to make this kind of story up. When it was time for her return, the guard came back. My youngster told the lawman what her mother did and he became suspicious. "You need to contact your attorney immediately", he told me. The policeman did accompany us when we brought my daughter home and followed me as I walked her up to the door. Cassie was furious when she answered and saw me standing there with Amanda. "I have a restraining order, he's not supposed to be here", she said loudly. The officer told her that when he is present, the order is invalid. My supervisors both agreed to continue with the visits only if we used a police escort. Brad's conduct and lack of self-control intimidated my sisters. I had to comply with them or risk losing their involvement altogether.

Seven days later was another weekday visit. We called the police from a restaurant that was nearby, for an escort. They were to meet us there and we'd all go to get Amanda. The officer went to the house first and then met Tabby and me at the restaurant. Deputy Fuller proceeded to speak at me in a rude, noisily way. "You need to understand, she has a restraining order against you, you're not allowed on her property", she yelled. When Tabby tried to tell her what the lawman told us previously, she was cut off, "you need to be quiet", the officer snapped. If Cassie portrayed her "trembling state of fear act" to this woman, this might be the reason she treated us this way. This woman styled her hair like a man. She was shaped like a man, sounded like a man and had a slight moustache. She had characteristics to insinuate that her sexual preference was women. We all went to the mother's house and attempted to get my daughter. Two male officers met the deputy there and they all went inside. The men came out shaking their heads and left the scene. Tabby waited on the sidewalk in front of the neighbor's house. Fuller came out and conversed with my sister, telling her the mother wasn't going to let the youngster go because the father was late on child support. I sat in my car and watched them as they talked. Their conversation appeared to be about me so I got out and joined in. "Have you been coming over to this house", the deputy asked as she pointed to Nat and Pam's place. "One time not long ago", I responded. "Well you're not suppose to be here, and you coming around is stirring up trouble, if you come here and I get the call, you're going to jail, do you understand", she asked? "Yeah, okay", I replied. "It's not in the judgement for him to be with the supervisors when they come to get the child"; she said looking at Tabby. "Where's Amanda", I asked. "She's not releasing the child, I can't force the mother to turn her over to you, we can't get involved in civil matters", the deputy said. We had no choice but to back down. The help we requested from police wasn't useful because they can't engage themselves in a domestic situation such as mine. If I went with my sisters to get Amanda or visited my neighbors, I took a chance on getting arrested. My court awarded privileges had now become tangled with confusion, making them more complicated.

The fifth weekend visit came and we decided to do the exchange differently. I'd wait around the corner at Mary's house while Tabby and her husband went to get my daughter. It seemed like a long time until they finally returned. I hurried out to meet them. “Where’s Amanda”, I asked? They told me that there was no car in the driveway. “We kept knocking on the door but no one would answer”, John said. We tried calling Cassie’s house several times and left messages on her answering machine. Eventually we had to give up. The next day was Sunday and I hoped Cassie would comply with the court order. We decided to do things the same way as the day before. I missed my little girl and Mary had a surprise waiting for her. Just like yesterday, it was a good while before they returned and I started to worry. I stared out the window anticipating their arrival. The truck pulled up and I quickly went outside. My little one wasn’t with them. I became very angry and couldn’t hold back the tears. “What happened this time, where’s Amanda”, I cried? “Cassie’s car’s in the driveway but she won’t answer neither one of her doors, I’m sorry”, Tabby said. Again we called repeatedly and left messages on the answering machine. She refused to answer the phone. Not knowing where Amanda was, not being able to see her or talk to her put me in a state of panic. I didn’t know what was happening and became filled with the awful feeling the something was dangerously wrong. It was hard to accept that I wasn’t going to see my little girl and was denied visitation for the fourth time. Everything we agreed upon in court was not being fulfilled. I lost two full days to be with my child and the mother would not make herself available to provide a reason, an excuse or any answers as to why she was denying me the opportunity to see my daughter. This was an injustice to Amanda and me. My anxiety was making me physically ill.

My post office box finally gave me some good news. The letters I requested from Provider Financial and Cell-U-Phone had finally arrived. Looking at the original application, I saw when Cassie signed my name that she printed the middle initial. All my checks and anything that involved money showed I never did this. The phone number to the nearest relative was Brad’s. It wasn’t hard to prove we weren’t related and I copied the page out of the phonebook to show that the number did belong to him. My flight itinerary and the stubs from my payroll checks revealed that the purchases made with this credit card occurred when I was working in Alaska. The mobile phone company also gave me the results of their investigation. The letter stated, “Please allow this letter to serve as confirmation that Cell-U-Phone has determined that the above referenced cellular accounts were established as a result of fraudulent use of your personal credit information". The letter ended with them stating they will remove this debt from my credit file. This evidence was turned into the police and they suggested I press charges for forgery. I now had a chance to put Cassie in jail. I thought about that but decided not to go through with it. She was our little girl's mother and no matter how upset or angry she made me, I refused to incarcerate her, I couldn't do that.

Faced with many decisions, it felt like I needed some advice. My old high school friend Jazzy was in a major custody battle long ago to free her two sons from the abuse of their father. Presenting all this evidence, I told her about Charlene. She was infuriated at what Cassie had done and denounced Jim's actions. "You have a new attorney, right", she asked. "Yeah", I replied. It took just about all my money and I still needed more. Kyle, Jazzy and I had been friends for a long time. They knew me when I was a teenager. She was going to talk things over with her husband and told me that if I needed help, to get back with her. "Don't let this woman walk all over you, what goes around, comes around", she said.

The time had come for my third visit with the evaluator. It was going to be with Amanda and me. I was delighted and couldn't wait to see my little girl. Upon arriving I saw Candy's red car, the one that Cassie had been driving. Opening the door, "daddy", Amanda called out as she ran towards me. I lowered myself to greet her as she lunged for me and wrapped her arms around my neck. I stood up with her and we moved over to a chair where she sat on my lap. Donnie and Candy had brought her for this session and appeared angry that they had to be here. We looked at the magazines and I showed pictures, telling her what each one of them was. The counselor came out and walked Amanda and me to the back. We had lots of fun and truly enjoyed ourselves. The lady was silent and observed me interact with my little girl. When I said, "daddy loves you", she responded, "I love you too", with a hug and a kiss. She had to go to the bathroom and I helped her. When we went back into the room and started playing with the toys, Amanda said, "I want to stay with you, daddy". Her statement broke my heart. The hour went by quickly and it was time to go. "Can we stay a little longer, please", I asked? "No, that's enough, I saw everything I needed to see", the woman said nicely. We brought Amanda out and she reluctantly went to Candy. We said our goodbyes and I watched my little girl walk away. I couldn't drive all the way home and had to stop. I didn't expect to start crying like this. This detachment made me feel like I was losing my mind.

Returning home, my dark apartment resembled the way I felt inside. Needing to take a shower, I flipped on the breaker to heat the water up. Leaving my hot water heater off lowered my energy bill and it'd be hot enough in a half-hour. Turning on the light in Amanda's empty room, I stared at the two portraits of her when she was younger. "Poppa's sorry boo, I am so sorry for all this", I cried. Turning the light off, I went to my room and sat on the bed. I began to think about everything. I remembered where I met Cassie, how we had sex on our second date, how her sons never knew their father, the drug and alcohol abuse, my relapses, all the places we lived, my investments on her new house, my financial catastrophe, the nightmare of losing my right to be Amanda's father, how she had everything and I had nothing. Suddenly I heard the echo of what momma always told me, "you can't live without God". The answer to all my problems came quickly. He led me to bible studies and I stopped going because it upset Cassie. He said to flee fornication, and she convinced me that it was okay. He removed my drug and alcohol addictions and I took them back. What I read and learned in the bible was ignored and her place became a house of torment. Scripture after scripture played through my mind like a tape recorder. I rolled off the bed and onto my knees. The pain in my heart was so intense. I repented for all. Sins came out with no excuses, I was wrong. My cries sounded like a man with two broken legs but the feeling was more excruciating. This experience lasted a long time. I turned my back and left my first love, Jesus. Because he loved me, I was being chastised for my willful disobedience. Like a child that was caught playing with matches, I got burnt. I'm sorry, forgive me, please Lord God, in the name of Jesus don't forsake me", I screamed. After saying this, I quit crying. It was peaceful and there was silence. "You will win"; I heard a voice say. Immediately, I sprang to my feet and looked in my closet. It was empty. I turned on every light in my apartment and searched everywhere. I was the only one here. Going into Amanda's room, I sat down by her pictures. Her happy little face made me smile. "It's going to be okay baby girl, Poppa loves you", I said. It was then that I knew who spoke to me. After taking a shower, everything was different. The warmth of forgiveness felt like assurance that things would be alright. Before going to sleep, in my prayers I thanked Him for sending the Comforter. This was the promise made to all who believe in His name.

The first appearance in court for criminal mischief arrived and I showed up expecting to face Candy and Cassie for a quarrelsome confrontation. When my name was called and I stood before the judge, he saw that my accusers did not show up. I was surprised at their absence. The prosecutor requested a continuance and I was given another date to come back.

Noble wouldn't work me and Top Lab worked one or two days a week, so I quit them both. Most of my jobs were at XIH and I stayed busy. The overtime was picking up and I was back working with my friend Marco. We'd do two or three assignments a day. This would give me the money I needed to get caught up on my child support. They told me that when it was time to see my daughter someone would fill in for me. It occurred to me that if workers had to keep taking my place, this would create the same problem I just got away from. To remain reliable and dependable, I'd have to miss some of my visits with Amanda. Most of the work here was on the weekends so I could have my time with her on the weekday.

The June bug month started and those critters made working at night miserable. When you'd look up at the big lights there were hundreds swarming about. The second day was a Wednesday visit and my sister called early to avoid the shenanigans. There was no answer as usual so she left a message on the machine. We were all about to leave when the phone rang. It was Cassie telling Tabby not to bother coming over, she wasn't releasing Amanda. "He's late on child support and I don't trust him", she said. We decided to go anyway and do the exchange the same way. I'd wait at Mary's house for them to bring my little girl to see me. It was the same old song and dance. After knocking several times, Tabby realized Cassie wasn't going to answer the door. They left and met me over at my sister's, with out my youngster. I had a feeling this was going to happen and it didn't upset me as much like the previous times. This was the fifth denial of visitation for me. It was time for me to make an appointment with my attorney. I needed to file papers against Cassie for contempt of court.

Just before my 37th birthday, I was in Charlene's office with a stack of evidence. Not being able to afford the amount of support I was ordered to pay caused me to refinance my car. I had two overdrafts from my bank. We were hoping to force Cassie to reveal where her settlement money went. Five denials of visitation, credit card fraud, fraudulent use of my personal credit information, two negative drug screens, were just some of the documents that were in my file. Charlene took a look at all my information. Three days later, the papers were filed for contempt of court and reduction of child support. Before this week was over we'd have the last session with the evaluator and her report would join us in court. Until we had her written summary, the supervision status would remain on my visitation.

After we filed the motions, Charlene called Tony to make him aware of Cassie's actions. He assured her that he'd make a phone call and address these issues with the mother. It was agreed between our attorneys that for the benefit of our little girl, we should act appropriately and be civil to one another. In my defense I tried to explain that none of this was my fault. My intention was to fulfill the privileges given to me in court. From this point on Cassie was a different person to my sister. Sometimes she was friendly and nice, and other times, grumpy. Tabby always made an effort to be polite for Amanda's sake. She and I both knew it was very important for my youngster to see we could all get along as grown ups should.

The time had come for the last session of our evaluation. When I arrived, the little red car was already there. As I walked in they were talking and we all walked to the back to start our meeting. I was sitting by myself on the couch, as they sat across from me in separate chairs. The lady began to ask us if we argued or was there any domestic violence. "No", both of us replied. Cassie accused me of mental abuse and claimed I pointed a loaded gun at her face. She looked like someone sitting on the North Pole in her underwear, with all the shivering, trembling and shaking. Trying to cry and act out of breath, she definitely was no actress. I've never seen this kind of play acting before. She became unresponsive at times due to her pretended state of fear for me. She admitted to denying me visitation because I was an unfit father and gave the names of two women who'd verify what a bad person I was. It became evident to the counselor that our talk was unproductive. Our time ended about ten minutes after it started because of Cassie's uncontrollable behavior. It was like a bad movie that ended abruptly, with everyone wanting a refund for his or her tickets. I had to remain in the office until it was certain that she was gone. She agreed to finish this part of the evaluation only if her safety could be assured. The evaluator was perplexed at what all just happened and said she never saw anyone act like that before. She told me that when the fee was paid, the report would be written and we'd both receive a copy. Enough time had passed and she let me go.

Going to the last game of the season, my team was in first place. Two of our players didn't show up and we lost our second game. We had the best record, winning 12 of 14. This made the little guys happy. A few asked if I'd be coaching next year and requested that I put them on my team. We had hamburgers and hot dogs afterwards. I had to leave early and said good-bye to all the kids. The commissioner stopped me in the hallway and asked if I could come back later in the week to pick up the trophies. They weren't ready yet. I could give them to the players at another time. I agreed to do this and he congratulated me on a job well done.

Like many times before, my employment became a financial rescue. X-ray has a way of giving you the feeling of success. It's a real test to see if the technician can perform to all the standards required and assure that the final product is satisfactory and acceptable. Learning simple tricks to this trade enabled me to complete some inspections that other people couldn't do. The operations went off without a hitch when I was able to concentrate on my work. Marco was a good worker and would sympathize with the details of my personal problems. "I've had women in the past that gave me a hard time but what Cassie's doing to you is like mental gymnastics, I don't see how you're able to do a good job like this with all that going on", he'd tell me. It was important to do above average work so they'd send me on more assignments. I wanted all the overtime I could get because the evaluation report was $750 and I needed it for our next court appearance.

Tabby and her husband John were getting a king-sized bed and called me to see if I wanted the double they didn't need anymore. This was good because Amanda could have the single I purchased after moving in. The new single bed had drawers in its base where I could put her clothes. My nephew's wife gave me a quilt with cartoon characters on it that added color to her room. My little girl and I now had beds to sleep on in our rooms.

It was the last weekend of the month for me and I had to work on Saturday. Tomorrow was father's day and I requested to have off to be with Amanda. Tabby had no more problems with Cassie since the conversation between our attorneys. When my little girl is with me, we always have a good time and I try to be educational to her. I was thankful for all my chances to see her. Making sure that she ate food instead of candy was hard to do. Sweets were a big part of her diet. Sometimes I had to bargain with her and it wasn't supposed to be this way. Rather than argue with her and spoil the little time we had together, I usually let her have her own way. When my situation improved I could be sturdier with her.

The week started with some terrific news from Mary. She had some friends that returned to the states from England. Their house was filled with furniture from when their daughter lived there. Many things had to be removed to make room for their belongings. If I could find a way to go get what they didn't want, it was mine to keep. I called Jazzy and told her about this. She was happy and told me of her friend who was getting rid of a small dining room set, if I was interested. I accepted the offer and thanked her. I asked her to see if Kyle wouldn't mind using his truck to go with me and gather up all these things my sister told me about and he agreed to help. We arrived at their place, which was an A-framed house made of cypress. We loaded enough furnishings to fill my entire living room. They gave me extras like flatware, kitchenware and a microwave. I was so thankful and told Kyle I'd pay him for moving these things. He told me not to worry about it and was glad he could help. Once everything was unloaded, my place didn't look as empty anymore. You could now tell someone lived here.

The next day I met Jazzy and we went to get the dining room set from her friend's house. It was in their garage next to a big dollhouse. After loading the table and chairs in the van I asked my friend about the large toy. She said they were going to get rid of it in their next garage sale. When I told her that Amanda would love to have it, she said, "I'll see if I can get it for you, for your little girl". We went over to my place and unloaded everything. Walking into my apartment, it had a homey look inside with the scent of cypress wood from all the furniture I put in the night before. Jazzy had to go and I thanked her for everything. As I sat on my couch I remembered reading, "your Father knows what you need before you ask him".

July came with a blow out on the first day of this month. We were doing some inspections in a plant nearby and prepared to get started.

When I lifted the camera it felt as though some one stabbed me in the side. I dropped the equipment and fell to the ground. It hurt too much to move. My helper called for help and an ambulance came out. After we arrived at the hospital, emergency room doctors examined the lump in my abdomen. The physician told me that my intestine ripped through my lower abdominal muscle and that's why I was experiencing so much pain. It was a hernia. This required surgery to repair. A representative from an agency came in to get a specimen for a drug screen due to the job-related injury. Later on that day my boss, Stanley came to pick me up. We discussed what happened and he brought me to my car. He asked if I wanted the rupture in my belly fixed and I told him yes. He put me on light duty after this incident. This injury caused me to lose money and miss visits with my daughter.

When I felt better and to help ease my worries, I attended the dance at a local AA club on Independence Day. Upon arriving I noticed Donny and Candy had followed me there. A friend of mine greeted me as I approached the entrance. Noise from behind caught our attention. Turning around I saw a very pregnant Candy trying to restrain her husband. He got away and ran towards me. "Come here you weasel", he shouted. My pal and I watched as he tripped over a cable that separated the property. His inebriated state became amusing. She persuaded him to get back in the car and they left. The police were summoned and an officer arrived. He told us not to let him in and to call the station immediately if Donny came back.

A week before our time to be in court, the evaluation report arrived. I was astonished with the observations this evaluator made. It was written in sections according to the order of those who participated. The additional people helped to provide information that would assist the counselor in making her recommendations. These were the substance abuse assessor, my two supervisors, a woman from the battered women's shelter and a woman from the victim's assistance shelter. It wasn't any surprise how Cassie recruited two strange women that never even knew me in an attempt to defame my character. I told the truth. Cassie fabricated stories and mixed in truth where she had to. At the end, the meeting between the mother and me was a joke. Our little girl's participation revealed how she is a product of her environment.

It's important to be truthful and I may have revealed too much information about myself. My job to job work history, the problem with drugs and alcohol I once had, how my arrest record was for misdemeanors and not convictions of criminal activity, my thoughts about the "Jezebel" spirit, where I met Cassie, what our relationship was like, the fraudulent use of my personal credit information filled the section written about me. I was surprised that the woman remembered when I told her that Cassie said, "no matter what happens, I'll never keep you from seeing your daughter". She ended this article stating that I seemed to be a good parent, voluntarily attending a parenting class, how I became a coach for a children's baseball team and expressing my deep concerns for the safety and wellbeing of Amanda.

In the section about the mother, Cassie spoke of her sons and how in twenty years they had no relationship with their father. She was married and divorced three times, had an accident, surgeries and was on pain medicine. Saying that I mentally abused her, how I pointed a loaded gun at her, and admitted that we had no history of domestic violence. She said that I'd come home drunk, smoke pot in the house and always go to AA meetings. She insisted of being tortured and threatened. Her stories sounded contradicting? Between interviews she sought help one time at the battered woman's shelter. She felt that I'd never hurt Amanda but after counseling at the shelter her story changed, saying I was "very crazy", and now she thought I would hurt our daughter or tell her things. This article ended with Cassie stating how I killed my sister's dog and that Mary wanted to commit me to a psychiatric institution.

In the section about Amanda, she was seen with Cassie first. She was nice and enjoyed playing with the toys. During their play, our little girl climbed on a chair and jumped off, hurting her nose. Cassie did nothing to prevent this accident. Amanda became upset and wanted to go home, taking the toys with her. When things didn't go her way, she'd get angry and holler. She often had brief tantrums. When playing with her mother, she had to be in control. She was used to getting her own way and demonstrated being the center of attention.

When seen alone, Amanda was very perfectionistic and easily frustrated. She was found to be a demanding child and threw many tantrums. She would often get upset. She did not like being questioned and was happy doing exactly what she wanted to do.

It was mentioned how Donnie and Candy brought Amanda for the meeting with me and they appeared unfriendly, angry and unresponsive to the counselor.

In the section when Amanda was seen with me, we immediately began playing happily with the toys. We had fun and were enjoying ourselves. I'd kiss her on top her head, telling her, "I miss this, boo". (the playing) When I said, "I love you", she reciprocated, "I love you too", and gave me a big hug and a kiss. As always, she was very affectionate and bonded to me. She needed to go to the bathroom and I helped her. Afterwards we returned to play and she spontaneously stated, "I want to stay home with you, daddy". This article ended with the evaluator noting that I appeared far calmer and "more normal" when seen with Amanda, displaying completely appropriate parenting skills and showing a lot of love towards her.

In the next section, the evaluator started this article with Cassie's noticeable trembling. Histrionic and forced, and exaggerated were the words the counselor used to describe this act of hers, the pretended state of fear for me. Stating that I rarely raised my voice at her, we both agreed that there was no history of domestic violence. She insisted that I mentally abused her and admitted to denying me visitation because I was an unfit father. She encouraged the lady to call the victim assistance shelter to verify what a bad person I was. All I could do was sit in amazement and watch Cassie portray herself to be someone she wasn't. We couldn't continue the session because she was shaking, crying and acting out of control.

The substance abuse assessment gave different results for both of us. I co-operated with the man, did not hide anything and openly discussed my past history with drugs and alcohol. He advised that I continue my program of recovery with the AA meetings. Cassie did co-operate but was "guarded and defensive", and showed evidence of substance abuse. He recommended that she enroll in a substance abuse education program.

Tabby admitted to us being denied visitation because I fell behind on child support. She talked about the problems with Brad and how we had to use a police escort for our safety. She agreed that I didn't handle this situation too well in the beginning but since becoming a coach, attending AA meetings and spending more time with my family, I'm managing the stress very well. She ended her conversation with the fact that she and Mary were feeding me because this case was draining all my money. In her opinion, she felt that Cassie was being unfair.

Mary told of her concerns for Amanda. She spoke of my love for kids and how I wanted to volunteer to work with abused children. She commented that her dog did get hurt but didn't know exactly what happened. She did not press charges and never tried to commit me. She ended her conversation with the belief that Cassie was unreasonably angry for something and punishing me by preventing my connection with Amanda.

Cassie went to see a woman at the battered women's shelter. Stating that she was terrified about the upcoming meeting with me, she asked this woman to call the evaluator and tell her about me. In the conversation she had with the counselor, the woman admitted that this might be a "ploy" on Cassie's part, but believed her situation to be a dangerous one.

Cassie asked the evaluator to call a woman at the victim's assistance shelter so she could get information about my arrest record. She went to see her as a witness to the charge pending against me for writing something on her daughter-in-law's car. The woman said that the last time I was arrested was nine years ago, in 1990.

After the counselor evaluated all this information, she ended the report with the reasons for her recommendations, and her actual recommendations. They went as follows:

Reasons

- Amanda appeared equally bonded with both parents but more physically affectionate and better behaved with her father.
- Cassie prefers keeping our child home with her and I prefer that she be in pre-school; she would benefit greatly from being with children her own age, learning to share and be part of a larger community.
- No one should use drugs, consume excessive amounts of alcohol, and engage in any illegal, fraudulent or violent activity at any time when the child is present.
- The mental health of each party needs further investigation; obsessive letters and postcards, and religious preoccupation from me, and; hysterical, seemingly manipulative behavior and

accusations from Cassie. A psychiatric examination is needed from both.

- It is important to Amanda's social and emotional development that she interacts regularly with other children her own age.
- Cassie has not shown the willingness and the ability to facilitate and encourage a close and continuing relationship with the other parent. She must realize that if she blocks a court ordered visitation, she will be in danger of facing a change in custody.

Recommendations

✓ We should have joint custody with Cassie being the domiciliary parent.

✓ A visitation facilitator should be appointed by the court to monitor visitation.

✓ I should remain on supervised visitation until the psychiatric evaluation, including psychological testing is complete. My current supervisors are adequate. Cassie should have Amanda ready and available for each scheduled visitation and her sons or their wives should not be present during any of the exchanges.

✓ I cannot accompany my supervisors to pick up or drop off Amanda.

✓ I should continue my recovery program and Cassie should enroll in a substance abuse and cross addiction education program.

✓ Amanda should be enrolled in a pre-school in order to gain the social and emotional maturity this experience would provide.

✓ Cassie should have a psychiatric evaluation, including psychological testing.

✓ Neither parent, nor anyone they are with, should use drugs or excessive alcohol while in the presence of Amanda.

It seemed as though that someone was finally on my side. A person in the middle saw that I wasn't a bad parent. Some good observations were made. The report became a tool for me to work with. Because of Cassie's behavior, the psychiatric/psychological examination sounded like a good idea. In less than a week we'd be in court and I had to get all this done.

My quest to find a doctor began immediately because our hearing was near. Looking in the phone book I found a renowned psychiatrist who operated out of his home, Dr. Rubin. I told him of my needs and expressed how this all had to be done quickly so I'd have a report for our court date. He was familiar with situations like mine and agreed to help me. Using money John and Tabby loaned me, I paid for his service. I met with him on Thursday and spent the afternoon testing. We talked, I took the very large test called the MMPI-2, and another examination and we were finished. In two days he'd have the document completed and it would be waiting for me in his mailbox on Sunday. This was on time for my agenda.

When my new attorney was told that I was a "code 6", sent Cassie post cards and letters, made a video tape, and that I was on supervised visitation, she must have thought something was wrong with me. I was a good father. When a man is desperate to see his child but access is denied, this action will sometimes produce very questionable behavior. The development of self-control and patience became powerful weapons that would help my defense. Too much aggressiveness would become unproductive. My documentation produced a large paper trail where occurrences could be traced and easily remembered. Daily incidents written on the calendar or in a notebook would serve as evidence. It was important for me to do all this paperwork, be able to answer any questions and remain informed on anything that pertained to my situation. We were preparing to go before a judge who would make a decision for the parents of a little girl that he didn't know.

On Sunday I went to the Dr. Rubin's house to get my test results. The envelope was addressed to Charlene. Curiosity and the fact that I paid for this exam made me feel like I had the right to read it first. The MMPI-2 test showed the lie scale, infrequency scale and the defensiveness scale to be in the acceptable range. The scales measuring abnormal personality traits were within normal range. The only factor that was showing abnormality was the scale measuring anxiety. In his words the doctor stated, "this anxiety level is so high that it may cause a deterioration in his efficiency under pressure, he feels tense, nervous, lacks confidence in himself, and will have difficulty in concentrating". The second test revealed that I had several positive characteristics and a sufficient number of responses to indicate contact with reality. He went on to say that I had the potential for above average intelligence and an effective level of creativity. It was also noted that I was socially responsive, empathetic, emotionally sensitive and exhibited good impulse control. Fundamental to my anxiety problem are strong feelings of social inferiority. The report ended stating that I was a mildly emotionally disturbed individual, the result of a General Anxiety Disorder. However, there were no indications of violent, irrational acting out behavior. Therefore, it is believed that I am not a threat to children. In fact, my relationship with children should be extremely positive in nature. I may be aggressive with adult female figures only. However, even then, I will not exhibit violent and irrational acting out behavior. The most significant factor in my case is that I have an abnormally high anxiety level. Now I knew why it felt like my world was crumbling around me. This diagnosis explained many things about myself and proved Cassie's allegations to be false. I was not the menace she wrongly accused me of being.

On the morning of our court date I arrived at Charlene's office early. She was surprised when I handed her the papers from the psychiatrist. After reading it, "this is good", she said. Tony didn't approve the doctor and the court hadn't ordered the examination yet so we could not use this report. This was credible information that'd defend me if Cassie continued with her slanderous accusations. We briefly went over my finance records and talked about what she had planned. I agreed with what she intended to do and we went to the courthouse.

John and Tabby met us outside the building and we all walked in together. Cassie and Tony were already there. I directed Charlene's attention to them and we went over for an introduction. There was no smiling and laughing like the last time. My counsel was forward, had good integrity and took my case very seriously. As we sat waiting, our attorneys were talking before it was time to go in and see the judge. They walked into the chamber and would soon come out with a new agreement. A good while later my counsel came to me with the decision they reached. "This is what we have, I think you'll like it", she told me. "Supervision status will remain until you both get a psychiatric examination and psychological testing by Dr. Watson, you'll keep your sisters as the supervisors, the exchange area will change to an arcade by the Redwood Mall, her sons cannot be present during any of the exchanges, your monthly support has been reduced to $280 and you'll have to maintain the health insurance", is that okay with you", she asked? "Wow, yes, that's great", I replied. As Charlene looked across the lobby she saw Cassie raging when the news was given to her about the reduction. We went before the judge and our lawyers put on record what was agreed. Tony made the comment on behalf of his client that she was totally disabled, receiving worker compensation. After that Cassie and I were sworn in and gave our consent to the new judgement. This was only the beginning. I was happy with this victory and pleased with my new counsel of record.

It was a bit satisfying that I could have more money in my pocket but with the supervision remaining, this would limit the freedom with my daughter. I was thankful for Tabby helping me. Her health condition hampered the outings my daughter and I could've had. We couldn't go to the park, the zoo or places where children played so she could make new friends. Due to what we agreed, wherever Amanda and I were, one of my sisters had to be with us. These arrangements were my fault because of the first court appearance when Jim led me to believe my visits had to be monitored and that I had no other choice. It wasn't too comfortable for me having to impose on Tabby to see my little girl. In my heart I knew that wasn't necessary. I was in no position to object to this situation and expressed my gratitude for being able to see my child. With patience I hoped that eventually things would change.

When there is a lack of consistent activity between you and your child, the youngster can become disinterested in spending time together with his or her parent. It's hard to provide warm and cheerful outings when you can't go anywhere or do anything. Good childhood memories are very important to a little one as they get bigger. It helps them learn, creates educational experiences and gives them something to grow on. What a real heartache it is to go from a full time parent to a visiting dad, with supervision required.

Although the evidence against my ex had accumulated greatly and I was happy with the work Charlene did, now wasn't the time to let my guard down. It was important to continue my investigations, the research and keep notes on events that happened. I'd also have to stay in contact with my associates. Considering all the events that occurred in the first five months of my separation from Cassie, the battle with her was far from being over.

With a new player in the game I had a better chance of winning. Tony must have known from the start that Charlene was a specialist who didn't back down like Jim did. It was my hope that this situation with Cassie would improve. Expecting an onslaught of more false allegations, wild accusations and the probability of new recruits, I recognized the need for having a strong defense. My plan was to continue documenting all that pertained and follow the orders of the court. I set my appointment with Dr. Watson.

It was time for my second court appearance for criminal mischief. Charlene wanted me to have a friend of hers represent me but I refused. Although this wasn't a major offense I was still expecting the worse. Walking into the courtroom I noticed that Cassie and Candy were not there again. When it was my turn to go before the judge, they found that my accusers had not shown up. Another continuance was issued and I'd have to return in the future.

The time had come for me to fix my hernia. This put me out of work for a while and prevented me from seeing Amanda. After the out patient surgery Tabby helped take care of me because I wasn't able to do much. While recuperating at their place I began learning how to use the computer. John gave me some helpful advice and I developed an interest. He made his living building and repairing this equipment. After working with the device for a while the operations became less complicated. I considered buying one of these for myself. At the end of July I was feeling better and it was time for me to go home.

There wasn't any problem getting Amanda for my visits. My attorney must have told Tony how contempt for denial of visitation is a serious offense when custody issues are concerned. If the man is late on his child support, that doesn't give the woman a right to stop him from seeing his child. The only time I didn't see my daughter was when I didn't have a supervisor, had to work, or my injury and the surgery. The days we'd spend together were going to be more consistent. This would help me develop a better relationship with my little girl. She enjoyed going to my sister's and was getting more used to being with me.

The psychiatric evaluation was near and I didn't have the money. I wasn't fully recovered from my surgery and hadn't been working. Jazzy and Kyle agreed to pay the fee for this visit. When I picked up the loan from her, she told me of a surprise in the van. We went outside and when the door was opened I saw the dollhouse from her friend, disassembled. I put the pieces in my car. This was Amanda's first big toy to put in our apartment.

It was time for my first session with the psychiatrist. His secretary did all the work, which was to have me take the MMPI-2 test again. This big exam had 564 questions and takes a while to complete. In addition to that was a "complete the statement" test. Dr. Watson talked to me briefly, asked a few questions and I was finished. The lady said my next visit would be with Amanda and the doctor. We scheduled our appointment for next week.

Almost a month after my surgery I was back in the field. Anyone who worked with me knew they had to carry the camera. Stanley would sometimes check with me to make sure I had no more pain from the injury. The money from this job was needed for our next court appearance after the sessions with Dr. Watson were complete. It was important to get all the hours I could for my attorney fees, the psychiatric evaluation and my personal bills. My financial status had to be kept up so my privilege to see Amanda would remain. It was important to make myself available for work. If people took my place at work so I could keep my visitations, this would jeopardize my position with XIH. This was the same problem I had at Noble. There'd be some times that I'd have to lose visits with my daughter.

At the end of August it was time for my second session with the doctor. Charlene sent Tony a letter to notify Cassie of the time and place we were to meet. Amanda was happy to see me but made to sit in the chair next to her mother. Our meeting started a short while later. It was the same as with the evaluator. Dr. Watson sat nearby and observed us interact with each other. We had fun playing together. I could see that my youngster was getting smarter as she would tell me colors and put numbers together in a puzzle. There were animal characters that I'd get the name wrong on purpose, so she could correct me. I'd ask her questions about all the toys. It seemed like we just got started and our time was over. We went out to the front and once again I had to watch my little girl walk away.

In September I started moonlighting. Mama Mia Pizza needed delivery drivers and I took a job doing that. A manager took me on a trial run as part of my training. Returning to the store we drove down Bloomington Street. Passing Cassie's house I noticed Brad and his friends loading up a truck with furniture. She was moving. It worried me that this might further detach my connection with Amanda. There was more than enough money from her lawsuit to keep that house. Bad decisions on her part may have caused a monetary problem.

My credit was somewhat cleared and I attempted to buy a computer. The application was denied due to a debt with Cell-U-Phone. Mailing them the letter stating the results of the phone company's investigation quickly cleared up the misunderstanding. Soon the new device arrived at my door. This piece of equipment would enable me to keep in contact with my associates and retrieve information. Saul was happy to hear about my new purchase. He's an activist for the rights of non-custodial parents and had plenty of documentation to send me. The Internet would allow me to get this data from him at a minimal expense.

Tabby received a call with bad news from Cassie. Being vague in her explanation, she said our daughter had fallen and suffered a laceration on the back of her head. The doctor at the emergency room put four staples in. Later in the week I saw my youngster at the market with her mother. "Daddy", she exclaimed! She turned and looked up at her mom, asking, "can I go see him"? "Yeah, it's okay", Cassie replied. She ran over and hugged me. "How are you doing, I heard you had an accident", I asked? At this time Cassie had come over closer to us. When I looked at Amanda's injury, her hair was caught in the staples. At the base of her skull was where this wound was located. Had it been any deeper, our child may have been paralyzed? The mother pulled a comb out of her purse and attempted to brush the hair away from the injury. I told her not to worry about it. Noticing that she had beer and diet coke in her basket made me wonder if that was the reason for our little girl getting hurt. If Cassie's too busy drinking, she can't be watching Amanda properly.

Having two jobs made it hard to find the time to do anything else. Working at XIH during the day and Mama Mia at night gave me a busy schedule. While delivering pizza in my neighborhood, several times I noticed Cassie's black Firebird and the red Stealth parked at the apartment complex next to mine. One day I saw Nat at the supermarket and asked him about this. He told me she moved two blocks away from her house, not too far from me. This seemed like a strange decision for her to make. She claimed to be so afraid of me but moves very close to where I lived. Although she was nearby, I still couldn't see my little girl without supervision and Tabby had to go to the mall to pick her up.

Sending out E-mails to family and friends help me get familiar with my new computer. A message came back from Saul informing me of the data he'd be sending. He said that it might be a little disturbing but very important that I know this information. He urged me to look it over. This made me curious of what he had. It would involve lots of reading and that was something I didn't have time for. I asked him to send it immediately. It'd take him a while to gather everything together and he'd send it to my mailbox.

The final session with the psychiatrist arrived. We sat in his office while he asked me questions about my childhood, family and the relationship I had with Cassie. He wanted to know if we fought or argued often, and the reason for our split. As always I told the truth and didn't hide anything. He spent most of his time writing notes and this meeting didn't last too long. At this time the evaluation cost me $450 and $850 would be needed to write the report. Asking the receptionist how many sessions Cassie had left, she replied, "she hasn't even called to set up an appointment". Without her participation, this examination couldn't be completed. She was now in contempt for refusing to follow court orders.

With work picking up and not having a supervisor, this caused me to lose visits with Amanda. The weekend is when I was allowed to have the most time with her. At XIH, most of their jobs were at the end of the week. I made good money doing x-ray jobs and tried not to pass up an opportunity to work. If I had a chance to see my little girl during the week, work at Mama Mia would be cancelled. Borrowing for the doctor visits had me owing money to family and friends. My financial status was improving and I'd soon have to pay my lawyer. To remove the supervision status, this required another court appearance.

In October a large E-mail came from Saul. His writings contained pages of information I knew nothing about. It was too much to read all at one time so I picked a subject and started with it. Fatherlessness, the nation's number one epidemic hurting children, teenagers and young adults. Kids living in single parent homes without any kind of relationship with their biological father can result in emotional, psychological, behavioral, and in later years, sexual disorders. Men must be involved in the lives of children they help produce to ensure a healthy lifestyle that contains obedience, self-discipline, self-control and self-respect. A mans participation has to start in the early stages of the child's development. The learning experience is an ongoing lesson both parents endure. This baby was born to a couple and they should equally share all the responsibilities. He should be the role model and set the example so the child will grow up morally fit. When bad habits are seen by the youngsters, they can evolve to possess similar or the same traits because it appears to be acceptable. Adult situations should stay in the grown up arena. If a man and woman split up, it's natural for him to try and remain in the life of his child regardless of what anyone says. Men are needed for guidance, correction, emotional support and discipline when necessary.

There are some guys that father children and don't want anything to do with them. With no remorse, men evade or abandon their youngsters. Where is the heart of this man? Does he proudly say, I haven't seen my child in years and helped destroy his or her life"? How can he not know that without his presence, his kid's life may be ruined? Can it be said that such a man has no conscience? His absence can cause low self-esteem, self-doubt and give the child a higher expectancy of being rejected. When the youngster grows up, drugs, alcohol or both might be used to relieve the pain from dad's inattentiveness in their earlier years. The moral stability in this young one may be dislodged or lost. Without interference from the mother, dad should remain the leader, the protector and the provider of his kids. When he gives no support, the mother usually has no choice but to seek assistance from welfare. These men who desert their children help the "low view" of the father remain.

There are many men that don't try and then there are some that will do all they can to instill their child's wellbeing. Fatherlessness can exist without the man realizing it. While some fathers live at home, not enough involvement with his children can cause them to feel unimportant or left out. If you often say, "after the ballgame is over, when I'm finished we will or I don't have time", your youngster may stop asking. He or she is left alone to play by him or herself. One of the most valuable gifts a dad can give his children is attention and affection. If the only thing the little ones want is your time, give it. Coloring books, puzzles, play-doe or any creative activity you can do together will show your love for them.

Alarming were the effects of Fatherlessness to kids, as they grow older. Starting with children, those who had learning disorders, the inability to concentrate, behavior or conduct problems, were easily intimidated, lacked confidence in themselves and showed mild emotional disorders mostly lived in single parent homes. Teenagers that, had unusually aggressive behavior, resented authority, displayed poor educational performance, are frequently absent from class, fail or drop out of school, commit delinquent acts, engage in premature sexual activities, have continued drug and alcohol use, experience depression, and contemplate suicide mostly came from single parent homes. Young adults who, could not hold a steady job, had no plans for their future, had habitual drug or alcohol usage, had children out of wedlock, neglected or abused their children, married or divorced early, suffer from poverty, displayed violent or irrational behavior, performed criminal acts, were often arrested, convicted and incarcerated grew up in single parent homes. Disturbing was that the amounts of people in all these age groups were unusually high. In conjunction with this was that both genders may have had physical illnesses, headaches, asthma attacks and mental problems related to the absence of their biological father. In some cases he was at home but didn't have a close and continuing relationship with his children. This is what can happen when there is neglect, abuse or an absence from dad. While observations like these don't pertain to everyone, the people for whom they do may have repercussions that can last a lifetime. Above are the results from a father who ignores instruction. (Ephesians 6:4)

Saul is an architect. Because of the traumatic bout that his ex put him through with their children when they were young, he does his research as a hobby. The information he sent amazed me. Donny and Brad resembled some of his findings and in some instances the description was exact. Cassie never bothered her sons with chores and did most everything for them, which helped to make them irresponsible. Because she decided many things for them, they weren't able to learn from the errors they might have made. This encouraged their dependence on her, which prevented them from becoming independently responsible. She often had to bail them out so they'd remain unaccountable for any mistakes or accidents that occurred. If she didn't, that might create anger in their relationship. She gave them a big allowance in the form of two sports cars and they didn't have to do anything for it. She'd always give in to Brad's bad temper. I sent my friend a letter of appreciation for all this data. He responded by telling me that there was more to send and the best was yet to come. The next packet of information would explain how some fathers get ejected from the lives of their children due to a phenomenon called Parental Alienation Syndrome.

The time for my appearance in court for criminal mischief arrived. The courtroom was full and I had to wait a long time. My name was called and I walked up to the front. The prosecuting attorney called for Cassie and Candy but there was no answer. They were not there again. This was the third time they did not show up. The counselor discussed this with the judge and then came over to me. "We're going to dismiss the charge, keep your nose clean and don't come back", he said with a smile. "You won't see me again", I responded.

It was my weekend visit and I couldn't wait to see my daughter. Work kept me very busy lately so our chances to see each other were few. I waited for John and Tabby to bring her back from the mall. When they arrived and Tabby got Amanda out of the truck, "daddy", she hollered! As she ran to me I lowered myself and she jumped into my arms. We hugged tightly. "I missed you", I told her. "I missed you too", she said. We all went inside. My little girl liked to pet my sister's dogs and sometimes we'd play outside. Watching television or playing games, anything we did was fun. It became worrisome to me how she wouldn't eat. Unless it was sweet, she didn't like it. I couldn't express my concern to Cassie because we weren't talking. The hours always went by quickly when we were together. It felt like our visits were too short. I was happy and thankful for being able to see her.

Once again, employment and not being able to fulfill the court requirements caused me to continue losing time with my daughter. Without either of my sisters, I couldn't see Amanda. My situation didn't give me much of a choice. The jobs were helping me get the funds I needed to make my predicament better. With all these hours stacking up I was able to save money for future legal events. Three months had passed since the judgement ordered us to see the doctor. I completed the psychiatric evaluation and Cassie didn't even call to make her first appointment. When I told Charlene about this, she suggested that we might have to force her to complete the sessions with Dr. Watson as ordered by the court.

The month of thanksgiving started and this brought cooler temperatures to the south. Knowing that I wouldn't be able to see Amanda for the holidays bothered me. Her mother and I had been separated for about nine months. First Cassie severed the communication line between us and then she filed a motion against me filled with false allegations. Jim did a lousy job when he represented me. This was a mess I had to clean up. My refusal to give up on Amanda became the driving force to proving my innocence. Evidence to show that I was not guilty of anything began to appear. By following the advice of my attorney and doing what the judge ordered us to do, I had a better chance of lifting the supervision off my visitations. This would enable us to go more places, creating joyful memories for both of us.

One night while delivering pizza I stopped at a convenience store near the Cablanka. As I paused at the exit of the parking lot and waited for traffic to clear, there was a jolt that shook my vehicle. Looking to my right I saw it was Brad. He was running from about ten feet back and kicking into the passenger side. Oncoming cars prevented me from leaving right away and he continued to kick two more times. After his last kick, he spit on that side of my car. Quickly pulling away, I drove to the end of the block and stopped. I got out and looked to see if anything was damaged. A man and his family saw this. They slowed down behind me and rolled down their window. "You alright, what's wrong with that guy", he asked? He saw what happened. Informing him that I've had trouble with that guy in the past, I asked if he'd mind telling the police what he witnessed in the parking lot. He was going to bring his wife and child home first and agreed to meet me at a nearby service station. I called an officer and they came out. We all looked at the damage. Brad cracked my side panel, chipped the paint and buckled the pinstripe. The force from his kicking damaged the controls inside the door that operated my power window, causing it not to work. The deputy told me the culprit was being detained at the lounge and we all had to return there to identify him. When we arrived they had Brad in handcuffs up against the squad car. The man who saw this criminal act was an investigator for the police. He got there first and had already identified the guilty one. They issued the delinquent a citation for simple criminal damage and he was allowed to go free. A lawman brought me to my car and suggested I get an estimate on the damages.

The next day I went to a repair shop to find out what it'd cost to fix my car. This vehicle has dent free flex panels made of fiberglass. That's why there appeared to be no damage on the outside. When the estimator found out that the power windows didn't work, this pushed the repair price up high. The total amount exceeded $1000. I presented the paperwork to the district attorney at the courthouse. The charge was then upgraded to felony criminal damage to private property. They set a court date and told me that a jury would try Brad. My hope was that this incident might help the son act like a grown up and develop some self-control.

My funds began to grow and I went shopping for clothes and toys to put in Amanda's room. There was a second hand store I knew about that was well stocked. Looking through the children's apparel I found some colorful dresses, shirts, pants and shoes. All these items looked new, in mint condition. In the toy section I found little dolls for her dollhouse. I made furniture out of the small boxes my checks come in. As time went on I had her room filled with plenty. Jazzy's friend gave me several outfits her daughter had out grown. Tabby told me that our cousin had an entire toy kitchen set for us to go get. I lowered the shelf and clothes rack in her closet so Amanda could see and reach everything. When I was finished she had her own wardrobe, several pairs of shoes, coloring books, a toy microwave and stove, plenty of toy pots, pans and eating utensils, stuffed animals and a variety of creative games to play with. She needed to start learning how to use a computer so I bought a compact disc loaded with some activities and games that would educate her. The CD would jumpstart her knowledge in colors, letters, shapes and sizes. Imagining all the excitement I'd see on her face when she saw her room would occupy most of my time.

A problem occurred at XIH that would lead to my dismissal. I was using the fax machine and Stanley walked in. The space I was in belonged to his wife Darla, the secretary. I was told to leave and go into his office. My boss apologized for being so rude. His reason for acting like that was because things were turning up missing. He and his wife were upset about this. "Did you take anything out of there", he asked? When I told him "no", he looked as though he didn't believe me. For him to insinuate that I was a thief made me very angry. I emptied my pockets and boots to prove I didn't take anything. It wasn't necessary for me to act like this. Marco and I had a job to go on and he came in as I was putting my boots back on. As Stanley was explaining to him what he and I were talking about, Darla walked in. Waving a pair of scissors at me, "If you go into my office one more time, I'll cut your head off", she angrily warned. This was too much for me. We gathered our equipment and headed for the job site. The tank we were to work in smelled like a gasoline can. I thought this was too dangerous for us. Marco wasn't feeling good and I was still thoroughly upset from what happened at the shop. We didn't even get prepared for the inspection and left the plant. The foreman phoned my boss and he called me. We talked briefly and Stanley told me to be in his office at 8am. I showed up at 9am, an hour late. He used that as the reason to fire me.

It was my last weekend visit for this month and I asked Tabby if we could take Amanda over to my place so she could see her new room. Everything was set in place and a good surprise for her was long overdue. "Please, I really want to do that for her", I asked her? She obliged and left to go get my daughter. Later in the afternoon we went to my apartment. "Where we going daddy", she asked? "I'm going to show you where your Poppa lives", I told her. I left the light on in her room so that'd be the first thing she saw when we walked in. She ran to her new play area and climbed in her dollhouse. With smiles and laughs she hugged her stuffed animals. There were too many toys and she didn't know what to do first. We had a puzzle to put together, coloring books and seven little dolls for their tiny mansion. When she got hungry I gave her chocolate mint ice cream. Now was not the time to argue about her eating habits? This was like a birthday party for my little girl. When it was time to go she began to cry. "We'll come back next time", I promised her. We drove to Tabby's house and they brought her to the mall to meet Cassie. This was surely the best time I had with my child. Now I was going to try and get the additional things she asked for.

The holidays weren't too joyful for me this time of the year. As of yet there wasn't one I got to spend with my little girl. When the occasion would arrive, she'd be with her mother. To me this wasn't fair so I had some kind of surprise for her whenever she came to see me. My records revealed that although my weekend visits consisted of two days, I never had a supervisor on Sundays and would only get to spend eight hours with her on Saturdays. All this lost time with my daughter started in August. I was in no position to complain. This situation became a burden on my sister Tabby and I could not rely on Mary to help me.

A new company called Allbell needed x-ray people and I went to talk with them. Their shop was a little far away, across the river. Their pay rates were higher than the places where I had been working. They had inspection contracts in nearby plants and fabrication shops. Work here was mostly during the day and that meant I could keep my pizza delivery job. The man I spoke with knew of my performance because we did jobs together in the past. The next day I started working for them. He had upcoming jobs in the future and would need more personnel. When that time came I knew just who to get, Marco.

The Santa Claus month was upon us and I wasn't too jolly because of all the commotion. Cassie's apartment nearby no longer had her sports cars parked by it. She moved away again with Amanda and I didn't know where they were. Because she was always on time at the mall, this had me thinking that she had to be living somewhere close. I couldn't talk to my little girl because there was no telephone communication. A close friend of mine who was helping me stay informed offered to look into this. He used to be a detective and assured me that this wouldn't be a problem. In a few days he'd give me a call with what he found out.

Not knowing how Amanda was began to affect my health. If I ate, it was once or twice a day. My weight dropped and I looked thin. A case of insomnia made its presence known and that helped me be late for work. I didn't like my job but needed the money. Although I was on a guaranteed 40-hour workweek, the attitude I had due to my personal problems made that unappreciated. I spent most of my nights compiling evidence and keeping tract of what was going on. My dilemma seemed like it was progressively getting worse.

It was cold making deliveries at night. One evening I stopped at a different convenient store. On my way in I noticed a black car but didn't know what kind it was. Once inside, I knew. I saw Cassie at the counter buying two cases of beer. Amanda turned around and didn't recognize me right away because I was in my Mama Mia uniform. When she saw my face, "Daddy", she exclaimed. She ran over to me and jumped into my arms. She hugged me tight and laid her head on my shoulder. "How are you doing", I asked her? "I'm fine", she said quietly. While holding my little girl I noticed that Cassie asked a strange man to help her by carrying the booze she bought out to her car. When he picked up the two 24-packs, the mother came over to me and peeled our little girl out of my arms. When she tried to hold on, "let go Amanda", her mother snapped. It broke my heart to see how this saddened my child. Cassie's action angered me. At the counter I bought a pack of smokes. "That's my little girl", I told the man behind register. "What's wrong with that woman", he asked? "I don't know", I replied. I waited a while before going out so there'd be no altercation with them. Walking out I saw Cassie doing her pretended state of fear act for the stranger. From a distance I saw her give him two beers, and she left. After she was gone I attempted to get in my car. The man appeared to be very angry as he approached me. When he got closer I could tell that he was drunk. "What's your problem, why do you scare that woman, she's afraid of you", he yelled. When I tried to explain, he interrupted me. "You go near her again, I'll kill you, you don't want to mess with me", he shouted. Looking behind him, I saw the people in the store at the door watching all this. I didn't respond to any of his threats and left the scene. This event had me shook up and I didn't feel much like working anymore. When I returned to the parlor my manager told me to take the night off, go back to that store and file a report with the police. Doing like he suggested, I went back and called for an officer. A while later Deputy Fuller came out. She remembered the last time we met and didn't like having to take this call. I told her Cassie was there, she befriended a man and gained his sympathy by acting scared, which resulted with verbal threats from him. The drunk was gone at the time but the witnesses here did confirmed what happened. As the paperwork was being written the boozer staggered his way back to the store. He had left his keys on the counter. I pointed him out and Fuller went over to speak with him. They talked briefly and he walked away. She came back, finished her work and gave me a number to get the report with. She saw nothing wrong with the man's actions and defended him because I frightened Cassie. It used to be that I only had Donny and Brad to watch out for. The "I'm so scared" act could now be used by their mother to recruit strangers, people I didn't even know. Knowing she could do this had me worried.

My detective friend called me at home with the news I had been waiting for. He looked into the disappearance of Cassie and found out that she had moved in a place two blocks away from the Cablanka. This was the same drug infested neighborhood where we lived at the time Amanda was born. This information was a big help to me and eased some of my anxiety. "Not knowing if my daughter was alright is making me sick", I told him. "I know exactly what you're going through", he said. Long ago he had the same problem. He told me to hang in there and try not to worry too much, remain strong and things would get better.

The next day I went to see Charlene. It was disturbing to me that I never had any holiday visits with my little girl, that my time with her on the weekends were one day instead of two due to the supervision status, that there was no phone communication and that Cassie had disobeyed the judge by not completing the psychiatric evaluation. My lawyer was going to prepare the motions for all of this and include the denial of visitation, which had been put on hold. We were going to use these contempt charges to seek incarceration if she didn't lift the supervision off my visitations. There wasn't much time left and we pushed for an expedited hearing in an attempt to gain a visit on the next holiday. I signed the papers and the next day they were rushed to the courthouse. Our court date was set four days before Christmas.

There were about ten days left and I had to be ready. I gathered my documentation for court. I had five negative drug screens that were two months apart from each other. My notes showed that I had little time to spend with my daughter due to the court required supervision status and the different incidents that occurred. I had the report from Dr. Rubin. My receipts served as proof that I completed the psychiatric evaluation as ordered by the judge. Tabby agreed to appear to confirm the five times I was denied visitation and tell of the harassment that we endured from Cassie and Brad when trying to do the exchanges of my daughter.

Calculating the amount of time I spent with Amanda irritated me. From April Fools Day when I was given the privilege to see her till our next court date was 262 days. That's 6288 hours. Counting all the hours from the visitation days granted to me in the first judgement came to 431 hours. The injury and my employment cost me 105 hours and no holiday visits added 16 more. Not having a supervisor caused me to lose 120 hours and Cassie denied me 30. This meant that in the last nine months of this year I got to spend 160 hours with my little girl. When you add the hours in a week, it comes to 168. This was an injustice to my daughter and me. To my Savior, with prayer I implored this unfair situation to change.

At Tabby's house, my niece and I began discussing the concerns I had for my daughter. She agreed with me that my youngster should be in pre-school. In two months my little girl would be four years old. A year later she would start kindergarten. If she had a structured environment and was punctual in her attendance, this may help develop an adequate routine that would prepare her for school. She would arrive at a scheduled time, learn, eat at a certain time, nap, play with her friends and return home. Being able to interact with kids her own age would improve her social skills. The teachers there would help expand her education level. Cassie wasn't talking to me so we couldn't discuss the benefits of pre-school. There was no way for me to find out exactly what Amanda's life was like over at her mother's house. I knew she watched a lot of television and sometimes played with her friend Diana next door.

It was time for my haircut and I went over to Jazzy's. With the court date approaching, I began to predict the outcome and that worried me. "You're gonna win, Cassie never did what the court ordered and that's contempt", she said. We talked about the things Amanda and I did when she is with me. When I spoke of our time together being too short and that I felt cheated, she suggested that I show more gratitude. "Some dads don't even get to see their kids", she said. We talked about the behaviors she developed at her mothers. I already saw how she acted a little spoiled and was only happy when things went her way. "Try to be selective in your activities, make them creative and educational, be the fun daddy and enjoy yourselves", Jazzy told me. That sounded like a great idea, easy to do and it was similar to what I had planned. Now wasn't the time to be concerned over petty issues.

On the morning of our hearing we all met at Charlene's office. We discussed all the evidence I had. John and Tabby talked about the contempt Cassie was in for denial of visitation and I explained in detail about all my documentation. Our plan was to get the supervision lifted off the visitation, gain holiday visits and I wanted to have telephone privileges. I also requested that the exchange area be moved to the other side of the Redwood Mall by the police station for safety reasons. I didn't want Brad making any surprise appearances. Because of my adherence to the previous judgement, I wasn't too worried. When it was time, we all walked over to the courthouse.

We walked in to find our opposition waiting. Cassie looked like she hadn't had any sleep and was not prepared for this occasion. We moved aside so our lawyers could talk amongst themselves about what they were going to present to the judge. When they were finished, my attorney came over and sat down by us. We saw Tony motion Cassie over to talk with her. Charlene tells us, “when I presented him the paper showing how you had only 160 hours with your daughter and 5 denial of visitations, he got angry and he didn’t know that she avoided the evaluation either”. We glanced over at our opponents and noticed him scolding her. A while later our counsels went in to see the judge. Their meeting didn’t last too long and they soon came out. Charlene sat down to confer with us. As John, Tabby and I listened, my lawyer told us of the long awaited news. “The supervision will be lifted, the exchange area will change to in front of the police station, she is to have the child call you at your home on Monday and Thursday between 7 and 8pm, there will be random drug screens to be done within 72 hours of notification and your holiday visitation will start in four days on Christmas, how’s that”, she asked. “That’s great, it’s everything I asked for”, I replied. We were overwhelmed with joy. John and Tabby were relieved and decided to go home because their help wouldn’t be needed. As I walked them out they expressed their happiness for me. “It’s about time”, John said with a smile. Tabby asked me to call her later and they both walked away. Before returning inside I stopped to pray, “O heavenly Father, thank you for what you’ve done for me, thank you Jesus, thank you Holy Spirit”. Since the night I prayed in my room and heard that voice, I became successful in whatever I needed to do. Walking in I saw our attorneys chatting again. When I sat down Charlene came to me and said, “we’re next”. A while later we went in and put our statements on record. My time with Amanda would start at 6pm on Friday until 7pm on Sunday, beginning after the holidays. “Thank you Jesus, thank you Jesus”, I kept saying to myself as I listened to this agreement. After we were finished I walked my lawyer to her office. We talked of the accomplishments from my last two hearings. Both of us had believed there would be no more court dates. She told me to call her in the event Cassie decided to disobey the new judgement. I shook her hand, thanked her and went home to relish our victory. I had no more worry about being denied an opportunity to see my child or suffer a confrontation with Donny or Brad. I’d be home when it was time for her to call. My visits no longer had to be monitored. We could go to the park, the zoo or church like I had been wanting to. Finally, my little girl and me, we were free at last.

Two days later I picked Amanda up for a Wednesday visit. As we drove away I informed her of how we wouldn’t be going to Aunt

Tabby's and that we'd be going over to Poppa's place. This news made her very happy. Upon arrival she ran over to the Christmas tree and looked at all her gifts. She wanted to start opening them. "No, not now", I told her. Using the method of distraction, we went to her room. She got lost in the excitement with all her toys and the closet full of clothes and shoes. I softened up a bit and took a gift from under tree and presented it to her. It was a CD for the computer. She opened it up and I showed her how to put it in, install it and do the activities. She caught on quickly and we spent the rest of our time playing the games. This became an educational experience for her. When it was time to go, she didn't want to leave. I assured her that she'd be back in two days and we'd have more fun because it'd be time to open all her gifts. She quickly agreed and we left.

Considering the information I received from Saul, it's important for dad and his children to be together. This is the needed time that most kids don't get. It helps to be the friend, not just the father. That is what I had been doing. When Amanda talks, I listen. When she asks a question, I provide answers the best way I can. With encouragement I try to incite her ability to do things. When I explain the outcome of a task she becomes more motivated to do it. If I'm not patient with her she can get discouraged or frustrated. It's important to her that I try and understand any problems she may have. She is rewarded for her accomplishments and that gets her to try harder. A prize is given for a job well done. The youngster will feel the same way you do when you get your paycheck at the end of the workweek for doing what's expected, or your job. This is a good way to raise a child but it has to start at an early age. It's a useful tool when it comes to enforcing the consequences for disobedience.

Everything was in place at my apartment for a holiday celebration. Her gifts were set under the tree and I hid her new bicycle in the closet. I knew she'd want to open everything as soon as she arrived and that's what we did. After it was all over we went to her bedroom. "There's one more surprise but you have to find it", I told her. When she opened the doors to her closet, "a new bicycle", she screamed. Immediately we went outside and she rode her bike for a while. When she got tired, we went inside and she wanted to get on the computer. I was impressed at how quickly she caught on. "Daddy, I love you", she said. Hearing her say this was soothing, like music to my heart. We had lots of fun and enjoyed our time together. I noticed that her eating habits were poor and she wanted only cakes and ice cream. I urged her to eat some yogurt and an apple. The time was coming when I'd have to explain to her the importance of proper nutrition and the benefits of having a healthy body. As for now we were content being together. She played with all her toys and we watched some television. We spent 16 hours together, the equivalence of a full weekends visit. This is how it should've been from the beginning but no one ever suspected that Cassie would be so selfish when it came to our daughter spending time with me. How could she not know that her crazy conflicts were an injustice to Amanda?

The judge granted me most everything I fought for in court. In time I would be able to tell if Cassie was going to obey and fulfill the agreement we made in court. It would have made me happier if I could have been guaranteed to have more time with Amanda. I remember how forgetful her mother is and wasn't sure that I'd get my phone privileges. A question that wasn't answered was the reason for Cassie's strange behavior. Because she didn't get the court ordered psychiatric evaluation, there was no way to tell if there was anything wrong with her. If the way she acted were due to a mental problem, my attorney and I needed to know about this for the safety of my daughter. It was my hope that things would finally settle down between us. These proceedings and the legal fees were too expensive for me.

After the last Wednesday visit of the year I began to prepare for the widely circulating rumors that the computers were going to crash worldwide. This was hard to believe. There are many million-dollar organizations operating everything through this device and they were not going to lose all they had due to a problem that could've been fixed. There were plenty of advertisements for generators, freeze dried foods and camping supplies. As the end of the year approached a lot of companies made plenty money off the fears of people who didn't know any better. Many thought it was the end of the world. We may endure some complications but surely the world as we know it, was not over. There are instances in the bible that had not come to pass, clearly indicating that the end was not near. If people would just read the word of God, that alone would prepare them for anything. Christians rely on the strength of their faith to carry them through tough times like this. (II Corinthians 5:7)

Chapter Seven

CHANGING THE RULES

Looking back on the previous year, what a relief it was to finally be over. The ball and chain around my ankle had been loosed and the predicament was different. Just because we reached a new agreement at our last court appearance didn't mean everything would go smoothly. If I had learned anything it was this; that no matter what the judge ruled or what was written, when we walked out of that courtroom Cassie would do what she wanted, when she wanted, however she wanted. The court's authority never did intimidate her. When things didn't go her way it was certain that she'd start throwing punches in the form of false allegations or whatever she could make up. Considering the type of person she was, I had to continue following my same routine as before. The paper trail and my notes written on the calendar would serve as a valuable referencing system for a strong defense.

On the day beginning the new millennium, predictions of a big computer failure were found to be false. Logging on to the Internet, I found out that nothing had changed. There were plenty of people that just didn't know and to be on the safe side, prepared themselves the best way they knew how. This wasn't the first time that someone made lots of money off the fears of many. We made it without computers before and would again if we had to. I saw that a large e-mail from Saul was waiting in my mailbox but I didn't have time to look at it. In the subject line it read, "Parental Alienation Syndrome". I had been waiting for this.

Also at this time the media told the American public about a popular Latino singer who they believed was gay. In this new year he was supposed to "come out of the closet". Radio, newspapers and magazines helped develop the hoax. Here was another example of how propaganda is used to mislead people and defame a person. Previously, a Degenerate had announced her homosexuality and she was embraced by many. A major television network encouraged her to display this abnormal lifestyle on the screen, portraying it to be normal. Intimate same sex relationships aren't natural, should be kept private and out of view. Our children don't deserve to be exposed to this kind of behavior. Homosexuality will remove the natural affection that attracts men and women to each other. (Romans 1:27)

It was time for me to go pick up Amanda at the mall for our New Years holiday visit. She spent a lot of time on the computer playing with her games. Eventually she'd be using one of these devices in school. I felt that now was a good time for her to become familiar with one. After using it a few times the operation became easier for her. We had fun doing about the same things we did on Christmas. We were happy just being together.

Work would soon be picking up because of the inspection contract we were getting from a nearby refinery. The job guaranteed us 12 hours a day, five days a week with weekends off. This was good for my visitation schedule. The boss was lenient towards my visits and asked me again about finding a reliable worker to help us. I worried that my continued absence would cause a grievance between the other employees and me. My finances were improving and I could now make plans to go places with my little girl. The next weekend would be my first unsupervised visit with her and we already had lots of things to do.

With a new judgement in place, Cassie began to act more civilized. We'd have small talk that didn't exist in the past. In the event that I'd have to miss a visit, it was my responsibility to call and cancel no less than 30 minutes before the time we were to meet. She gave me her phone number and said that it was registered in the name of her fiancé. I was happy that she found a man, was in love and going to get married. My little girl called me a couple of times but our conversations were brief. According to my caller ID, the phone number was in her brother Wendell's name, not her fiancé. It was hard to understand why she had so much trouble telling the truth. It worried me that if she continued to be dishonest in front of Amanda, then our little girl may grow up thinking that this is acceptable behavior and start fibbing. I didn't want to be the one having to sort through all the lies to get to the truth. It was my hope that my youngster wouldn't pick up on these bad habits of her mother's.

My job became more consistent. Everyday we'd go in and get out at the same time. Usually at an inspection company, the schedule is so erratic you don't know when you're going to be working or not. Most of the time it's impossible to make any plans. It became tiresome for me because of my other part time job. Trying to be at home for when Amanda called made me late delivering pizza more times than they appreciated. If this continued I'd have to talk with Cassie about it and hope this matter could be settled between us. I didn't want to contact Charlene about not getting my phone calls and it'd look childish to go back into court for something this minor. I decided to wait and see if this action would change.

My first weekend with Amanda was filled with excitement. We stayed up late playing. I began to wonder if she had too many toys. We ate almost a whole pizza by ourselves. She had these two babies and would pretend to cook for them with play food. When she was finished I'd have to feed them. After they ate I had to read them a bedtime story and she'd put them in bed to sleep. We'd tip toe out her room, turn off the light and close the door. To the living room we'd go and eat some ice cream while we watched a video. The next day was about the same. She wanted to visit her Aunt Tabby so we did. It was easy to find something for us to do. Creative activities and games on the computer kept us busy.

Cassie had a doctor's appointment and allowed Amanda to come over to my place. When I explained to my youngster that we'd be spending more time together, this made her happy. She didn't like the sodas too much and often asked for water to drink because it tasted better. The Brita filter I use may have been the reason for this. It filters out both the chemicals and the sediments and my little girl could taste the difference. There were lots of things for us to do. Coloring with crayons, playing with play-doe or using the computer was just some of the things we'd do. I reminded her to call me at the time her mommy tells her to and she said, "okay daddy". It'd make our daughter happier if her mother and I could find a way to get along. Little ones can sense when there's friction between dad and mom. Friendly, polite and helpful were the ways I would try to present myself to Cassie anytime Amanda was present.

It was still cool in the evenings at this time of the year and on a weekday visit I decided to take Amanda to City Park in New Orleans. There were amusement rides here for the kids and I knew she'd like this. Our time was limited so we hurried throughout the park. She was excited with all the lights and sounds. When it was time to leave, she didn't want to go. It was hard to explain my reasons so I said that her mommy was waiting and promised we'd come back another time. She understood and from here we left to meet Cassie at the mall.

The first month passed quickly and a new one was upon us. Being able to do more things and go places would help create joyful memories for us. I was thankful she was with me to celebrate her fourth birthday. With another CD for the computer and some games, we had a wonderful time. I noticed how she'd get unusually upset when she couldn't do something right. "I'm better than everybody else", I heard Amanda say. "Who told you that", I asked? "My mommy did", she replied. "That's not true, we're all the same, just different in some ways, some people are better at things than others, that's why you need to practice", I said to her. If a child is taught to believe that he or she is superior to others, that's setting them up for disaster. When a challenge arises and the child can't successfully accomplish the task, it'll be a contradiction to what they were taught. They might think, "if I'm better than everyone else, why can't I do this"? Being unable to succeed will frustrate the child and the end result may be anger. To constantly criticize other people may also cause a child to believe that he or she is better than everyone else is. It was a Wednesday and we had only three hours to be together. She didn't want to go home but I explained to her that we'd see each other again soon. She accepted that and we got ready to go meet her mother at the mall.

There was a second hand store I often went to because of the inexpensive prices on their clothes. I had picked out a couple pairs of blue jeans and was waiting in line. The woman in front of me had an infant in a stroller and I peered over to see the child. "He looks tired", I said, after noticing the baby was asleep. When the mother turned around I saw it was Candy. "Hi, how are you", I asked? "I'm fine, how have you been", she asked? I didn't expect her to be so friendly. After paying for our merchandise we continued to talk outside. She asked if I did anything about the forged credit card episode and I answered her. She wanted to know the outcome of the criminal mischief charge and I told her why it was thrown out of court. "Good, I would've showed up for one reason, to dismiss the charges", she said. She went on to tell me of the fistfight she had with her mother in law, two weeks after her son was born. Cassie spent a lot of time at their house and would often smoke around the baby. She repeatedly asked her stop and urged Donny to do something about it. One thing led to another and when she wasn't looking, Cassie popped her in the mouth, busted her lip and pulled a handful of hair out of her head. Wendell had to stop the fight. This hurt her badly and she insisted on her husband that his mother had to go. Amanda was there at the time and saw all this occur. This was an astounding conversation and it surprised me that Cassie did this to the mother of her grandson. I was convinced that this wasn't a story Candy made up.

The hours with my daughter were adding up. We had more time together near the end of this second month then all of last year. It was peaceful and sometimes quiet. The, "I want to go to my mommy's", remark, when she didn't get what she wanted, had stopped. It became a necessity to structure all our events. Playing at a certain time, eating at a certain time, bathing and sleeping at a certain time all became part of our routine. So there wouldn't be any surprise, I'd tell her of what she would be doing thirty minutes or so before it happened. This way she'd be prepared and get used to doing things at a specific time. If there were any problems, I'd know about them beforehand. Things got easier as time went on.

On the first weekend visit of this new month, it was Barbara I met at the mall to get Amanda instead of Cassie. I found it to be unusual for her mother to be absent from the exchange. I figured it'd be best to leave this one alone and didn't ask any questions. Aside from doing things here at my place, we began to visit Tabby, Mary and my friend Jazzy. We were always doing something. My little girl told me of the new daycare she was attending called "Tumbling Blocks", and how she didn't like it there. "I get there in the daytime and leave at the night time", she said. This was a 24-hour daycare. I didn't know what to make of this and became curious as to why our little girl had to spend so much time there.

According to the court judgement, my little girl was to call me at home on Monday and Thursday. Waiting at home for these phone calls caused me to be late for my part time job. To date, of the 24 times she was to call, there were only 6. This made me wonder why her mother wasn't doing what we agreed upon in court. During deliveries I often noticed the black firebird in front of the Cablanka. One evening at work I called Tumbling Blocks to see if Amanda was there. They told me she wasn't. After my shift was over and I went home, the daycare called Mama Mias Pizza to say that Amanda was there and she told them that her daddy was supposed to come pick her up. It was 10:30 at night when the manager called me with this information. I arrived at the daycare and they said that the mother had already picked her up. They also told me that if I'm going to be picking her up from there, I need to be put on the pick up list, otherwise they can't release her to me. I agreed with what the woman said and returned home. This occurrence left a lot of unanswered questions.

Work slowed down and some of us couldn't be kept at Allbell. They reduced the personnel to a skeleton crew and I was let go. This bad news was turned around when Cassie called and asked if I wanted my little one to come over. "Sure", I replied. Now was a good time to see if she'd notice the new clean air machine I purchased. This device worked excellent and I could smell the difference. It electronically removes odors and airborne dust particles from the air. Usually, I never smoke in my apartment but if I lit up a cigarette, this device would eliminate the smell and make the air fresh for her little lungs. In addition to this, some days I'd open up all my windows for a few hours to let fresh air in from outside. We came home, watched a video on television and ate pizza. We spent time doing her computer lessons. Later on her mother called and said Amanda had to come home. We met at the mall and traded off. That was the end of our evening. I enjoyed spending more time with my daughter on the days I wasn't supposed to get her. Cassie was being unusually nice. This made me a little suspicious. In the past, she normally doesn't act this way unless she's up to something. For that reason it was important for me to keep my eyes open for anything that might occur.

Different people continued to show up at the exchanges. Brad's girlfriend Tina drove the black firebird while Cassie appeared to be drunk and wouldn't get out of the car. When she opened the car door, Amanda would climb in and they'd drive off. The exchange area had changed to a nearby drug store for convenience purposes. I didn't ask any questions and agreed to meet there. I'd do whatever her mother instructed me to if it meant gaining the opportunity to have an unscheduled visit with my daughter. Before the legal proceedings started, all I ever wanted was to spend more time with Amanda.

When I was told to go pick up my daughter from Tumbling Blocks, it was here that I had a problem. Amanda had a busted lip because a little girl pushed her down. From the look of this place, it seemed like the youngsters weren't properly looked after. Most of the caretakers were teenagers and I saw two of them watching television while the kids were running wild. It disturbed me that Cassie put our daughter in a place like this where it was kids watching kids. I was on the pick up list for Wednesday only and this was my weekend. They made one phone call to Cassie and changed all that. No more was said and we hurried out.

Top Lab hired me back but warned that when an assignment is scheduled, I'd have to forfeit the visits with my daughter. I agreed to their terms and started work. They didn't have the jobs they used to and not too many people were employed here anymore. I was glad that my part time job delivering pizzas was there to provide an income. This inspection company was near its end. There wasn't too much work to keep everyone busy. By not having enough hours, this meant that my check would be small. My bills had to be paid so I'd soon be looking for employment elsewhere. When the time was right, I'd have to go.

It was good that I got to see my daughter more than we agreed in court. This was a vast improvement for me. My concern was that Cassie took it upon herself to move the swapping area and appeared to be under the influence of something or drunk when I'd see her. When I called the daycare two times and found out that my little girl was there at 8pm, this raised the question, "what was she doing there so late"? Knowing her mother wouldn't answer, I informed her that she was in contempt for not giving me my phone privileges with Amanda. "I'm not going to make her call you, if you want to talk to her, you can call her over at my house", she said. I figured that because she gave me permission, it'd be okay to call there. It was my guess that this would be the only way I'd get to talk with my daughter.

Allbell had that contract starting up and I went back to work over there. With a high pay rate, my boss and I lured Marco over from XIH. Our crew consisted of three people. The job was just as they described. We worked 12 hours a day, five days a week. None of us could believe how easy this work was. It felt like they were giving money away. Completing our project in less time, allowed us to leave when finished. This enabled us to get out early. That was like a bonus for this job. In NDT it's either feast or famine. As always, you have to get it when the getting is good. We may not be working next month.

One evening I called to speak to Amanda. She didn't want to talk so Cassie and me was chatting a little. At first we started talking about our little girl and how smart she was. The conversation drifted to reminiscing about events from the past. The places we'd go and things we'd do with our daughter became topics. When I slipped and finished one of my statements with, "when we loved each other", she responded, "no, I never did". "What", I exclaimed! "I never loved you", she says. "You mean to tell me the entire five years we were together, you never loved me", I asked her? "Nope, I never did", she said. "You didn't have to say that", I told her. "Well I'm not gonna to lie", she chuckled. Although it may be hard to swallow, a dose of truth is always the best medicine. Here she used it to reveal her true feelings for me. Her comment made my impression towards women change. It was hard to accept that they were not all the same. I didn't want to speak with Cassie at all anymore on the phone. If my little girl wasn't there to talk then I'd hang up after saying good-bye. I knew now, more than ever that it was true when my friends said how she was using me. I'll never forget the way she tried to poison me with these words out of her mouth. (James 3:8)

The next evening while checking my mailbox I got to read some of the large e-mail that Saul sent. His letter began saying that these were things I should get familiar with in case some of the symptoms began to appear in my daughter. PAS, (Parental Alienation Syndrome) is a condition that can develop in the form of psychological damage to a child whose parents are in a high conflict divorce, or a separation that involves plenty of controversy. When grown-ups allow their kids to witness occurrences in the adult arena, the pain from this memory can last a lifetime. He continued to write that of the two parents, the woman is considered to be the nurturer. This fact ensures that she will be the domiciliary or custodial parent and in most all cases, will remain in control of the kids. Here is where it becomes a power struggle between the couple through the use of their youngsters. If the father truly loves his children, the mother knows he won't be far behind as long as she has them. Because the little ones spend most of their time with mom, a loyalty tie will grow and they become bound to her. It's not healthy when kids find themselves having to choose which parent they will love more. At her discretion, mommy may decide to brainwash the children with comments about their daddy being a bad person. Due to monetary reasons, if mom gets angry enough she may do all she can to exclude dad from the lives of his children. When uncontrolled bitterness sets in, with the use of derogatory statements, harsh criticism and degrading remarks, the mother can destroy the relationship they once had with their father and the love bond between them is replaced with one of disrespect or hate. If she can have it her way, with the help of the court she can limit the access he has with his own children. He is made to go away and pay. Because of the love and natural affection he has for his children, this kind of situation causes dad to stumble, fall, feel insecure and humble himself before their mother. If mom tries real hard, dad will give up and the children are left to suffer the consequences. Battles like these become too emotionally exhausting for some men and they forfeit their rights. Saul also stated that the courts do not recognize PAS as a form of child abuse and listed numerous signs to indicate whether or not a child is affected by such treatment. He ended his note with encouragement as he urged me not to give up and remain focused on doing what's in the best interest of Amanda. Now I pondered the best way to handle this.

Kim's daughter Kayla, my niece came to visit. I met her and Marie at Tabby's house where we talked about the upcoming Easter holiday. "Isn't this your holiday", they asked. "Yeah, it is", I told them. Kayla had never met Amanda and asked me to bring her over. When I explained my situation with the mother, they understood how much trouble I have when it came to making plans. They were all surprised when I told them how nice Cassie had been lately and we all agreed that she must be up to something. With the holiday being two weeks away, I offered to try and bring Amanda over so Kayla could meet her. We sat and had a long talk about what my little girl and I had been doing during our visits. They were impressed at how well she was doing with her computer lessons and the things I taught her. When summer comes and the pool is open I would teach her how to swim. In the evenings we ride our bikes and go to the nearby playground. She really enjoys that.

It was my weekend visit before Easter that I picked Amanda up and asked Cassie about my holiday visitation. She said that they might have plans and she'd let me know at the end of our visit on Sunday evening. When I reminded her that it was my turn, she said that we were to alternate the holidays. From the tone of her voice, it sounded like an argument was about to start. I backed away from the discussion because it's important to me that we conduct ourselves properly in the presence of our daughter. Lately we have set a good example for her by being friendly with each other and I wanted to keep it that way.

During our time together, the relationship with my little girl had grown beautifully. We'd play games, make things out of play-doe, she enjoyed pretending to cook for me on her toy stove, the coloring books and her computer lessons would fill up our time. The next day I told Amanda that she had a cousin who wanted to meet her. We went over to Mary's house and she got to meet Kayla. Later that evening we went to the skating rink. I didn't skate but that didn't stop them two. It made me nervous to watch them skate amongst all these bigger kids. Linda, a Christian friend of mine was there with her two daughters. She and I used to attend bible studies together. There was an area outside the rink for the little ones and mine was learning to skate. We watched the kids have fun and talked a while. She asked about the ordeal with my ex. I told her that Cassie changed a little and my situation with her had improved. Long ago, Linda warned me about the trouble my former girlfriend would cause. She also told me about the spirit of Jezebel. We all had a good time. It was getting late and I decided we better go. My youngster was tired from all the excitement and ready for bed.

Amanda and I went to the mall for the exchange on Sunday evening. Cassie was a little late and we waited outside. When she arrived, I walked my little girl over to her vehicle. She stopped the car and got out. When she bent over to move the seat forward so our little girl could climb in the back, I was shocked to see what she was wearing. There she was in a very short dress that barely covered her butt. She pulled it down over her buns and it hiked back up again. Quickly she got in her car and I asked about the upcoming holiday. "I don't know yet, I'll let you know on Wednesday", she replied. Looking at Amanda, "daddy loves you boo, I'll see you real soon", I told her. After they drove off, the last time I saw Cassie dressed like that was when she worked at the Cablanka. Her outfit had me suspicious.

On Wednesday I went to the mall to pick up my daughter. Tina arrived and said Cassie had a doctor's appointment. "That's okay", I said, walked my little girl over to the car and we got in. On the way to my place I passed by the Cablanka. Amanda recognized it right away. "That's where my mommy and Donny work, she don't let me go in there, but Mitch brings me in", she said. "So you've been in there", I asked? "Uh huh", she replied. She wanted to play on the computer when we got home and I helped her get started. She was getting good at all the activities. "I'm so proud of you boo", I told her. She did almost everything by herself and didn't need much help. There were few mistakes and I explained to her what went wrong so she wouldn't get upset. "No one's perfect, sometimes daddy slips up too", I told her. It's not good to stress upon a child to achieve something that's not adequate for their age. At four years old, she was doing things most kids her age didn't even know about. It made me happy to see her learn new things with these educational activities.

Upon returning to the mall I found Cassie there with one of the friends she used to work with in the lounge. Both had skimpy dresses on and looked like they had a shift to pull. I walked over and asked about the holiday. "You can pick her up on Friday but she has to be back on Saturday because we're going on a Easter egg hunt, Sunday morning, it's very important that you have her back", she said. This sounded fair to me. I promised to pick her up and have her back at the time I was told. As I was leaving, seeing her mother dressed this way two times made me wonder what she was up to. If she wanted to work, that's fine but I wanted Amanda with me while she's at the lounge and I didn't want our little girl in that place again. I knew this was a touchy subject and to ask about it would be a huge mistake. In due time and with the help of my associates, I'd find out what's really going on.

According to the news, it had been a year since the massacre occurred at a high school in Colorado. Listening to this horrible event, I wondered about the parents of these two boys who ended their spree in suicide. It's not what dad and mom say that ruins their child; it's what they don't say that ruins their child. How often did either parent ask questions starting with the words, "what, where, when, who, why"? How could they not know what their sons were planning? Who allowed them access to those weapons? What was the relationship like between these boys and their father? Why aren't the parents held accountable for the actions of these two teens that murdered their classmates and a teacher? Where is the justice for the ones who suffered? When a young girl admitted that she believed in God, she was executed?

Here is the evidence of what happens when parents do not get involved in the lives of their youngsters, especially teenagers. When dad and mom don't take the time to find out what their kids are watching, how their kids feel about what they see and hear, and what their kids are thinking, the wiles of this world will do the teaching. Park them in front of the television and let the media program their minds with violence and lawlessness. Don't pay attention to the dangerous video games they play. At a young age, they're allowed to dress up and express themselves any way they want. Living an unrestrained life, the children grow up to become delinquents. Adolescents must be monitored because of their exposure to the garbage produced by the media. Parents, who don't ask children enough questions and demand truth in the answers, are rewarded with uncontrollable kids. Proper communication in the family is vitally important. Absence of guidance and correction will leave a household in disarray. Lastly, disciplinary action may have to serve as a consequence for disobedience.

Early on Friday I picked Amanda up for the holiday. At my place I had a basket for her filled with candy and surprises. We went to Tabby's house so she could visit with her cousins. I wanted her to get acquainted with our relatives so she'd know who everyone is. All this attention excited her and she had lots of fun. She was too young for me to tell her the true meaning of Easter. When she gets older I'd explain to her that Christians regard this time as a celebration of redemption and atonement. It's the time God our father reconciles with man through the death of his son, Jesus Christ. Long ago in 1620 a document was written that clearly reveals the intention for the formation of the foundation of this country. Since that time many have gone astray and a large number of people helped to dilute the truth. Freedom of religion allows people to choose any god they want to follow. The Ten Commandments, which aren't allowed in most schools, begins with one God. It is here that I'll start to teach my daughter what I've learned and provide proof of the truth. (John 14:6)

On Saturday we spent some time at Mary's house. In the evening we went home and I told Amanda that later on we had to go meet her mommy at the mall. I was supposed to be there at 9pm. Shortly before it was time to leave Kayla came over. She decided to take a ride with us to go meet Cassie. When I arrived at the mall no one was there. We waited for about 30 minutes and left. On our way home I saw her black Firebird parked in front the Cablanka. Remembering the promise I made to return my daughter, we stopped to see if her mother was there. As I went in, she was seen hurrying from behind the bar and sneaking out the back door. "Cassie", I yelled, and she was gone. Turning around to leave I was faced with Brad who had a pool stick in his hand. Dodging him in an attempt to get away, I was hit in the mouth with the cue. It busted my lip. He let it fall from his hands and made the gesture for a fistfight. I didn't have time for a scuffle. I ducked down as he approached and with my shoulder, lifted and tossed him into the jukebox. He grabbed my ear when I did this and felt like he ripped it off. My car was still running when I got in and the noise woke my daughter up. They noticed that I had some injuries. As we were leaving I saw a squad car in the far corner of the parking lot. Going over to the officer, he immediately noticed I was bleeding from my mouth and ear. When I told what happened, he called for a back up. The police went in and got the guilty one out the bar. They ran our records and told us if they were going to arrest anyone, it'd be both of us. "This won't look good when we go to court", Brad said. "What are you talking about", the lawman asked? "We're going to court soon, he's being tried for criminal property damage to my car", I told him. This was my choice, go to jail or drop everything. I withdrew and we all went our separate ways. My niece was scared so she left and went to Mary's house. This incident would have me do some investigation.

Returning home, I found four messages on my answering machine. The caller ID showed that it was Cassie and the calls were only a couple minutes apart. Repeatedly she claimed to be so worried and concerned because she had been to the mall and didn't see us there. When I called her she sounded like nothing was wrong. I told her she was not there at the time we agreed and she denied it. Regardless of what the judgement said, it seemed like she was in total control. If I didn't listen to her, the extra time with my daughter might stop. She told me to go back to the mall with our daughter. Amanda was upset from all of this. "I'm sorry, boo, daddy don't know what's going on but we have to go", I told her. When we arrived, the mother was there with a strange old woman. As we made the swap I urged her to be on time from now on. She looked shaky as I watched her put our child in the woman's truck.

As the week rolled by I prepared for this weekend with my little girl. When the time was near for me to pick her up, her mother called. She informed me that if I wanted to keep my visit I'd have to pick Amanda up from Mayes, the daycare we enrolled her in after moving into Cassie's house. "That won't be a problem", I said, and she told me what time to be there. The receptionist recognized me when I walked in. She asked me to wait and began looking in a nearby file cabinet. With a folder in her hand she told me they couldn't release my daughter to me because I wasn't on the pick up list. When I told them that it was her mother that sent me, they needed to make a phone call for verification. I waited out front until the lady came back. She apologized for having to do that. "I'm sorry, I remember you registered her but our policy allows only the listed people to leave with the child", she said. I didn't object to what she did and walked to the classroom to get my youngster.

Although our time together was consistent and usually did the same things, we always had fun. There was so much to do. The creative activities were good. We were happy to make something and this helped her learn. Play a game, go to the playground, eat pizza or ice cream, ride our bikes, use the computer, watch a video, making things with play doe, visit someone, by juggling all these activities around, this would occupy our time and there was never a dull moment. This is the way I wanted to raise her that was different from my childhood. We had many members in my family and dad didn't spend much time with us. It was important to me that I take every possible opportunity to be with Amanda.

Our weekend was over and I met Cassie at the mall. "You want to pick her up tomorrow at the daycare, I put you on the pick up list", she asked. "Yeah, thanks", I replied. With a smile I left. This was great. It started to look like I was going to have plenty of time with my little girl. Her mother was being very fair but I still had to keep my guard up. I was still sore from the encounter with Brad a week ago and in two days I'd be in court against him for the damage he did to my car. Could that be the reason Cassie was being so nice to me?

The next day I picked Amanda up. She always did like this preschool and was enjoying her time there. We watched a new video I bought and ate some pizza. She didn't want to do any computer lessons so we played some games instead. Late in the evening her mother called and it was time to go to the mall. Cassie was there with Moe, a friend she introduced me to when we were together. He once owned a lounge called "The Glass Beagle" and was good to her before she met me. "I'll always love him", Cassie once told me. I assumed that he was this new fiancé she told me about. Now wasn't a time to ask any questions.

The occasion for Brad and me to appear in court had arrived. He had with him a barmaid from the Cablanka and the friend who helped Cassie escape out the back of the lounge that night. I remember this guy was out there with him when he kicked in the side of my car. It was my guess that these were his witnesses. They had been there a while before me and the accused gave his statements to the judge and jury. When asked, three of the jurors believed he was guilty before they even heard my side of the story. Immediately they were dismissed. My help came from the investigator and the officer who was at the scene. To confirm what happened, they were subpoenaed. The proceedings started with the people on my side and me being questioned by the two attorneys. Then we were made to wait outside. Brad had his friends come in next to help defend him. Afterwards it was time for the jury to leave and make their decision. All except one had to wait outside. The judge had the culprit sit in the courtroom. The district attorney came out later to speak with the officers and me saying that they were caught in several lies and couldn't answer the critical questions. The verdict was reached and everyone was called back in. "Guilty", he said and now we'd hear his sentence. It was ordered that Brad pay all court costs and was put on probation for 18 months. He'd have to pay a monthly supervision fee for his meetings with a probation officer that the court would appoint. Added in was a fine of $400 and the deductible for my car insurance. Another stipulation was that he stays away from my family and me. "If you see him, you better run the other way", the judge told him as he was smiling and laughing. Here was the justice I had been waiting for. By having a copy of this judgement I'd be protected from any abuse he may try to administer. Presenting this paper after an altercation would put him in trouble because he was ordered to stay away from me. It was a relief not having to worry about him anymore. This is the event that was needed to make Cassie's son leave me alone.

Regularly I began to pick Amanda up from Mayes. Late in the evening I'd have to meet her mother at the mall. It soon became an inconvenience for me because the exchanges were getting later at night. In the middle of this month Cassie and Moe arrived here at my place to pick our little one up at 2:30 in the morning and she was staggering drunk. As time went on she remained pickled when I saw her. On a couple occasions she didn't show up at the mall and had to be called. The outfits she wore and her intoxication began to bother me. It eased my worry when I was able to call and know they made it home safely. She arrived one night at the mall in a new white convertible and I was bold enough to ask if she was working in the lounge. "No, I don't have to, my fiancé puts $2000 in my account the first of every month for me to pay bills with, he's a boat captain and makes a hundred thousand dollars a year", she told me. "Is it Moe", I asked? "No", she said. This was enough interrogation for me. It felt like this was none of my business anyway. There was a better way to get the correct answers. I was thankful for her allowing me to see more of my daughter.

Mamma Mias and me had a mutual agreement, which led to the loss of my job. If there were a chance to be with Amanda I wouldn't go in. Too often I was late and they didn't like that. When the manager and I spoke she used a very familiar phrase, "you're too unreliable, we can't depend on you", she told me. I couldn't deny that this was true and had a better job anyhow. This was part time work I didn't need because I had recovered financially.

An accident at the refinery resulting in an injury to one of our crewmembers caused Allbell to get run out of the plant. This was bad news because there wasn't much work available at the time. Marco and I spent a lot of time at the shop until a job was called in. He told me how Stanley over at XIH was under pressure from the other employees about the time I took off for my visitations. That was part of the reason why he dismissed me. I kind of expected that because Noble let me go for the same cause. I soon realized that no matter where I worked, there'd be a problem with me trying to keep the time I was granted to be with my daughter. On the first day of June in an unexpected layoff, I was let go.

Being temporarily unemployed was nothing new and this would give me time to arrange a new game plan. I wanted to find an answer to my new question. Contacting several friends and explaining what I knew gave me a variety of choices. Many of my associates had the same intentions I did and two of them insisted that they be used as plants in the Cablanka. My informants would find out who worked there and then get back to me. A few days later one called to tell me Cassie does work there and she had the day shift from noon to 8pm. He wasn't sure how often she was there but assured me that she was an employee. At the end of her shift she would sit at the bar with friends and drink on her tab. How could she think I wouldn't find out about this? Now my child was in the care of an alcoholic.

There wasn't much work available here at the local inspection companies. My reputation had become that of a worker who had too many personal problems. The few leads I found weren't paying the technician what he's worth. As always, the good jobs were away from this area. A friend from my crew at Allbell found a job working up north. The company was inspecting a natural gas pipeline that stretched across two states. I had the qualifications and he urged me to give them a call. Everything he said was appealing but I couldn't just pack up and go. It'd take a while before I could leave because of the necessary arrangements I have to make. After I informed Cassie, preparations would be made to go back to work.

On my way home from the store I was involved in an accident. A van had hit me in the back and did some body damage. This was the second time I had a wreck with a woman who wasn't paying attention. The police arrived and I heard her tell him that she didn't know how this happened. Our automobiles were insured at the same company and I was issued a check to pay for the repairs. Soon I'd be going out of town for work and needed my car. I put the money in my bank until the time came when my vehicle could be fixed.

My hours with Amanda accumulated and our relationship was great. The pool had been open and I was teaching her to swim. Her arm floats let her paddle to the deep end and she liked that. When I told Cassie about the upcoming job she said it'd be okay for me to see my little girl on the time I had off. All I had to do was call and let her know. This was too good to be true. It seemed like I was dealing with a totally different person. I couldn't figure out why she was being so nice to me. Maybe she came to the realization that our little one needs both of us. Hopefully this was her concern and there wouldn't be a catch to this courtesy.

A phone call was made to that northern company to inquire about the work they had. Head to Toe X-ray, (HTX) was known for their thorough inspections and treated their employees like family. Where I come from, that was unheard of. They were impressed with my résumé and hired me immediately. It was no surprise to them when I told of my ongoing custody battle. There were other workers here that had the same problem. For a month I worked there locally until they were comfortable with my job performance. When my trial period was over they sent me to Beaumont Texas on the pipeline my friend told me about. The section of this project that they put me on was in the swamp and we would travel by boat to get there. It felt like the mosquitoes followed me here from Louisiana. I didn't have to worry about not being busy because they had plenty of work at this company.

Whenever work wasn't available I'd travel home to be with my little girl. With a phone call I could make arrangements to see her. The different exchange area was closer and more convenient. I became accustomed to these changes although they were not in the judgement. Amanda and me would swim every chance we had. "You're my hero"; she'd tell me. Cassie moved back into her house on Bloomington Street and this made her happy. She had been out of it for about ten months. I was pleased to have my daughter closer to me. My job kept me busy and helped the months of July and August pass quickly. The only time I'd get to see my daughter was on the weekends when I could make it into town. Beaumont was four hours away. All the traveling was too much. At times our connection was the telephone.

In September the pipeline job was near its end and this gave me more time to be at home. Cassie would bring Amanda here to my apartment and pick her up later. She never came to my door so I'd meet her outside in the parking lot. Her drinking problem became obvious. My youngster became disinterested in her computer lessons so we spent lots of time doing other things. I talked with Saul and told him how she didn't like the device anymore. "I hate to tell you this, she's going to need her own computer", he told me. After he said this I went to John, the expert in our family. I gave him the money he needed to start building one. It'd take him a few weeks and he'd have Tabby call me when it was finished.

During one of our visits Amanda spoke of the new preschool she had been attending called "Kids Cottage". The following Friday I had to go there and pick her up because it was my weekend. The receptionist I befriended had one of the coordinators gave me a tour of the school. I was impressed at how clean this facility was. Here was an organized school that had a structured environment to benefit its students. The kids were to arrive at a certain time, learn basic skills, eat and nap, then in the afternoon, play. They had different activities every day of the week and qualified teachers that took an interest in the children. A system was installed for the parents to watch their little ones in the classroom via the Internet. I asked my guide how long had my little girl been going here. She didn't know. We went to pull the records and have a look. Her file showed she started near the end of July. My daughter had been in this school almost two months and Cassie never told me anything.

It felt like I was being kept in the dark and this didn't surprise me. Most of the time I knew only what Cassie wanted me to know. She had no empathy for what it was like when issues about Amanda were hid from me. There was no way to find out what my daughter's life was like at her mother's house. One thing I never did was asking my little girl a bunch of questions about what was going on over there. As children get older, they get smarter. It was my hope that if something were terribly wrong, my youngster would tell me. In my prayers I always asked God to protect her. For now that was all I could do.

We continued trading off at the drugstore or my apartment. The first Saturday in October Cassie brought Donny with her for the fourth time and both were drunk from a festival they attended earlier. The judgement stated that neither of her sons were to be present during an exchange. In the past I didn't say anything about this. It troubled me how she drove with our youngster in the car while she was intoxicated. It was evident that the safety of our daughter wasn't one of her concerns. Amanda had been with me consecutively for weeks now. It was to my advantage not to say anything if I wanted these unscheduled visits to continue. I'd have to be returning to work in a week and my time with her would be put on hold.

When I called one day to talk with my daughter I found a new player had been enlisted. Her name was Lacey, the live-in babysitter. In a somewhat lengthy conversation she told me a little about herself and how she happened to be there. She was a friend of Tina's and that it was Brad who first asked her if she wanted the job. She didn't know Cassie but needed a place to stay and accepted the offer. She had kids of her own who would come over and play with my little girl. Her friendliness brought me a little comfort but I still didn't know anything about this woman. She didn't hesitate to allow Amanda and me to chat.

My daughter was dropped off here Wednesday night and in the morning I brought her to school. She told me of all the fun that was had while there. The next day was Friday the 13th, a time of superstition for most. My weekend started at noon and we did the swap by a local car wash. I was told she didn't have to be in school today. Later that day Kids Cottage called to tell me that Amanda would no longer be attending that preschool. They told me how our child was often late, frequently absent and that Cassie paid the tuition with two checks that came back because of non-sufficient funds. In an attempt to help the mother they suggested that she find a babysitter. Here was a facility that helped prepare kids for kindergarten. It was a requirement that they be there on time and have a good attendance record. This kind of routine and being with her little friends would help our youngster. I promised to take care of this and went to see them. When we got there Amanda went to her class and I talked with some of the faculty. Using money from my car accident I paid a month's tuition. I assured the administrator that I'd talk with her mother so our little one would be punctual from now on. Looking at her records we found that Amanda was present 28 of the 56 days she was to be there, half the time. They let me see the registration form and I found a large pick up list. Moe, Donny, Brad or Tina, a woman I didn't know and Lacey were allowed to get my little girl from here. My name was added at the bottom. The spaces to provide information about our child on the back of the page were empty. They asked me to bring the immunization records her mother wouldn't provide. Amanda stayed in class while I went to a department store to get her school supplies on the list they gave me. It became apparent to me that Cassie was too busy with her personal life and our daughter was a secondary responsibility.

On the last day of our weekend together we went to City Park in New Orleans and all the amusement rides had tired her out. At the end of the day we were both exhausted from all the fun and she took a small nap when we got home. When it was near the time to meet her mommy at the mall, I woke Amanda up. We arrived to find that her mother was not there. I decided to return home and bring her to school in the morning. When I called Cassie to tell her my intentions, she was upset and demanded that I return to the mall. I refused and hung up the phone. We settled in and started watching a video. A while later there was a knock on my door. I opened it to find the police there with Cassie in the background shaking, doing her pretended state of fear act for the officers. They informed me that I had to release my daughter and she went out to meet her mother. "She needs to be at school for 8 o'clock in the morning" I said as they were leaving. One of the lawmen stayed behind to tell me that we should try to get along for the sake of our little girl. Without being told, I knew that this occurrence would obstruct my chances to see and talk to Amanda again.

On Tuesday I traveled 16 hours away to work in Barbourville Kentucky. HTX had a job for a gas company that was refurbishing their plant with a compressor and new piping. We were needed to remain onsite until a weld was ready to be x-rayed. I couldn't pick and choose my assignments and had to take what they gave me. The mess I left back home put me in a bad mood and I didn't want to be here. It felt like this was all my fault and that made me feel bad. I called Kids Cottage and they said my daughter had not been going there. I told the administrator if she wasn't there by the end of the week that she probably won't be attending. When the weekend came I called Amanda. She was happy to hear my voice. Lacey told her, "your mommy don't want him calling here anymore", and she began to cry. I tried to console her. She had to get off the phone and asked me to call her back. I attempted to call and heard Cassie's answering machine. Finally after three times I gave up. This action showed me that from now on they would impede my contact with Amanda.

We had a four-day weekend come up and I drove home to keep my scheduled visit. My daughter's computer was finished and I picked it up from John and Tabby's. At the mall I found a large woman with an earring in her nose and littered with tattoos waiting with my daughter. It was Lacey, the new babysitter. Before we could leave she was quick to make Amanda give her a kiss good-bye. Seeing this reminded me how Cassie always pulls our little one close and whispers something in her ear before she is allowed to leave with me. We left and went home. I anticipated plenty of excitement when my youngster saw her new toy. As we walked in she ran to her room. "A new computer, for me", she screeched! "That's right baby girl, poppa knew you needed one", I told her. Later we went to the local department store to buy a desk to put it on. After I got the shopping cart, we were heading down the isle when Lacey walks over and tells Amanda hello. She happened to be at this store with two men I didn't know. We found our item and went to the check out counter. The babysitter and her two friends were a few aisles over. They were talking about me and one man made a hand motion to instigate a brawl. I ignored them all and looked the other way. We returned home and I set up everything for my little girl. She started doing her lessons again and that made me happy. Saul was right when he said she had to have her own computer. We had a fun time. Because of the confrontation at the store, I called Cassie to tell her that she'd be the only one I'd release Amanda to. Donny said she was at work so I relayed this message to him. On Sunday evening Cassie was alone to do the exchange.

It was cold up here in November and signs of the changing seasons were visible. The feeling of being disconnected from my daughter, both past and present was too much for me to handle. When I tried to call Amanda, Cassie put a block on her phone. This prevents calls from my number from going through. In the evening I would have to find a pay phone if I wanted to talk with my little girl. I had only one chance to try and get through. The second time I called there would be a block on the number I was calling from. This had me traveling around looking for a phone to use. One night when I was able to get through, Cassie tells our daughter, "you can talk for five minutes". Another night Mitch answers and he doesn't know where my little one is. A few nights later her mother answers and is hesitant to let us chat, saying, "let me see if she's here". Rapidly my indignation grew. When I called at the middle of the month, Lacey answered. I could hear my youngster there but was told that she was asleep. When I asked what time would she be awake, the caretaker hung up. I called back to ask if that was her I heard in the background. Filled with obscenities, the babysitter replied, "yeah, that's her, I was lying when I said she was asleep, now leave me alone you *_*"! To hear Lacey talk like that in front of our daughter enraged me. I took offense to this profanity and called back to leave a message for Cassie. "I didn't appreciate the babysitter's name calling and decided to quit this job, I will be driving home in the morning and would be there on time to keep my Wednesday visit", I said. Informing our client that I had an emergency back home, he allowed us to leave. He and a few other people on this job were aware of my situation. Some of them once had circumstances like mine and could relate to what I was going through. Their advice was helpful but I had to go now. We left Kentucky and I was home on Wednesday at three o'clock in the morning.

At five o'clock I was inside the mall by the police station waiting to do our exchange. Cassie didn't show up. I called and the babysitter answered. She knew nothing about this meeting. She needed to make a phone call and asked me get back with her. When I called back there was no answer and the machine picked up. When I realized that no one was going to show, I went home. This was the sixth time that I was denied visitation and there was nothing I could do. It was no use to ask the police to help me; they can't get involved in civil matters. Later that night I went to a lounge next to the Cablanka to inquire about the work schedule Cassie had. The barmaid here knew her and said she works five days a week, Monday through Friday, noon to 8pm. If she was getting $2000 a month from Moe for her bills, a monthly compensation check for her injury in the car accident and a support check from me, I wondered why did she have to work at the lounge? It may have been wrong for me to look into her personal business but when it affects our daughter, I feel that's my responsibility. Now I knew why she wasn't always at the mall but this didn't explain why she couldn't get Amanda to school on time. All this chaos began when I stepped in to help our little girl stay at Kids Cottage. Considering that event, I was sure that things were going to get worse. I wouldn't be able to see my child as much and our opportunity to talk would be hampered. It'd take another court appearance to get my privileges back and that still might not work. It was depressing to know that from square one, I had to start all over.

Kids Cottage had to be informed that Amanda wouldn't be attending. The administrator wanted to know why her mother would deprive our youngster of a chance to learn? When I went to the classroom to get her school supplies, this news saddened her teacher. She really liked my daughter. We both knew my little girl would excel academically at their school. She told me of some exercises we could do together at home. Before leaving I met with the owner. She wanted my advice on how to get reimbursed for the cancelled checks Cassie issued. I encouraged her to use their normal procedure. She agreed to send me a letter explaining the financial negligence on Cassie's behalf and a copy of the attendance record. They were honest about refunding me most of the money I paid to keep Amanda here. A week's tuition was subtracted because a spot was held open in case my daughter returned.

Remembering the conversation we had about the love that didn't exist in our relationship made me feel used. I couldn't figure out what it was that had her attracted to me. I'm not a very handsome man so I knew it wasn't my looks. It's not like we didn't spend enough time together. When I was free from work, both before and after Amanda was born, we were either at home or out somewhere. There were many times we went out to eat so neither of us would have to cook. The occupation I have keeps me very busy and the locations of the projects vary. I have to go where they send me. Most of my jobs paid well and nothing was ever turned off or disconnected. I made sure we had all the things we needed. My little girl meant the world to me and Cassie knew that. The fact that she was in control and I sat helpless felt like big weights pulling me down. I began to feel self-conscious about myself and depression became the emotion that wasn't invited. I went to see my doctor about this and he put me on some anti depressants that would make me feel better. The medicine helped me cope with these troubles and afterwards my problems didn't worry me that much anymore.

For a while everything was fine as long as Cassie got to do what she wanted to. All my snooping around revealed too much information. She wasn't aware that I knew about her working in the Cablanka. Being there and the excessive drinking made it impossible for her to be a good mother. She had recruited strangers to help watch our little one and that was annoying to me. The preschool Cassie put our child in was good but not making sure she attended was bad. Because I wanted more time with my little girl, I never did ask many questions. Were my actions in the best interest of Amanda? Should I have bowed down to the demands of her mother? I'd have to reconstruct my attitude towards this situation and remain calm. I was in no position to be forceful about anything and could not voice my opinion on the events that concerned my daughter. My number one priority was to keep Amanda out the middle of this controversy. She was not at fault for the discrepancy between Cassie and me.

The next Wednesday I was expecting a confrontation with whoever showed up at the mall and brought my video camera. Upon arriving to pick up my daughter I saw it was Lacey. She was friendly and asked what time I would be back. "Eight o'clock", she asked and I nodded. It surprised her to see my camcorder. I was hoping their behaviors would be normal by having it with me; and it worked.

Amanda was very happy with her computer and we'd spend most of our time together doing her lessons on it. She had many CDs now and was learning a lot. I bought some sketching tablets and we'd draw pictures of houses, cars, trees and people. The water washable markers in her school supplies came in handy. It was surprising to her when I showed how easy it was to clean up. I was trying to teach her the things she'd be learning at Kids Cottage. She was happy when I showed her how to spell her name. This visit is only for three hours. She got upset when it was time to go.

When we arrived to do the swap I found the babysitter waiting. The judgement states that the parties, meaning Cassie and me shall exchange the child. I refused to release Amanda to Lacey. In the police station the caretaker vented her anger at my decision to do this. Using profanity, she called me "a psycho", and other names in front of my daughter. She continued with accusations of me drawing crosses on my little girl, killing dogs and hating Halloween. When she admitted that the mother was at work in the Cablanka, the officer made her go call. Cassie had to come to the mall for the exchange. From now on she'd have to be the one to pick Amanda up. I had my camcorder sitting on the counter adjacent to where we stood and everything, including the frenzied behavior of this babysitter was recorded on film. Now I had proof of her true colors. This was my way of keeping the new opponent in check.

The next day was thanksgiving. Cassie has Halloween and this holiday was mine. We had planned to go over by John and Tabby's to be with family. No one came to the mall so I called to find out what happened. There was no answer. To stay at home would have been too depressing. I went to my sister's and tried to act like this didn't bother me. Amanda would be with me this weekend and I had that to look forward to. This was the seventh time her mother denied me visitation and I had to wonder, how long would this go on.

On Friday evening I took my video camera with me to the exchange area. A while later the fiancé arrived with my youngster. Happy to see me, she ran over and gave me a hug. As we turned to leave, Moe motioned for me to wait because there was something he wanted to say. "You're causing unnecessary problems for Cassie and me, knock it off", he warned me. "We don't talk anymore", I told him. I bent down, picked up my little girl and left. At home we ordered a pizza and watched some cartoons. After we ate she wanted to go play in her room. Her two babies were hungry so she had to cook for them. She pretended to cook and I had to feed them. "I'm their mommy and you're their daddy", she said. I'd read them a bedtime story and she laid them down to sleep. "Can I have some ice cream", she asked? We both had a bowl full and watched a video. Our weekends were always filled with things to do. In the daytime I began to spend more time away from home with her. It was better to be outside with the fresh air and sunshine. The next day we went to City Park again. She was more used to the amusement rides and didn't get tired as quick. There are many other parks around here with swings and slides. I enjoyed pushing her on the swing and knew that one day she'd be too old for me to do this. It gave me a warm pleasant feeling in my soul to hear her tell me, "daddy, I love you". She helped me realize that I was a good parent.

On Sunday morning I was in the kitchen fixing breakfast for my little girl. I got a chair for her to stand on so she could see me do this. As she stood watching I said, "I love you baby girl, daddy didn't draw any crosses on you, you know that". "I know, my step dad did", she replied. "What", I exclaimed! She told me that Moe lifted up her nightgown and drew an "X" on her chest. She continued to tell me how he's mean and yells at her. It was important that I didn't make indecent remarks about any of them. I apologized for him doing this to her and explained that there was nothing I could do. "It's not good for daddy to fight with them, it's not right and I'll get in trouble", I told her. I was very angry but had enough self-control to step back and develop a strategy. My objective was to educate Amanda and teach her to be perceptive so that one day she would figure them out on her own.

Later in the day while Amanda was playing I called a friend of mine Jerry, who used to work for a judge. I gave him enough identifying information on Moe and asked that he do a criminal background check. After hearing what he did to my little girl it worried me that he might be a child molester and this was something my attorney and I needed to know. My associate said it would take a while because he didn't have access to the computers like he used to. If he couldn't find out what I wanted to know, he had a friend that worked for the Drug Enforcement Agency and they had a better system for this.

In the evening we saw the fiancé waiting in the area to do the trade. Several times her mother was not at the mall and it disappointed my little girl when unrelated adults were there to get her. On a few occasions when I walked in with her I'd hear her ask, "where's my mommy"? I was determined to stop all these different people from being involved in this civil matter between Cassie and me. While Amanda sat outside on the bench I went in the police station and handed a copy of the judgement to the officer. I told him how we were supposed to be conducting the exchange. He took the paperwork, walked to the back and talked with some one. "You need to back off, you don't know who you're messing with", Moe threatened. The lieutenant came out and sided with me. "He's a code 6, a psycho, look in your computer", Moe shouted! Without delay I went out to sit with my daughter. A while later they made the fiancé leave and go get Cassie. No matter whom it was that brought Amanda to meet me, I made sure the mother was there when it was time to pick her up.

In December, problems with my visits continued. I'd arrive to pick Amanda up and no one would be at the exchange area. They were often late or in a different section of the mall. One day I found Lacey and Moe by the food court when they were supposed to be waiting in front of the police station. If the swap don't take place within 30 minutes of the appointed time we are to meet, they can leave and the visit is lost. Cassie would be by herself or with her fiancé when she came to pick our little girl up. "I have nothing to say to you", her mother said. This was not a good way for her to behave in the presence of our daughter.

With the status of my predicament worsening, it was necessary for me to stay closer to home. NDT has a way of separating you from your family. For a long time I made sacrifices to be with my little girl. Our togetherness was important and helped us remain close. All the jobs at HTX were out of state so I chose to resign my position there. This was the fifth job I lost due to the complications with her mother and the visitation schedule. Noble, XIH, Top Lab and Allbell wouldn't hire me back because my personal problems. I was too unreliable and undependable.

On strips of paper I wrote in two rows of 50, the numbers 1 through 100 and taped them on Amanda's wall. Odd numbers were red and the even numbers were blue. I would use this as our new game and teach her to count to 100. I'd say 1; she'd say 2, I'd say 3, she'd say 4, and we'd continue until we reached 100. After this I taught her to count by fives and tens.

Christmas was beautiful for Amanda and me. She referred to this holiday as the time we get presents. When she is older I'd teach her about the true meaning. She knew this was the birthday of baby Jesus and for now that was good enough. I began to run out of things to get for her. A couple of games, plenty of clothes and a printer for her computer were the things I chose to buy. She was delighted and we enjoyed each other's company. Our time together was short because this was Cassie's holiday. I was surprised when her mother let me drop our youngster off at her house. This was the only time she allowed me to go near her place on Bloomington.

On the last Wednesday visit of this month Amanda asked her mother if she could spend the night. Cassie turned to get permission from Moe. It bothered me that she let him decide what our youngster was going to do. In a friendly way he said yes. This upset his fiancée and the look on her face was a bit amusing. For her to pull him into our personal affair may have been the burden he didn't want. Our little girl kissed her mommy good-bye and we left.

At the end of the year I prepared to get my daughter for our New Years holiday. I arrived a little early and sat patiently on the bench in front the police station. It was cold out and looked like it was about to rain. I didn't have a good feeling about this. After a while I began to worry that no one was going to show up. The waiting time expired and I had to make the phone call. There was no answer so I left a message. The thought occurred to me that they may have been out somewhere and I went home to wait for Cassie's call. My phone never rang. For the eighth time her mother denied me visitation.

The mother's non-compliance suggested that it was time for another court appearance. Hopefully the judge would force Cassie to stop doing whatever she wanted to. My phone records indicated the many times I called to speak with Amanda and got the machine. Some of my documents were a letter from Kids Cottage that showed her financial irresponsibility, her inability to have our little one to school on time and copies of the negative results from all my drug tests. She was in contempt for denying me my court awarded phone privileges and visitations. The previous times we went to court, none of my paperwork was ever looked at. All this information was put together and I planned for a meeting with Charlene. I didn't know how serious it was to disregard a valid court order, but I was going to find out.

Chapter Eight

SURVIVING THE CRASH

On the first Wednesday of the new year I went to see my attorney. She became flustered after hearing the latest events. She got upset because I strayed away from what was written in the judgement. Calling Cassie's house to talk with Amanda and changing the exchange area were things that had to be agreed upon in court. We both felt that the blocks on the phone used to stop my communication were unfair. My documentation and the additional evidence I had served as the reason to set another court appearance. After we reviewed my information, the papers would be drawn up. There'd be a different judge for this hearing because our issues were no longer domestics. This was about Cassie not following court orders.

For a short while my impossible dream had become a reality. The previous year gave me a calculated 1506 hours with my little girl. That's almost ten times the amount of the year before. The realization that dad and mom are the influential backbone of their children made me do my best to be a shining example for Amanda. My parenting is a strong impact on my daughter but there was much work to be done. It helped to forget the times Cassie forced me to succumb to her demands. My ability to practice self-control and patience had to remain intact. Retaliation in any way was not an option. Two wrongs don't make it right. In order to find peace, it was necessary to forgive the injustices she inflicted upon me. (Matthew 6:15)

In the evening I picked Amanda up. Our Wednesday visits consisted of doing the same things. We'd make stuff with play doe or play with her toys, ride our bikes or go to the park, and her computer lessons were mostly what we did. Sometimes she or we would dance to her favorite music. Of course we had to have pizza or ice cream. On the weekends I made her eat more nutritional foods. Three hours isn't a lot of time so our activities were limited. She began to be a little too demanding of the things that she wanted to do. "My mommy lets me do whatever I want to", she said. I refused to give in to her statement. "Well, I'm not your mommy and you're not going to do whatever you want to here", I told her. She knew I was serious about this matter. Had I not said anything about this she may have grown to think that she'd always get her way. If left uncorrected, this could expand to her telling me what she's going to do and when she's going to do it. Here is when the child is allowed to run the life of their parent instead of it being the other way around.

At the time my papers were filed for another day in court, my opponent's were too. A different attorney had been introduced to our proceedings. It was my guess that Charlene was too much for Cassie's former counsel and Tony dropped out. A year ago was the last time we saw him and it looked like he didn't approve of his client's actions. With the help of that barmaid I spoke with, the night I went in that lounge next to the Cablanka, Cassie invented a new allegation. She claimed that I threatened to kill her with a stun gun and was seeking a restraining order. Our new court date was set for the end of the month.

Although the exchanges were somewhat troublesome, I refused to give up on my little girl. She came over on Friday with grass stains on her face and knees. Lacey's boyfriend pushed her down hard and she landed face first on the ground in the backyard. She also told me how this babysitter is mean and slaps her in the face like her mommy does. I failed to understand why this caretaker was needed when I lived less than three blocks away? On the Wednesday visits Amanda would start crying when it was time to go home. This made me suspicious of what's going on over there. Our youngster wasn't in school so we'd ask her mother if she could spend the night. Cassie would make up some kind of excuse or Moe would say "no".

Without having a job to go on, this gave me time to read some of the e-mail from Saul. His research can be disturbing at times. For a while I couldn't look at this because of my irritation with everything going on. "When it's intentional, parental alienation is usually implemented in a disguising way for personal gain and to convince the children of something that may not be true", he wrote. When couples split up and the separation embitters the mother, she might use tactics involving the children as her form of revenge. It's not often realized that this parent's actions will have a negative impact on her kids. When a man does not recognize the signs, the mother can successfully abuse his children both emotionally and psychologically. If a child is persuaded to believe that he or she doesn't need their father, the damage is already done. He suggested that I become aware of some things Cassie might try to do. She'll strengthen her bond with my trusting youngster by debasing me with insulting words or statements. She will try to extinguish the natural affection Amanda has for me. She may find people to help turn my child against me or leave her in the care of others. She can neglect to tell me about emergencies or school events and disallow me access to medical or school records. Important decisions concerning my daughter are made without me knowing. Disapproval of the attire I dress her in is common and the clothes may sometimes be thrown away. It's possible that she may select unrelated people to become pretended family members such as an uncle, aunt, father, brother or sister. Communication will be monitored or obstructed. There can be attempts to relocate, move away or change her last name. The mother may lash out at you in front of the child or in public for no legitimate reason. Cassie's disobedience for the courts ruling will escalate.

How does this happen? The courts theory, "in the best interest of the children", does not regard the father as the primary role in the family. Nowadays dad is secondary. Mom rises to a position of making the decisions in her family. As time went on the media assisted in this tragedy when they made dad a figure of incompetence and belittled him on many of their sitcoms. In the later part of the last century, most all magazines for parenting were written specifically for and addressed to the mothers, pushing fathers out of the family picture. The masculine character in most schools are practically non existent because they're dominated by women. In this industrialized country, some men have to travel away from home for work. When employment isn't the reason, a defective family court system can banish him away from his children. Socially and emotionally, he becomes less involved because he is made to feel unimportant or unneeded, moving him farther away. Many of the problems in society today reflect the catastrophe of a missing dad. Guidance, correction and education in a manly fashion are not provided when the father is absent. (Proverbs 15:5)

My friend Jerry called and left a message for me to contact him. He had something to tell me about Moe. When I called him he was glad to hear from me. He told me that this man had been arrested for both minor and major offenses. Criminal trespassing, theft, driving under the influence and cruelty to a juvenile were the only charges he found. He once had a lawsuit from a confrontation with the police and the permanent address of this mysterious fiancé was near my place. His date of birth revealed that he was 24 years older than I was and 15 years older than Cassie was. He was old enough too be a grandpa and near the legal age to retire. After hearing all this, we talked about how everything was going. My friend told me the reasons why he couldn't give me this information in writing. His help was very much appreciated and I thanked him for it. I called Charlene and told her about all this.

As time went on, things remained the same. Lacey would bring my daughter to the mall and Cassie was always there to pick her up. On the times her mother was late, Amanda would start to cry because she thought mommy didn't want to come get her. The blocks were still on the phone so I couldn't talk with my youngster. "My mommy says you're a nut", she told me one Friday evening as we drove to my place for a weekend visit. "That's okay", I said. Cassie put dark red lipstick on her again and I didn't like that. The mother knew that letting our little girl wear make-up and lipstick irritated me. Her fingernails were dirty so I decided to clean them when we got home. Blue, green and dark red were colors of the nail polish she had on. "Amanda, who's putting three coats of nail polish on your nails", I asked? "My mommy is", she replied. After finishing, I'd paint them her favorite color, pink.

Near the end of the month my youngster called. We were happy to hear each other's voice. She wanted to come over and see me. I said yes but Cassie said no. Suddenly her mommy wanted to read a story to her and our chat ended abruptly.

On a bright sunny morning it was time for our hearing. We arrived to find our opponents already there. My attorney suggested that I wait at the other end of the hall while she talked with them. Charlene, Cassie, and her new counsel Misty sat on a bench to discuss what we'd present to the court. A while later I was called down there to hear what they agreed. When I was introduced to the new lawyer, she looked frightened as she greeted me with a quick glance. Very pale and wide-eyed, she appeared to be scared. Without being told, I knew her ears had been filled with things about me that weren't true. The compromise was fair for now and we waited to see Judge Armstrong. In the courtroom our attorneys dictated the new agenda. A mutual restraining order prohibiting abuse or harassment of any kind when we were alone or in the presence of our child was put into affect. The blocks on the telephone are to be removed immediately and my access switched to 7 days a week, between 6 and 8pm. There'd be no having unrelated overnight guests of the opposite sex while Amanda is with either of us. Our little girl was to have her own room and bed to sleep in. Evaluations from Dr. Watson were deferred for a period of 60 days or until it was determined that his services would be necessary. In two months these issues would be brought up for review.

My funds were low and the search for a job became a troublesome task. No employment for over two months now had swallowed up most all of my finances. Before I left to go on an interview the phone rang. It was the owner of SWX. "Are you working", he asked? "No", I replied. His offer was sufficient and I needed to be earning money. This job started at the first of the month. It was important to inform them of my situation with Cassie and they were shocked to hear that this was still going on. Wayne, a close friend of mine was still working here. We both had daughters and very similar circumstances. His insight about how things would turn out were correct. He warned me not to let the mother walk all over me.

On my first weekend in February I took Amanda to City Park in New Orleans again. She liked going here because of all the amusement rides. We'd walk through Storyville, which was next to the park. A recreation area was on the other side that had a pond with some ducks to feed. I knew about these places because as a child I came here with my school on field trips. I began to teach my little girl about God and told her about Noah's Ark. She liked the music I had that sang about the Christian faith. We made up a dance of our own. Joining hands, we'd swing side to side, I'd pick her up and hang her upside down, turn around two times and then gently toss her on the beanbag chair. She laughed and giggled when we did this. "Do that again, daddy", she asked? After doing this a few times I had to have a rest. This was our little jitterbug and she loved it. We started to cut and glue construction paper together for a new activity. "You have to be very careful with the scissors", I told her. When it was time for her to go home, as usual she didn't want to leave. It upset me to see her cry.

After our hearing the blocks remained on the phone. When they were removed her machine still answered my calls. On Amanda's fifth birthday I called to chat with her. She was not there. "Cassie didn't tell you, they went to Disney World", Lacey said. "No, she didn't", I replied. It was good that my little girl went and I was happy for her but the mother could have told me. On the weekday I went to the mall for our visit and no one was there. Calling to find out what happened, the number was disconnected. Almost three weeks after our court appearance, Cassie denies me visitation for the ninth time.

When my weekend came, I arrived to find Moe waiting with Amanda. "Hey boo, I missed you", I said to her as she ran over to greet me. Saturday morning at my place, she says, "my mommy says you're a psycho, what is that daddy"? "I don't know, boo, I don't know what that is", I replied. To quickly change the subject and act like this wasn't something to worry about became my way of preventing her from knowing how I felt. Using other examples, I could take this opportunity to teach her that name-calling is wrong. At first this was hard to do because cartoon characters call each other "stupid". "It's not nice when people use bad words to hurt the feelings of other people, you should treat other people the same way you'd want them to treat you", I told her. It didn't take long for her to understand what I was talking about. She told me that her brother Donny calls her names and makes her cry.

On the last Friday of the month I called the local hospital and asked to have copies of my little girl's medical records. After they were found the nurse called me and said I could pick them up. This wasn't free and I had to pay for the paperwork. Reviewing these reports I found my name to be missing. It was like I didn't exist. Cassie was the guarantor, the parent, and the one to notify in case of an emergency. Amanda had been to the emergency room twice. One time for a laceration and the other was for having a foreign object in her ear. I remember being blamed for that because the mother said the earplug was mine. The trips to this hospital were 3 months apart with the first one occurring 7 months after I moved out.

Arriving at the exchange area for our weekday visit I noticed an unfamiliar man sitting with my daughter. Walking in I noticed it was Terry, Cassie's nephew. He was friendly and that was nothing unusual. He was always kind to me. Amanda told me her mother got a computer. She wanted to do some lessons so I got her started. While she was busy doing that I put together some of her school pictures taken at Kids Cottage. I had these photos for a long time and thought that giving her mother some copies would be a nice thing to do. I put three in little frames and was looking for a box to set them in. My little girl came and asked me to fix her some ice cream. I made her a bowl and put a video in for her to watch. When she was finished eating it was almost time for us to meet at the mall. As we did our trade I handed the box to Cassie and told her what was in it. "These are for you and your friends, they're her school pictures from Kids Cottage", I said.

The next day I went on a job with SWX that lasted all night. After working these long hours, I went home in the morning and was trying to relax. It's hard for me to sleep in the daytime. After taking a shower, I was climbing into bed when the phone rang. A woman from the child protection agency requested that I come in and meet with her. She needed to speak with me about allegations of abuse to Amanda. "What kind of abuse", I snapped? "I can't discuss that over the phone", she said. "Look, I've been up working all night, I'm tired and I'm going to bed", I told her and hung up. News of this accusation perplexed me and sleeping was something I couldn't do. Calling her back at the number she left, I apologized for being so rude and agreed to see her. It was urgent that I bring in evidence to prove they made a mistake. I put pictures, CDs and some paperwork in a folder and drove to their office. Two ladies came out and we walked to a room in the back. We sat down and they told me that this was a sexual abuse case. They began to ask me about the relationship I had with my little girl. They were impressed with the lessons I was teaching. The ladies liked the pictures of her at the park, on her computer or in the pool. I took the time to tell them of my Christian faith and expressed the importance for Amanda to know about it. I gave them their own copies of the wrongdoings on Cassie's behalf and asked if she was the accuser? They couldn't reveal that information. Their inquiries were simple, direct and I could sense that they were satisfied with the way I elaborated on all my responses. We had been talking for a while and this gathering was centered on a question that neither one of them wanted to ask. "Do you bounce your little girl's head up and down on your lap until your pants get hard", she asked. "No, absolutely not", I responded. Our little jitterbug was the next topic of our discussion and I showed both ladies how we did it. They didn't see anything sexual about our dance. I wanted to know what procedure did they use for their investigations. "After we're finished talking with everyone, we evaluate whether or not further action needs to be taken, if there's not enough evidence, we close the case and send you a letter confirming that", she said. Enough questions were asked and I answered all of them. Our time together was over. I handled this meeting in a calm, cool and collected manner. There was nothing to hide and they both knew it. I called Charlene and told her what happened. “What”, she exclaimed! The tone of her voice let me know how she felt. After my attorney heard some of the questions they asked, we both knew Cassie was behind all this.

My weekend arrived and I went to pick Amanda up. It was set in my mind not to say anything about the meeting yesterday. My waiting time expired and I made the call. No one picked up and my message was left on the machine. At my apartment I tried to call a few more times. I got in my car and passed by Cassie’s house. Her vehicle and Moe’s truck was parked out front. She wasn’t going to answer the phone or bring my daughter to the mall. For the tenth time she denied my visitation. I lost the entire weekend to be with my child.

On Saturday evening I called to speak to my little girl on the phone. It was a miracle that I got through. We talked for a good while. Amanda told me to hold on so she could ask her mother a question, “Mommy, tomorrow can I go to my daddy’s house”? “No, you’re sick”, I heard Cassie say. My daughter was sad from her mother’s answer. We chatted a little more and Amanda asked again. “No, you’re sick, you have diarrhea”, her mother yelled. “I do not, there’s nothing wrong with me, please, mommy please can I go to my daddy’s tomorrow”, she begged. Something bad happened and all I heard was Amanda screaming. Suddenly the phone hung up and the line was dead. On my answering machine I recorded all this. When I listened to the recording, it sounded like my daughter was being abused and I became filled with anxiety. To hear this and not be able to do anything about it was sickening.

The following Wednesday I went to get my little girl from the mall. The exchange area was empty so I sat on the bench to wait. This was a somber event for me when I’d arrive and find no one here waiting. At half past five I called to see what the hold up was. The machine picked up and I left a message telling of the meeting with my attorney tomorrow because I was tired of all this foolishness. It was my hope that by saying this, it would make Cassie follow the orders of the court. This made the eleventh time she denied me visitation.

Charlene was disturbed when I told her of these recent events. She decided to send a letter to Misty. In this note she expressed our discontent with the false allegations to child protection, the continuing denial of visitations and phone privileges. In a nice way she said that we were seeking sanctions in the form of incarceration for disregard of a valid court order. She ended suggesting that Cassie's attorney cooperate by correcting this situation.

All this commotion had to be affecting my daughter. I wanted to do something nice and decided to get her two CDs that had learning activities from a cartoon character she liked, Clifford the big red dog. I set them on her bed where they could be seen when she walked in. I'd have to meet at the mall tomorrow to pick her up and was hoping not to have any problems. I trusted that my attorney had straightened everything out. In the past I saw how she was very good at making sure that our instructions from the court were followed.

On time I arrived to find her white convertible parked, waiting at the entrance to the mall. I walked up and my little girl's eyes lit up when she saw me. She hurried to get out but Cassie pulled her close and whispered something in her ear. Whatever the mother said made her sad. As we were driving to my place she tells me, "my mommy says you're a psycho, what is that daddy"? "I don't know boo but I don't think it's nice", I replied. Quickly changing the subject, I told of a surprise for her at home. This excited her. We walked in, "Clifford", she screeched. She ran to her bed and looked at the boxes. I opened them up and took the discs out. It delighted me to see her this happy. She turned on her computer and let it warm up. Afterwards she selected a CD to play. All her software mainly consisted of learning activities in the form of games. I didn't buy anything that wouldn't teach her something. Amanda's education had always been my first priority and responsibility.

For a long time now, the exchanges had become peculiar. Whenever I drove up and saw Cassie waiting outside, she'd quickly turn around, hurry into the mall and wait in front of the police station. If someone were with her, she'd urge him or her to follow. I'd have to get out my car and walk our daughter to the entrance. The doors were heavy so I told my little girl to let me open it. As she went inside, I'd tell her, "daddy loves you boo and I'll see you real soon". After this, I'd leave right away so there wouldn't be a confrontation. In stead of her mother waiting until I stopped and from inside opened the car door, where she could take Amanda by the hand and help her out of my vehicle, Cassie runs the other way. Actions like this made me impose on Charlene to mail my support check to Tony or Misty because I couldn't get close enough to hand it to the mother myself.

Since the beginning, Cassie could not be trusted. For this reason, my monthly payments were handled through our lawyers.

At a department store I met a nice lady named Lana. We talked for a long time and did some shopping together. Hoping to meet again, we exchanged phone numbers. This was the second woman that I dated since my break up with Cassie. The first, Shelly worked at the children's hospital and had a degree in child psychology. Our courtship ended as quickly as it started. After a couple of dates I felt that she asked to many questions. We both had too much baggage from previous relationships. Lana seemed to be different. She owned a beauty shop and worked lots of hours. After we got to know each other I noticed how she often talked about money and the things she'd like to have? I figured that this was just small talk to her and didn't take her comments too seriously. My years with Cassie and the torment she put me through made it necessary to keep my guard up when it came being friendly with another woman. It was in my best interest to do this so I wouldn't be taken advantage of, again.

Off and on my phone privileges were being granted. The answering machine took many of my calls. Our chats were usually brief due to distractions or because Amanda was always being called away to do something. Several times this happened. "My mommy needs me to help in the garden, my mommy wants to read me a story, my mommy says I have to eat now, were some of the reasons Cassie used to get her get off the phone. Most of the time our conversations would only last a few minutes. Her mother wasn't aware that I had phone records which would show all my attempts to call and reveal the small amount of time she allowed my little girl to talk with me. This documentation would serve as evidence in court.

On the last Wednesday of this month I was awakened with another disturbing call from the child protection agency. A different social worker requested that I come in and answer to allegations of abuse. I put together the same file from my previous appointment and went to see her. She greeted me and we walked back to the same room as before. Our conversation started with her telling me that this was a case of physical abuse. The interrogation didn't last long. She admitted to conversing with her colleagues about the meeting with them on the first of this month and enjoyed looking at Amanda's pictures and my paperwork. Finally the question which served as the reason for our gathering came out. "Are you hitting your daughter in the head with your fist", she asked? "No I am not, not only to my child, but to any child, I wouldn't do that", I replied. Quickly she shut her folder and our time together was over. She offered to send me a letter of confirmation when the case was closed. When I informed Charlene of this, she sounded furious. Because of an upcoming job, I couldn't go see her. "On your next available moment, you get into my office", she demanded.

In the evening I picked my daughter up. We went home and started doing our regular activities. She was hungry so I ordered a pizza for us. As we sat eating I began to ask her a question. I made a fist and asked her if she knew what that was. "A fist", she replied. "Has daddy ever hit you with this", I asked? "No", she responded. "Has anyone ever hit you with their fist", I asked her. "Lacy did, she hit me here", Amanda said pointing to the top of her head. "I'm sorry boo, I'm sorry she did that to you but there's nothing daddy can do about that right now, be real nice to them from now on so they won't do that again", I told her. This was a young woman whom I didn't know too well and here she was, striking my little girl with her fist. This would be an issue that I hoped we could bring up in court.

Arriving at the mall on the last Friday of the month for my weekend I didn't see anyone waiting. I parked my car and was heading for the front doors. Walking towards the entrance I saw Cassie carrying Amanda and walking fast. It looked as though she was hurrying to get in the mall. Twice I waved to my daughter and she saw me. They quickly made it inside and I followed behind them. Cassie stopped between the two benches that were in front of the police station. There were people sitting on the seats and others standing by. I went over and said, "come on Amanda, lets go". She looked at me and laid her head back on her mother's shoulder. As I reached for my little girl Cassie increased the distance between us by turning her body. This movement put the mother closer to me, almost face to face. "She don't want to go with you, can you tell me why, I'll tell you why, you're molesting my daughter, you pervert", Cassie loudly proclaimed. Many of the bystanders started to ooh and ah, some were laughing and some moved away. I threw my hands up as the gesture of surrendering and said, "I don't have to take this". As I turned to walk into the sheriff's office the mother followed saying, "yeah, you go in there, she wants to talk to a detective". Looking through the window, I told the officer behind the desk that this was my weekend and the mother won't release our daughter to me, and I moved away. Immediately Cassie walked up and set Amanda on the counter, "he's molesting my daughter and she don't want to go with him", she told the officer. "Would you like to speak to the sergeant", the man asked? "Yeah, she does", the mother replied. The sergeant came out and took Amanda to the back to ask her some questions. After our little one left Cassie started to argue in a tone of voice that could be heard by the officer behind the window. I tried to ignore her. "How could you force my daughter to put her head in your lap and go up and down until your pants get hard", the wild mother accused? "I never did that", I replied. "Yeah, right, she tells me everything, you're not there, she has bad dreams, won't eat and cries in her sleep", this frantic woman told me. "She don't do that at my place, Jesus lives there", I said. "Oh yeah, is that why you call me Jezebel", she asked? "Why do you always bring that up, you're only hanging yourself", I said to her. "You're hanging yourself, you're going to have to answer a lot of questions, you pervert", she responded. "You two are going to knock it off now, now be quiet and I don't want to hear another word", the officer hollered. Suddenly the lawman came out to tell the mother that he asked Amanda three questions. "I asked her if she was afraid of her dad, and she said no; is your dad hurting you, and she said no; do you want to go with your dad, and she said no", said the sergeant. Pointing at me, Cassie assures, "he's guilty of sexual and physical abuse and he's being investigated by the child protection agency". "Have you seen any bruises", the sergeant asked the mother? "No", she replied. Looking at me, he then asked, "is he the father"? "I'm not sure, yes, I think, unfortunately", Cassie responds. "Well, you don't have to let her go with him if you think he's hurting her", says the sergeant. It was then that I stood up and blurted out a statement that Charlene told me about. This really upset the mother. "Child protection is involved because if she can get them to side with her on these false allegations of abuse, she can leave the state with our daughter", I said. With rage, "I can leave now if I want to and there's nothing you can do about it", Cassie shouts! The sergeant asked that she calms down and said it was her choice if Amanda was to leave with me. "You two need to try and get along, and stop acting like little kids", he said. When our daughter came out, she was happy with the two stuffed animals that the lawman gave her. Immediately the mother started to ask her questions. "Tell me why you don't want to go with him", Cassie asks? Our little girl looks very confused and stares at the ground. I told my little one not to be afraid and asked if she was scared of me? "No" she responded. Cassie gets more upset, looking at me, she asks, "why do you keep asking her to play mommy and daddy"? "She asks me to play that", I replied. When Amanda looked at me, I asked her, "at daddy's house you have two babies, one of them you can put your hand into and it becomes what"? "A puppet", she answered with a smile. "And the other one is a little bigger, huh", I asked? "Yeah", she answers. "Who's their mommy", I asked her? "I am", she replied. "And who's their daddy", I asked? "You are", she replies. I looked at her mother and said, "that's how we play mommy and daddy". "Why didn't you tell me that", Cassie asked Amanda? She didn't answer and just stared at the ground. The mother says, "well you can take her, kicking and screaming". She gets up and quickly walks out the police station. As we walked to my car I saw Cassie flip her middle finger at me. She almost got hit by a car as she sped away. On our way home Amanda asks, "daddy, what's a pervert"? "I don't know boo, but your daddy's not a pervert". "Yes you are", she says. "Baby girl, who's telling you this", I asked? "My mommy", she replied. Amanda was being brainwashed. When inappropriate subjects came up again, right away I tried to change them. I wasn't comfortable with the turmoil Cassie put our youngster in the middle of. It was to my better advantage that I handle this situation in a gentle manner. The more unshaken I looked, the angrier Cassie would get. Once again she tried to overthrow me with her slanderous false allegations. My shield of faith in God reflected the daggers coming out of her mouth. (Isaiah 54:17)

The April showers month was upon me and it felt like I had been rained on enough. Moe began to accompany Cassie on all the exchanges when he wasn't working. It was easy to see that he didn't want to be here. On my second weekday visit of this new month I noticed that Amanda was getting too fast for her games. As soon as possible I'd get a bigger hard drive and an extra memory chip installed in her computer. This was necessary so the device would stop freezing up when she does her activities. "I'm so proud of you, let me go get you a treat", I told her. Her rewards for completing the tasks were gummi lifesavers or a miniature peppermint patty. On our way to meet her mother at the mall she said something funny and it made me laugh. In return I'd make a funny face and she'd giggle. I had a talent for making a silly face or funny voice and she'd laugh so hard at me that sometimes she got the hiccups. "You're silly daddy"; she'd tell me. "Yeah I know, but I'm only silly for one person", I'd tell her. "Mmmeeeeeee", she'd say. She enjoyed my clowning around and it was a way of showing my love for her. When we arrived I gave her a small kiss or smooch before opening the door to the entrance of the mall. She became hesitant to show her affection for me this way. "I love you boo and I'll see you real soon", I said to her. In my younger years when I was her age, I'd give my parents a kiss as a sign of love. To me, it was natural to do this.

The next day Amanda called me. As always, I was happy to hear her voice. "I can't kiss you on the mouth anymore, my mommy don't like that, I can kiss you on your cheek, that's all", she told me. It hurt to hear her say this to me. I heard her mother in the background telling her what to say. This was just another one of the ways Cassie attempted to destroy the bond I had with my daughter. She was trying to disrupt the natural affection a child has for his or her parent. Her deceptive methods were not that of a normal mother. This strange behavior of hers is the reason I wanted to pursue the psychiatric evaluation by Dr. Watson. Hopefully he'd be able to tell us what's wrong with her and why she did these things.

In the morning I went to see my attorney. She was anxious to see me so we could make arrangements for another court appearance. We both had enough of Cassie's shenanigans. With this mother going to a state funded organization like the child protection and continue with her false accusations was a huge mistake. This agency can come to your house, take your kids away, place them in foster care and there's nothing you can do about it. We carefully went over everything that happened recently and the papers were drawn up. Some of our issues were denial of visitation and phone privileges which were held over from the previous, Moe was staying at Cassie's house, I insisted that the evaluation with Dr. Watson be completed and we were seeking court costs and attorney fees. After we were finished I signed the paperwork and it was submitted. Charlene said that she'd try to get our court date set for the beginning of May. "You may not get much of a notice", she told me.

On the Saturday of our first weekend we went to the zoo. The temperature and humidity down here can exhaust you. We found ourselves often seeking shade to stay somewhat cool. Both of us were worn out when we got home and needed a nap. Waking up with hunger I ordered us a pizza. I was happy to see that Amanda was eating better. "Daddy, Moe's whipping me with his hands and leaving marks", she told me as we ate. "Baby girl, try to be nicer to him so he won't do that anymore, I'm going to see if I can do something about that", I told her. "Okay", she said sadly. Our little rest energized us and we went to her room to do some lessons. She was too quick with the activities and her computer continued to freeze up. I decided to get the components needed to fix this device when our visit was over.

On Sunday we started going to a Christian Outreach church that was on the Manhattan. To hear preaching and teaching come out of the bible is what I am used to. My daughter would participate in the children's ministry while I joined the congregation to worship. Fervently praying to God, I asked him to protect Amanda in his love and make these people stop abusing her. Having faith that my Heavenly Father would do this was relieving to me.

There were times when I wasn't at home to call my daughter. If I tried to reach her from someplace else, there'd be no record of my attempt on the phone bill. I opened up a mobile phone account specifically for continuing my communication with Amanda. I requested to have detailed billing on my statement so this would give me a complete list of all the calls made and received. From this cell phone I was able to call my little girl at the appointed time from anywhere. I was hoping that Cassie would soften up and let me to talk to her.

The following Wednesday I picked up my little girl's computer from Tabby's house. John installed a bigger hard drive and an extra memory chip. He told me that freezing up was one thing it wasn't going to do anymore. In the evening I picked up Amanda and we decided to stop and eat some beignets at a nearby café in the mall. As we sat eating our snack my little girl said her milk tasted like beer. It shocked me to hear her say this. "How do you know what beer tastes like", I snapped. "I smelled it at my mommy's house", she responded quietly. "That's okay, that's okay, don't worry about it boo, but let me tell you something, people who drink lots of beer usually turn into alcoholics and ruin their lives", I told her. She understood the words I spoke and we finished our meal. As we were leaving in my car I asked, "hey boo, do you know anyone that drinks beer"? My youngster named everyone she knew, including Cassie. Most were family or friends that went by her mother's house. Donny was currently staying there and she told me that he's a big drinker. This was something I already knew. Now it was my job to educate Amanda that alcoholism is a bad habit. If she saw first hand the adverse effects of this self-inflicted abuse and how it can make you sick, then this wouldn't be a hard lesson for me to teach her. It worried me that she wouldn't be able to recognize when their drinking created an unsuitable environment for her.

The next day I called child protection and requested to speak with a supervisor to find out if the investigations were complete. I also wanted advice on the situation my daughter was in at her mother's house. When I told about the suspected abuse from Moe and how I wasn't comfortable with the excessive alcohol consumption, this was her response. "Just because someone drinks, it doesn't make them a bad parent, if the child is left with a person the mother feels comfortable with, then he or she can correct or discipline any way they see fit", she said. These remarks sounded ignorant. It seemed like she was defending the actions of Moe and Cassie. When I mentioned how we figured that the mother planned to leave the state but needed their help in believing these false allegations, the supervisor changed her attitude. I told the woman about our upcoming court date and asked about the paperwork that gave the results from my previous two meetings with the social workers. She offered to find out what the hold up was. "If they're finished with their investigations, I'll see to it that they get the reports out to you", she said. It offended me to see my tax dollars wasted on this agency's incompetence.

On my last weekend of this month we went to see my niece Marie at her house. On our way there Amanda told me how her mother keeps calling me a pervert. "What's that daddy", she asked? "I don't know boo", I replied. One day she's going to learn the meaning of this word and realize that it doesn't apply to me. This is when she'll know that Cassie was lying to her. My little girl and her cousin were doing different things around the house. My sister and her husband were here visiting at the same time and we sat at the kitchen table. My youngster took a rest from the pretend chores she was doing and sat down to talk with us. Marie motioned for me to go with her and look at something in another room. My niece started to tell me what Amanda had just told her. "My mommy has a house in Ohio and we're going to be moving soon, I won't see my daddy anymore", she told Marie. "Why didn't she tell me this", I asked? "Because she knew you'd get upset and she asked me not to say anything, she's not happy about this, you need to go to Charlene right away or Cassie's going to leave the state with her and you'll never see your daughter again", my niece said. When I returned to the kitchen, my little girl had just finished telling John and Tabby about the home up north. "Uh, what's she talking about", my sister asked? "I'm not sure", I replied. I asked my youngster about this and she began to cry as she told us about the plans her mother had. I picked her up, hugged her and wiped the tears away. "Don't worry about anything baby girl, you're not going anywhere, daddy loves you and I'm not letting you go", I told her. This made her happy and she smiled. She gave everyone a big hug and we all changed the subject. Cassie's threat to flee will be addressed first in court.

On the second day of May, I found letters from child protection in my mailbox. They didn't have enough sufficient evidence that a finding of abuse or neglect to a child in my care was justified and both cases were closed. Cassie's false allegations were of no avail. Charlene was successful in setting our court date for this month and our appearance was to occur in five days. These two letters would show how I had to meet with this state-funded agency and prove that I was not guilty of the accusations the mother made against me.

It was another bright sunny day for us to see the judge. We arrived to find Cassie and Misty already there. I waited down the hall and Charlene went to talk with them. A while later my attorney motioned me to join in and discuss the terms they reached. They granted me extended summer visitation that included a full week in both June and July. The week in June was to include my birthday. Amanda would be with me on Fathers Day and Cassie on Mother's Day. Appointments to do the evaluation with the psychiatrist were to be set within 72 hours of this hearing. Our legal proceedings would not continue until the sessions with Dr. Watson were completed and he sends his report. Notification was now required for all future out of state vacations. Neither party can or will remove Amanda from this jurisdiction for the purpose of relocation. This was about the extent of our compromise. We waited our turn to go before Judge Armstrong and put our agreement on record. It surprised me when the judge took a moment to tell Cassie and me how disturbed he was with our behaviors. "First of all, let me say this to you two, I've had suggestions made to this Court regarding misconduct of both of you, and I am not excited over what I've heard". "I am trying to stifle my comments because the truth of the matter is, I am very upset". "If I see that you are not obeying the orders of this Court, I will lock you up, whether it be momma or poppa, I will lock you up". "Last week I was five minutes away from taking a five year old from her mother and father and putting that child in foster care, because of the misconduct of those two parents were such that they were destroying that poor child", Judge Armstrong told us. "It wasn't me", I blurted out. Charlene quickly grabbed my arm as though to say, "shut up". He continued, saying that he wasn't talking specifically to one person but did direct most of his comments to Cassie. With this warning, he allowed us to leave. My biggest fear had now become a reality. We were before a judge who would decide the fate of our daughter, a child that he didn't even know. Once again, my paperwork wasn't looked at. When we got to Charlene's office, immediately I called and made arrangements to start my sessions with the psychiatrist.

Lana and me continued dating. We had been together for a while and were comfortable with each other. Often she'd ask about my occupation and wanted to know if it was a well paying job. It seemed like most of our conversations were about financial issues. When she started to boldly ask me to loan her money, I put the brakes on. The truth came out that all she wanted was a sugar daddy. We didn't have much of a relationship and it was here that it ended. Agreeing to keep in touch and remain friends, we went our separate ways. Not being able to trust females told me I had a serious problem that needed to be addressed.

The obstruction with my phone privileges continued. When the machine didn't answer my calls, distractions from Cassie or the people in her house hindered my opportunity to chat with Amanda. Many times her mother found something for my little girl to do when it was our time to talk. Enduring this cruelty was difficult for me especially when I was far away on a job out of town. Even after I quit doing the long distance assignments and lived less than three blocks away, I still couldn't talk with my daughter. It seemed like her mother was enjoying this. The excruciation of being disconnected from Amanda was hard to bear.

Horrifying news from Mary to Tabby trickled down to my ears. Hanna was found to be with child and made a decision. With massive amounts of cocaine, she tried to end the pregnancy herself. From the excessive drug abuse, she was certain that her baby would be deformed. Her father escorted her down here to New Orleans to have the fetus vacuumed out of her womb. When a woman chooses to abdicate her biological purpose this way, it can result in severely harmful medical consequences. To Christians this is known as, "the shedding of innocent blood", and we do not approve. When the sperm cell penetrates the egg and it starts dividing, life for that being begins. To stop this process by any means other than natural is murder. In many cases women don't even have to specify a reason and make the final decision to slaughter the child. Before this little baby has her first breath, before her mother can hear her helpless cry, her life is snuffed out as though it never existed and her limp body is thrown in the trash can. When you think about abortion for what it is, women are the only ones that can legally slay another human and are not prosecuted. When medical reasons don't apply, the pro-choice belief allows the, "I chose to kill it", option for females. Leaders in this country refuse to acknowledge this as self-destruction therefore no one in the United States of America will ever be able to stop the WAR. (Women Against Reproduction)

Overlooked is the fact that many mothers have a litter of kids from fathers that scatter. Some women do this for the big welfare check that enables them to remain unemployed. Support for these abandoned youngsters comes from the taxpayers or some other state-funded organization. The children may feed off a small part of this money and a large portion might be used to satisfy the wants and desires of a self-centered parent. No one knows where dad is. The kids live in poverty, suffer from the neglect of his absence and grow up unrestrained. When the media is used as a tool to program or raise the juveniles in their early years, violence, sex, and drugs can become topics of their discussions. Whether it's heard over the airwaves or seen on the screen, physically violent acts, homosexual or sexually explicit innuendoes, profanity or vulgarity fills their minds with curiosity and confusion. Boldness pushes them to try the things they hear and see. With a blurry sense of right and wrong they make incorrect and irresponsible choices in their life. Hollyweird and many record companies specialize in producing this immoral propaganda because it earns them lots of money and it's easy to deceive the young impressionable adolescent minds of their audience. In some cases young boys grow up to become predators and young girls inherit an aggressiveness that challenges them to lose their virginity before the teen years expire. A female that gives up her innocence prematurely has nothing to look forward to when she is married. She may find herself on a lifelong quest to satisfy an appetite that can't be filled. Sexual promiscuity and the wrongful exploitation of others don't belong in the lives of teenagers. Self-control is the gift one can possess that will assist in preventing these disorderly behaviors or dangerous actions from occurring. The sad part is this, not enough parents teach that to their youngsters. If teens do not have any motivation or guidance from their father and all they see is a parent that won't work, it's likely that this will be the path they choose to follow. They expect something for nothing and everything to be given to them. (II Thessalonians 3:10)

On a weekday visit near the end of the month we went to a toy store in the mall. As we walked around looking, Amanda found something she really wanted. It was Clifford the big red dog. "Can we get it daddy, please", she asked. "Okay baby girl, you can have it", I told her. She loved it. The stuffed animal was a bit too big so I carried it to the car for her. When we got home she made a special spot for the dog on her bed. She told him to watch while she played on her computer. Our time went by quickly and we had to go meet her mother at the mall. "Can I take Clifford home for a sleepover, please", she asked? "I guess that'll be okay", I replied. We left with her toy and met Cassie for the exchange.

The last weekend of the month was mine and I went to get Amanda. When I walked in the mall, Cassie got up off the bench and hurried away. "Come on baby girl, lets go", I said. My youngster was happy to see me. She came over, gave her red dog for me to carry and we went out the doors. This new toy I bought last Wednesday smelled awful and had something all over it. "Amanda, what's this stuff on Clifford", I asked? "My mommy said he needed to be groomed so we had to put some styling gels on him", she said. "That's okay, daddy will clean him up when we get home", I told her. After I set my little girl up on her computer, I washed Clifford. It took several washings to remove the sticky substance from his fur. It looked like Cassie tried to destroy Amanda's toy. Normally, an adult wouldn't purposely damage a toy that belongs to their child. When I thought about what kind of person her mother is, I should've expected this to happen.

That's why Cassie was so quick to get up and leave the area when I walked in. None of Amanda's toys would leave my place again.

At a local department store I bought an electric toothbrush. This would be nice for Amanda to try when she came over. After it was charged up I decided to see how well it worked. Surprising was the way it knocked off all the tarter that a normal brush wouldn't. It left my teeth smooth and clean like I had just made a visit to the dentist. For less than half the price of an office visit, I purchased a device that would clean my teeth just as good as the hygienist and it didn't take a long time. I knew my little girl would love this.

The full week that was awarded to me in court started at the beginning of June. Cassie was not at the exchange area and had to be called. There was a new addition to Amanda's bedroom. I had a picture of her mother and me holding our child when she was three days old enlarged. It was framed and hung on the wall by her computer. "Daddy why'd you do that daddy", she asked? "Because you need to know that you have two parents, both a daddy and a mommy who love you very much", I told her. In the bathroom she saw a new electric toothbrush and was curious about it. It tickled her gums when she used it and that made her laugh. I knew it did a good job on my teeth and was sure that it'd do the same for her.

The next day we went to see the levees that line the Mississippi River. I had a piece of cardboard and was going to show her how we used to slide down the dyke when we were kids. I ran and jumped on the hard paper, sliding down to the bottom. She wasn't impressed at all. We walked down by the water and strolled under the willow trees. I showed boats pushing barges and explained to her how they moved things to different cities along the river. From here we went to a nearby park where I pushed her on the swing. In the evening we went home to eat some pizza and watch a video. She could count to 100 easily from the numbers I taped on her wall. My goofy faces and silly voices made her laugh. To act funny like this was something she enjoyed. Every night I read her three bedtime stories before she went to sleep. She would be snoozing before I finished reading them. We stayed busy through out the week. We'd visit my sisters or her cousins to occupy some of our time. A trip to City Park and the zoo in New Orleans was on our agenda. If we weren't swimming, there were plenty of activities for us to do at my place. We had fun doing the things we always did. She was happy and content with just us being together.

It was time for my first appointment with Dr. Watson. I arrived to take the very large MMPI-2 test for the third time. I had taken this exam on my initial appointment with this psychiatrist long ago and at the meeting with Dr. Rubin. It takes a long time to answer all the 564 questions. When finished, before leaving I asked the receptionist if the mother set up her appointments. Looking at the book she saw Cassie had scheduled her sessions. I left their office and would have to return next week to meet with the doctor.

The next day Amanda called and asked to come over so she could go swimming. I told her yes but Cassie said no. She got upset with her mother's answer. I consoled her by saying that I'd have her tomorrow for Fathers day. On Saturday evening I picked her up and we headed to my place. "Daddy, my mommy's a alcoholic, she drinks a lot of beer with a red dog on it", she said. When I told my little girl that people who drink a lot of beer usually turn into alcoholics and ruin their lives, I didn't mention any names. This statement she made came from her personal observation. Cassie chose to live a lifestyle that would show our daughter the malady this self-inflicted abuse can cause. Not knowing what Amanda was being exposed to really had me worried. This only added to my anxiety.

On my second meeting with the doctor I expressed my concern with Cassie's drinking. I told him of several occurrences when she worked at the lounge that were disturbing. It was me that insisted we finish our evaluation with him because of her obnoxious behavior. There was no reason for her to be scared of me and yet, she was. When I told him that the main reason for completing our sessions was to be granted more time with my daughter and that I was seeking a 50/50 joint custody, a week with me and a week with her mother, he wanted to know why? "Because I love her and she's my daughter", I said. "I need to teach her about God and Jesus, she's not going to learn that in school", "Our routine is filled with activities and I have provided a good learning environment for her", I added. "I want to be there when she needs me, that is why I want more time with her", I told him. He asked me a few more questions and our meeting was over. Amanda would be with us for my session next week.

It was the weekday to be with my daughter and we spent a lot of time swimming. Lately I found Cassie to be alone at the area to do the exchange. Moe and the babysitter had faded out of the picture. My little girl would pull away from her mommy and run over to me when I arrived. For a long time now I noticed Amanda had been wearing clothes that were too small for her. When she came over, one of the first things she did was take her shoes off and change into something else. She liked the clothes I bought and was happy to go in her closet and choose a comfortable outfit to wear. The garments she came over in would be folded up in a bag and given back when we traded at the mall. I didn't mind her wearing the attire from my place to her mother's house. I supposed that Cassie would return them when we met at the mall next time.

On our weekend visit my youngster told me of the continued name calling from her mother. It went in one ear and out the other. It was important not to say anything about this and I rarely mentioned Cassie's name. Amanda didn't hesitate to tell me what her mother was saying as though she wanted to know if what she heard, was true. My daughter revealed the newest lie her mother told her. "My mommy says you're going to hurt me", she said. "That's not true, poppa would never hurt you, I love ya boo", I said. The persistence of this mother to brainwash our little girl was not appreciated. It became evident that she wasn't going to stop. How could she not know that kids get smarter as they grow older? One day Amanda's going to find out that Cassie was untruthful in an attempt to mislead her. If the feeling of distrust develops, our little girl may not believe anything her mother has to say.

At my last session with the doctor our gathering started out the same way as the one long ago. Dr. Watson sat in silence and observed how I interacted with Amanda. By this time she was very smart and answered any question I asked. When the psychiatrist had seen enough, he called my little girl to another room to talk with her. While they were gone I straightened out our play area and put the toys away. A short time later they returned and I showed my daughter how everything was put away, just like her room at home. I gave her a treat for being good and she went out to meet her mother. Before I left the doctor told of a fourth meeting with me would be necessary. It was my guess that he needed to discuss some of the statements that Cassie had made about me. These sessions were $125 each and the cost for his final report was $875. I must complete this requirement of the court before the judge would even consider granting me the privilege to spend more time with my daughter. This was part of our legal proceedings. The cost for my half of the evaluation was $1375.

It was my last weekday visit of the month. A neighboring little friend named Kristy came over to see Amanda. While they played in her room I sat on the couch and watched television. Suddenly my youngster came to me with her tooth in hand. This was the second time at my place that one of her baby teeth came out and she was unusually upset. I told her this was normal and that everything would be fine. As she gets older it'll grow back. "We need to put it under your pillow for when the tooth fairy comes", I told her. The bleeding that normally accompanies this loss stopped a short while later. She remained frightened about this incident and I asked her why. "My mommy's going to be angry again, like she was the last time, she's going to make me go to the dentist", she said. "Don't worry about that boo, that's not going to happen, you can go play with Kristy now if you want to", I said. Amanda doesn't like having to go see a doctor or a dentist and the mentioning of either really scares her. As we headed over to meet her mother, my youngster sat in silence. When I asked what was wrong she admitted to being worried about having to tell her mommy about the missing tooth. When we arrived at the exchange area she ran over to her mother, opened her mouth and showed what happened. The resentment on Cassie's face was noticed immediately. "I'm taking you to the dentist tomorrow", she told Amanda. "No mommy, I don't want to go to the dentist", she cried. "She don't need to go see a dentist, it was one of her baby teeth", I exclaimed! All I could do was sit on the bench and watch as this mother pulled our unwilling child by her wrist to the exit of the mall. Cassie didn't have to say or do what she did. Long ago it was her who discovered that saying the doctor's name or to talk about having to go visit him would create a state of fear in our daughter. This threat she made to our little one had me sick to my stomach and created a memory I'll never forget.

July started with a weekday visit and I arrived at the mall to find the mother waiting in her car with Amanda. As I approached the vehicle, Donny got out so he could sit in the front seat. This was the sixth time Cassie brought her son to the exchange, which is against what the judgement ordered. Looking at him I saw he had an earring in his eyebrow. I took my youngster by the hand as he watched. "You have something stuck by your eye", I said jokingly. "I have one here too", he responded as he pulled his shirt up to reveal that he had his nipple pierced. His action was improper and I quickly turned away with my daughter. She didn't have to see him do that. "Daddy, Donny has an earring in his noonie, that's nasty", my little girl said after we got in my car. It made me feel good to hear her say this. "That's right baby girl, God doesn't give us a body to poke holes in it or litter it with tattoos that don't wash off", I told her. My lecture continued when we got home. When she saw the scar from when my ear was pierced, I admitted to making that mistake a long time ago as a teenager. I didn't like the way it looked and took it out. It was never put it back in. "God gives us a body to take care of, we shouldn't treat it like a pin cushion or a drawing board, using ink that doesn't wash off, tattoos mark you for life", I told her. Your nose is to smell with and your tongue to taste with, not to poke a hole in and stick in a piece of metal. Two earrings, one in each earlobe is fine. To have 4, 5 or 6 holes in your ear is a little too much. A person can desecrate their body when they poke a lot of holes in it or decorate with ink. "Some people pierce themselves in silly places, your brother might accidentally get hurt in his sleep with that thing in his eyebrow", I said. Tattoos can become undesirable to someone when they get older. "The ones you play with are okay because they wash off, real tattoos do not wash off", I said. Everyone has a different opinion about this. A person may copycat another and get painted. Sometimes it's hard to make a good first impression when you have metal in your nose, tongue or eyebrow. A company may have second thoughts about hiring you when they see that. I didn't stop until Amanda understood what I was talking about. "We only have one body and it's important that we treat it with respect". (I Corinthians 6:19-20)

Our weekend was great. Something we hadn't done in a long time was play a game of volleyball. Using a balloon so nothing would get broken, we'd sit down and pat it to each other. We'd take her tablet and open it up. She'd draw on one side and I drew on the other. I had much of her artwork hanging in different places around my apartment. "Good girl, I'm so proud of you boo, your Poppa loves you very much", I said. With a hug, "You're my hero", she replied. She wanted to dance and turned on the stereo. CDs by "Point of Grace, Rebecca St. James and Zoe Girl", had her favorite songs on it. Of course we had to have the usual pizza and ice cream. Her eating habits were getting better. She started to eat yogurt, fish sticks, bananas and other foods I had her try. Our relationship strengthened because of the routine activities we did. It was me that helped teach her to make stuff out of play doe, use the crayons and markers, swim and ride our bikes, the flashcards and the computer lessons. It's me that reads her the bedtime stories. My Christian music she listens to and our church are the things we like. It's me that sits on the couch with her to watch a video and share a chocolate bar. If she needs to know an answer, I give it. When she tries to do a task and don't succeed, "that's my fault boo, I'm not trying hard enough, lets try this", I'd say. If my child is doing the best she can, it's not good to tell her that she's not trying hard enough. I pay enough attention to know her capabilities. With encouragement and compliments I help to build her self-esteem. As her father, it's my responsibility to do all I can to help her learn.

Growing up as children, we relied heavily on our parents. Dependence like this is only natural. We did what they told us and knew better than to ask any questions. Explanations for the need to do right and not do wrong weren't given too often. "Because I said so" and "I don't owe you an explanation", is normally what we heard. It was the "children are to be seen and not heard", era. Dad and mom's endless drug and alcohol abuse affected the whole family. My older siblings weren't ready for the parenting job bestowed upon them. When I was a kid my father used to tell me, "go play in the traffic" and when I was a teenager he packed everything up and wouldn't disclose where they moved. My mother knew nothing about this. She was in the hospital being detoxified from her prescription drugs at the time. Us kids were in no position to say anything about their abusive habits. We're adults now and can see how this prevented their ability to be good parents. Dad was our leader that couldn't lead. There was no denying the fact that we were a dysfunctional family. When youngsters grow up watching their models get drunk and take drugs, they may see that as an acceptable lifestyle for them to follow. That's what happened to all of us. We all developed the habits of our folks. Some of my siblings still drink or smoke pot. Mary is addicted to her prescription narcotics like mom was and Mick is a heavy drinker like dad was. I'm grateful it doesn't have to be that way for me anymore. Tabby and I are the only two in our family that doesn't booze it up or do drugs. Alcoholics Anonymous pushed me into God and He never did let go. There are many unfortunate times in the lives of my family. We all agree that our parents didn't raise us properly. That doesn't give any of us the right to strike out at anyone for anything. We can't change the past but can learn from it, to avoid the same adversities from reoccurring. Just because my childhood was miserable doesn't mean Amanda's has to be.

Amanda and me would talk about what we did together on our way to meet Cassie. It was better to do this than see her look gloomy because she had to go back to her mother. "Did you have fun boo"; I'd ask her? "Yeah", she said. Amanda understood that I had no choice in this matter and we had to go when it was time. Just as we were approaching the parking lot, "daddy, hurry, give me a kiss", she said. I looked over to see her puckering up for the smooch that used to end all our visits. I gave her a kiss and then drove to the entrance of the mall. My little girl was afraid to let Cassie see her showing affection for me this way. It made me feel awful to know my daughter was fearful of her mother about this.

The week awarded in court to be with my daughter was taken near the end of the month. I had two new CDs waiting for her. They taught science and spelling. Together we installed them on her computer. These were subjects Amanda didn't know too much about. Together we played the activities. Always doing something to keep us busy was the routine that we had developed. By this time her library of storybooks had grown. At bedtime, her favorites were "Little Red Riding Hood, The Three Little Pigs and The Boy Who Cried Wolf. At the middle of the week I asked my little girl if she wanted to call her mother and say hello? This sounded like a good idea. I happen to over hear that their conversation was unpleasant. She looked troubled from the talk afterwards. "What's the matter boo", I asked her? "Mommy and Moe said you're stupid", she replied. "That's okay, we know that's not true", I told her. I gave her a hug and we ordered a pizza. She didn't want to call there anymore.

It was time for my final session with Dr. Watson. I paid the $875 he required to write his report. Amanda sat out front talking with the secretary while they looked at magazines. The psychiatrist asked me if I leave my daughter with strangers or alone? "No", I answered. He asked if I belong to a cult? "No I do not", I replied. He continued to interrogate me with questions that came from the false allegations Cassie made. Our session didn't last long. I went out to find my daughter enjoying herself. The lady was impressed with how smart my little one was. Before leaving I quietly asked the receptionist if

Cassie was through with her meetings. "She has her last appointment and then she's finished, after she pays the fee, the doctor will write his report and send it to the judge and the attorneys", she responded.

At the end of the week Amanda and me needed go out somewhere. I called Pookie, Kristy's mother and asked if she could go to the "Aquarium of the Americas", with us in New Orleans. She liked having her pal with us and we all had a good time. Afterwards we went home for pizza and ice cream. The little ones would play in her room until it got late. When it was time for bed my youngster would pick the stories she wanted me to read her. I have a big bed and she always slept in it with me. Tonight I was going to see if she'd sleep in her own bed. After she fell asleep I gently picked her up and went to her room. When I laid her down, she was wide-awake. Right away she started crying. "Please daddy, I'm scared to be alone, let me sleep in bed with you", she cried. I said okay and we went back to my room. The next night I tried this again. I put a night light in her room so she could see. The same thing happened. "Please daddy, I'm scared", she cried. I got the beanbag from the living room and set it next to her bed. "Daddy's right here, I'm not leaving you", I told her. She watched me as I began to read some more bedtime stories. Before I was finished she climbed out of bed and laid on the beanbag next to me. I asked her what she was so afraid of. "My mommy watches movies with vampires that drink blood in it and that makes me have bad dreams, she has pictures of a werewolf, a ghost and a headless horseman hanging on her wall and that scares me", she replied. "I have pictures of Jesus and you on my walls, you don't have to be scared here, baby girl", I told her. She was too frightened to sleep by herself so we slept in my bed. I needed to find a solution that'd help her grow out of this fear she had.

The next day I took her to eat at a hamburger and seafood place. She tried some of the food on my plate and liked it. I had the waitress bring us some ice cream. We talked a little about why she was scared to sleep in her own bed. This made her sad so our conversation had to stop. If my daughter was afraid to be alone in the next room for a long length of time, this may be a symptom of Separation Anxiety Disorder. (SAD) This is when a youngster becomes terrified when he or she is separated from a major attachment figure, such as dad or mom. Certain occurrences will cause a child to behave like this. My sister Cindy used to work with children at a psychiatric hospital. She had a special gift of being able to befriend and talk to almost anyone. She may be able to tell me how to find out if my little girl was suffering from this disorder. We hadn't spoke in a long time and I didn't know how to get in touch with her. If anyone knew, Tabby could tell me how to reach her.

It was our last day to be together. In the evening after we were through with the lessons on her computer, Amanda wanted to play dress up. There was a pink dress that she really liked. She put it on and was dancing to her music. "Can I wear this to my mommy's", she asked? "Sure boo, if you want to", I told her. "What about your other clothes at your mom's, have you seen them lately", I asked her? "No, I don't know what happened to them", she answered. Soon we had to leave and go meet at the mall. I walked over with my daughter and asked her mother about the garments from my place. Cassie acted like I wasn't even there and ignored my question. She quickly walked away pulling Amanda with her. I refused to chase after her mother. All I could do was ask her again the next time we met.

Calling to see if I could talk with my daughter, Cassie answered the phone. "Can you send her clothes back next time we go to the mall", I asked? "Yeah, don't worry, I'm not going to keep something you paid 35 cents for at a thrifty store", she said. I don't remember doing anything for her to be so sarcastic with me. Amanda got on the phone and we started out with a happy chat. I could hear her mother in the background talking to our youngster. "I have to get off the phone daddy, mommy says I have to look for something" she said softly. "Okay boo, whatcha gotta go look for", I asked? "I don't know, I have to go now", she said. It upset me to know that the mother made our little girl sad like this and we hung up.

A new month started and all the memories from everything that happened thus far had me puzzled. We were a couple that had a child, a little girl. Things didn't work out between us. I couldn't be a good parent living in the environment her mother created and felt it was necessary to leave. My little girl is very precious to me and her mother knew that. Portraying herself to be so terrified me; the mother tried to manipulate the police and the legal system. Several questions came to mind and I became curious about what she was actually afraid of. I knew one day we'd be back in court. On a piece of paper I wrote many inquiries for my attorney to ask Cassie in court. I worded the questions to be answered briefly, with either a "Yes", or a "No".

Her responses could serve as an admission of guilt and we might find out why she did these things to me. Charlene and I already knew most of these answers.

AFRAID OF WHAT and FAIRNESS > answer Yes or No

- Do you feel that because your child had only 160 hours of supervised visitation with her father in the last 10 months of 1999 that it might have damaged their relationship?
- Did you deny your child's father visitation with the child 5 times in 1999, even with supervision present?
- Are you rigid with the communication and visitation schedule?
- Did you knowingly interfere with the relationship between your child and her father?
- If your child were happy being with her father, would it be nice to let her spend more time with him?
- Are you more comfortable leaving your child in the care of a babysitter rather than with her father?
- Do you think your child's father is being a friendly parent as far as working with you when it relates to your child's best interest and wellbeing?
- Are you a friendly parent toward the other parent when it concerns your child?
- Does your child have easy access to her father other than what was ordered by the court in terms of communication and visitation?
- Are you thankful that your child's father shows great concern for her?
- Do you encourage a positive relationship between your child and her father?
- Is your child happy spending time with her father?
- Are you lenient with the schedule of communication and visitation to the extent where your child and her father have more contact than what the court ordered?
- Do you think it's psychologically or emotionally healthy for your child to hear or see any animosity towards her father from you, your family or anyone else?
- If your child were to ask if she could go see her father, what would your answer be?

- Do you hold back information concerning your child from her father?
- Are you pleased with the education your child's father is trying to teach her?
- Do you feel that you are the only parent when it comes to the decision making and doing what's in the best interest of your child?
- Do you allow your child to talk about her father any time she wants to?
- In the event of an emergency, do you allow your child's father to be contacted?
- Do you think your child might be afraid to express her true feelings about her father because she knows that you, your family or friends will get offended?
- Does your child ever ask to increase the length of time she spends with her father?
- Do you value the relationship your child has with her father?
- Is it important to have your child be with someone else instead of her father?
- Do you feel that by consistently leaving your child with unrelated adults, it could emotionally hurt or confuse the relationship between your child and her father?
- Does your child's father have involvement in any decisions made concerning her?
- Are you comfortable when your child is with her father?
- Do you allow your child's father to participate in the selection of her school?
- Do you believe your child should have contact with both her real dad and mom?
- Does your child become excited when she sees her parents talking and being friendly?
- Do you believe that it is psychologically and emotionally important for your child to see her parents get along and are friendly with each other?
- Have you encouraged anyone to verbally assault or threaten your child's father?

- Do you sometimes act frightened, hysterically out of control or cry to gain the favor of, arouse the anger of, or get sympathy from another person?
- In your opinion, does your child's father handle his financial matters well?
- Do you consider yourself to handle your own financial matters well?
- Did you ever try to persuade your sons or anyone else to attack your child's father?
- Have you ever fraudulently used someone's personal credit information to obtain an item or open an account?
- Are you aware that stalking is a criminal offense?
- Have you ever forged a credit card application in someone else's name?
- Did you bring allegations against your child's father to the child protection agency?
- Do you still feel that your child's father is "very crazy" or an "unfit father"?
- In the substance abuse assessment, is it true that you showed evidence of substance abuse?
- While you and your child's father resided together, was there any domestic violence?
- Are you aware of the cruel attacks your sons made on your child's father?

Charlene was impressed with all these questions. We both knew that she couldn't ask all of them. I relied on my attorney to pick and choose the ones she needed. The problem was that we didn't know when the judge would put either of us on the stand. We had been to court five times already and our issues were always decided before we went in. The report from Dr. Watson was needed to continue our legal proceedings. If Cassie continued to deny me phone communication and visitation, she'd have a tough time at the hearing. She's the one who started all this. All I ever wanted was to spend more time with Amanda.

School was going to be starting soon and I didn't know which one my daughter would be going to. I called to speak with Nat or Pam hoping that one of their kids knew because Amanda plays with their daughter Diana. One of their kids Jasmine answered. She told me that my youngster was enrolled at "Top of the Hill Academy". I thanked her for the telling me and hung up. This was a school that required tuition. I wondered how Cassie was able to afford this. I made a phone call to inquire about their facility. The receptionist I spoke with said that the monthly expense was $450. After introducing myself and informing the lady that my little girl would be going there, I asked if the fee was paid quarterly or annually. She told me it was paid. "Her mother got a loan from the only bank we deal with", she said. It pleased me to know that Amanda was going to a good school. She wouldn't be a product of our faulty public school system like I am, however; my budget wouldn't allow me to afford a large expense like this. Cassie's credit must have been better than I thought or she got Moe to co-sign that loan for her. It was none of my business to ask any questions. I couldn't express my gratitude to her for doing this for our daughter because we weren't talking.

The long awaited call from Cindy came. "Hey stranger, how ya doing", she asked? We talked for a while and then I started to tell her why Amanda wouldn't sleep in her bed. Sis was familiar with SAD. In situations like mine, separation can cause a child to feel insecure. There was brief silence. Suddenly, "I bet I know what it is, when she's playing in her room and thinks Cassie's in another part of the house, she comes out and finds that her mother is gone and she's left with people she don't want to be with; now she thinks you're going to do that to her", Cindy told me. This sounded logical. She suggested if I ask about this to do it tenderly and don't be too inquisitive. "Let me know what you find out", my sister asked?

Our visits continued without interruption. I bought a new chair for Amanda to sit on while she did her computer lessons. When I asked about her clothes, "my mommy throwed it away", she told me. "Are you sure, what about your pink dress", I asked? "She didn't like it, I can't find it", my little girl told me. "That's okay, we can get another one, don't worry about it boo, daddy loves you", I said. She gave me a big hug. "I love you daddy", she said with a kiss. She put one of her Clifford discs in and started playing an activity. Amanda enjoys wearing the clothes I buy for her. If I wanted to keep these garments, they'd have to stay here from now on. When it was time for her to go back to her mother's, she'd have to change back into the clothes she came over in. It was a disheartening to hear how Cassie discarded clothes that our youngster liked. She had no reason to do something like this. I decided to call Dr Watson set an appointment for him to see my daughter. Before the day of their session, he'd get a letter from me telling him all the things that I knew and why I felt the need to arrange for their meeting. It was important that he know how Amanda was being treated at her mother's house. This added session pushed his cost up to $1500.

The phone rang one morning and it was Tabby. She told me of an e-mail she received from our niece. Kayla sent my sister a letter announcing that she was gay. Her new lifestyle may have been a consequence from the maltreatment in her younger years from her parents. Long ago, Mary and I went to court to testify in an attempt to remove the young children from our sister. Kim didn't show up and was found to be an unfit mother. We won. Kayla, her younger brother and the two sisters were moved here from Texas to live with family. None of these kids had a good relationship with either of their parents. Their father was a boat captain and a drug addict. He had no bond with any of the kids. Their mother was in a wheel chair due to a drug overdose and we were told how she physically abused all the kids. Both parents were incapable of properly tending to these little ones. These four kids are now teenagers. Kayla is the oldest and moved near us, just across the river. She came to see me after an all night binge on a drug called ecstasy. After taking 3 "tabs" and dancing to techno music for hours, she was worn out. I warned her how that stuff is no good for her. We talked about people being gay was abnormal and she agreed. "I hope it's just a phase you're going through", I told her. "Me too", she replied. "It was Adam and Eve in the Garden of Eden, not Adam and Steve", I said. She seemed disinterested in talking about God so I left that one alone. Kim and her husband had addictions that disabled their ability to be parents and now their kids were paying for it. It was sad to see our family history repeating itself.

The acts of homosexuality and abortion are seen by some to be a method of population control. These acts are allowed to flourish because the highest court in the land protects them and the Anti-Christian Litigation Unit guards them. For obvious reasons, babies aren't born to homosexuals. If the government allows innocent trusting children to be given to same sex couples, these people can groom the youngster to believe that two dads or two moms in the same bed is a normal lifestyle. Condoning politicians who ignore the time when God burnt the sodomites to ashes in the land of Sodom and Gomorrah have been working hard to give these degenerates more privileges. The excuse, "I was born this way", has been proven to be false. Just ask someone who used to be gay. Men and women who choose to practice this strange behavior forfeit their natural affection, which produces the attraction of one sex to the other. Everyone has a free will but to misuse it breeds spiritual death and can land you a spot in Gehenna. From the rib of man, God created woman and instituted the first marriage with Adam and Eve. Both genders are designed for a specific purpose. Together, the man and the woman produce offspring, and they raise the child. Here is the fundamental plan for a family. This is some of what I learned as a Christian. One day I'll explain to Amanda why God gives kids both a dad and mom, because if I don't, our secular media will try to teach her that same sex perversion parenting is acceptable and normal. The lesbians don't like men, don't want men, don't need men but they want to be like men. While this is true, these females can't deny that they need a replica of the male genitalia to internally stimulate each other. Gay men who don't like women, don't want women, don't need women and give up the natural use for a woman choose to find sexual satisfaction in the orifice of another man. (Romans 1:24-32)

To a normal man, the most beautiful creation God made is woman. She was created for him, not him for her. Since she was made from the rib of man, that makes her part of him. Why the rib? Could it be that when a man and woman unite, at that part of the body they are to be joined so their hearts remain close to each other? Side by side, they are to walk together through the trials of life, not one in front of the other or one behind the other. This is why a man isn't to trample over the woman he loves, like she was formed from a bone in his foot. She is to be loved, honored, protected, provided for, and in a secure relationship. A man, who hurts his wife or the mother of his child, whether it is emotionally, verbally or physically, brings a curse upon himself. If a man truly loves his woman, he will never do anything to hurt her. The family circle of man, woman and child should never be broken or dangerous consequences can occur for the entire family. A real man needs a real woman. In love she brings forth his child. This youngster needs him, the one whom he or she calls daddy. Men are to be spiritual leaders for their children. It's vitally important that parents always remember they are setting the example.

In our nation there is an organization made up of women, specifically for women where it's members brainwash their new recruits, convincing them that marriage is when a woman submits herself to a lifetime of slavery. The main objective of these feminists is to persuade it's members that men aren't needed in all aspects of family life and should be excluded. The only thing that's needed from him is his reproductive ingredient. Laws are set in place where the sperm donor, when fighting to see his kids will never win against the human incubator and she knows it. When I was born women were burning their bras in protest, demanding liberation and equality. Since that movement occurred, their position escalated to a status that progressively demotes a man from his role in the household. Supported strongly by the Anti-Christian Litigation Unit and backed by thousands of lesbians, this regime will not stop until they have enough control to dominate their opponent. The man, the woman and the children make up the family. Freedom that allows the disruption of this union is the infection that will force the moral foundation in this nation, where these families live, to crumble.

Near the end of the month I continued trying to contact my daughter. The last time we spoke she told me that her mother don't like us talking on the phone. One evening on the third try, Amanda answered. "Hello boo, how ya doing", I asked? "Shh, my mommy's in the shower, if she sees me on the phone, she'll know I'm talking to you, I have to be real quiet or I'll get in trouble", she whispered. We talked for just a little while and then hung up. I didn't want to be the one to cause any problems for her. It was dreadful to imagine what her mother would do if she caught our youngster talking to me. My little girl already told me how her mommy slaps her in the face and makes her cry. Cassie has a drinking problem. If she gets too upset and loses her temper, it will be unpleasant for my daughter.

Returning home from the store I saw Kristy's godfather, Frank waiting out in the parking lot. As we talked for a little while I couldn't help but notice how familiar he looked. In our conversation he revealed that he was actually Kristy's father. This explained why they had such a striking resemblance. Although it was none of my business I asked why his little girl didn't have his last name. Pookie gave her the last name of some rich guy while Frank was at work offshore. "I think she's trying to collect back child support from him", he told me. He gets to see his daughter once or twice a month. I noticed Kristy, her mother and the boyfriend coming out and we hushed our little chat. I said hello to them, good bye to Frank and went inside. This sounded so much like my insensitive custody situation. Pookie was in control, not working, wanting money and depriving their daughter of the right to have a consistent relationship with her father. My little girl likes her pal and they have fun together. If Kristy ever discovers her mother's deceitfulness, she'll be hurt and angry.

September started with a weekend for us. At home I heard my youngster was singing something. Listening closer, I recognized it. I asked her where she heard that song? "I heard it on the radio at my mommy's house", she replied. I carefully explained to her about this diva and that a good girl wouldn't dress and act like that to lure money and friends. Amanda sang a song made by a young misguided prancer who wasn't at the legal drinking age yet Her voice sounds nice but the lyrics she sings are suggestive to her male audience. This singer, who hasn't even lost her baby fat yet, woos the admiration of her fans by the over exposure of her sexuality. Her powerful seduction ensnares devotees. A news clip from one of her concerts showed the outfit she wore was trying to let it all hang out. At the checkout counter in the grocery store she was on the front cover of a magazine with her top barely covered, showing the world that she had developed a cleavage. She gave up her dignity for fortune and fame. Her parents should be very proud that their daughter has become a sex symbol and wealthy. Nowadays some musical groups seek to influence young boys and girls to rebel against authority. An eroding conscience makes it easy to reject the right and do the wrong. Immoral thoughts trigger their hormones to pump prematurely and we find our youth looking to fulfill the habits and desires of an adult, ignoring the consequences. Most of the teenagers and young adults today rather attend a concert than go to church. It's important to educate my child that today's music can embed filthiness in her thoughts and emotions. To deter her now from music that can contaminate the spirit will enable her faith in God to strengthen. The spirituality in all secular music can pollute young minds to an extent that engulfs their heart. (Proverbs 4:23)

On Sunday we went to our church on the Manhattan. Afterwards my youngster wanted to go to City Park. It's still hot down here at this time of the year but we went anyway. We invited Kristy to come with us. It was better for Amanda to have a friend to get on the rides with.

The heat was a little too much and we left after staying a few hours. At home the girls played while I watched the news. I happened to catch a story that sounded so familiar. In the courtroom there was a girl that was still being tried for killing her newborn a while back. This was in New Jersey that a teenager aborted her baby in the bathroom at her senior prom. She strangled him, threw him in the trash bin and went out to be with her classmates. I have a file with newspaper clippings in it and went to have look. The article was on infanticide. It listed a variety of reasons ranging from public embarrassment, fear of their parents, to the interference with their college/careers, why unmarried women under the age of 20 kill their own infants. My file is for the day when I have to show Amanda the craziness in America.

Work at SWX had become irregular. The jobs had long hours but there weren't too many of them throughout the week. My funds were shrinking. I began to contact the out of state inspection companies looking for a better opportunity. There were two I became interested in and because of my qualifications, they wanted to hire me immediately. I couldn't make a commitment due to my custody situation. Lately at the exchanges when I could get close enough to Cassie, without talking I would hand her the monthly support check. If Charlene gave me clearance to go out of town for work, she'd have to handle these monetary issues.

On this date, the day before my weekday visit, terrorist hijacked two commercial jets and used them to bring down two of the tallest buildings in America. Thousands of people lost their lives. The future of many families is forever changed. Our revolving door policy, which allows anyone to enter this country, brought devastating consequences to all. In our face, innocent men and women were murdered and there was nothing we could do about it. We had to reluctantly realize that we were no longer an untouchable nation. There are no weapons to prevent surprise attacks like this. My television displayed confusion and fear. There was talk of an economic disaster. In panic I watched this horrifying event unfold. The ensuing investigation promised to reveal who did this to the United States of America.

Immediately I accepted an offer made by one of the out of state inspection companies. National X-ray Performance (NXP) had the contract for a power plant that was being built. In one week I would be leaving for Fort Myers, Florida, 780 miles away. I had to make the necessary arrangements with my attorney. Charlene recommended that I return as soon as the job was finished. We anticipated that Cassie would make false allegations if I missed too many of my visits. Long ago, I completed my sessions with Dr. Watson. He also met with my daughter. The mother did not comply with what the court instructed. Another hearing would be needed to compel her to follow through with what the judge ordered. At this time I couldn't afford my lawyer. I needed more money and was running out of options.

In the evening I called my daughter to see how she was doing. Amanda was speaking very low and I couldn't hear her too well. "What's the matter, boo, you not feeling good", I asked? "Mommy will wake up soon, if she sees me on the phone, she'll know I'm talking to you, if she wakes up, I'll have to hang up, okay", she whispered. I began to feel her worry and knew we shouldn't be chatting. I told her that I'd see her tomorrow and ended our short conversation. Appalling it was to think of what Cassie would do to her for talking to me. To save my little girl from being abused, I knew it was time for me to stop calling over there.

On Wednesday I arrived at the exchange area and saw Cassie getting Amanda out her car. As the mother was heading towards the entrance, from approximately 20 feet away I called her name so we could make the swap. Ignoring the two times I called, she continued walking. At the door I met her and had the support check in my left hand. "Didn't you hear me calling you", I asked? "You're supposed to be waiting inside", she growled. She was holding Amanda and turned her body as though she was handing our child to me. With my right hand I attempted to get my youngster when Cassie shouted, "RAPE", twice. In shock, I raised my hands and backed away. She opened the door, went inside and I followed. When Amanda reached for me, with my hands under her arms; I began to ease her into my arms. The mother, with both hands wrapped around our little one's thighs, then tried to pull her out of my hands and away from me, shouting, "HELP"! Amanda started kicking her legs in an attempt to free herself from Cassie. Had I let my youngster go, she would have fallen directly to the ground, face first. Quickly we left. I looked back to see the mother heading to the police station. I set my little girl down and watched. "Hold on boo, daddy might have to go answer some questions", I told her. "My leg hurts daddy, lets go, don't go back in there", she cried. Hearing this, I picked up my daughter and departed from the scene.

Amanda was still upset when we got home. I made us some ice cream and she calmed down. Afterwards we played on her computer. She did all the activities with ease. "Good girl, I'm so proud of you", I told her. "Daddy, I want to come live with you", she told me. "Poppa's trying boo, I want you to come live here too", I said. She wanted some pizza so I ordered us one. While we were eating I decided to ask her what Cindy told me about. "Hey boo, when mommy's at home, and you're playing in your room, do you ever come out and find out she's gone and you're left there with somebody else", I asked? "Uh huh, she does that all the time", she said. "Okay, who she leave you with", I asked her? "She leaves me with Moe or Donny", she said sadly. "You don't like that, huh, being there with them", I asked her? "No, Moe watches football", she replied. "Poppa's gonna see what he can do about that boo, always remember, Jesus loves you and you can't live without God in your life and be happy", I told her. My sister was correct. Now I understood why she was afraid to be alone. On the weekends when Amanda was with me I'd let her sleep wherever she wanted. Until she felt comfortable, I didn't mention that she sleep in her own bed.

Her little pal called and asked to come over. I told her yes and asked to speak with her mother. Pookie got angry about what I told her and they both came over. While our kids played, we talked. She offered to ride with us to the mall so Cassie would act more civil. "I need to tell you something, Kristy had head lice and I treated her but you need to check and make sure Amanda don't have it", Pookie said. I never saw this before so she checked my daughter's head. My little girl had it. Now I was worried about having to go meet her mother.

At the mall we saw Cassie in the station complaining to the police. My neighbors sat outside on the benches with my daughter while I went inside. I walked in to hear the mother telling them that I was a code 6 and I tried to throw her down. She asked the lieutenant for an officer to escort her to the car. I told the mother that our little girl needed to be treated for head lice. Turning around to check on Amanda, I saw her hiding behind a pole outside the station. The lawman came out to walk Cassie and our daughter to the car. When she left the lieutenant asked, "if you tried to throw her down three hours ago, why did she wait until now to make the complaint"?

"Because she's lying", I said. I apologized to the officers and went out to meet my neighbors. On our way home Pookie told me what my youngster said which indicated how scared she is of her mother. "She's mad and it's all my fault, I knew this was a mistake yall coming here, I'm gonna be in so much trouble when I get home, this is all my fault, everything's always my fault, I'm probably gonna get a spanking when I get home", Amanda told them as she hid behind the pole. "I know what's going on, I can tell, by what she says and the way she clings to me, she's longing for the love of her mother, and she's not getting it, I went through that when I was a little", Pookie said. For a long time I could see that my little girl was being neglected and now my neighbor saw it too. Instantly my anxiety level went through the roof. The defective family court system forced me to sit by helplessly and watch my daughter suffer. At home it was hard for me to sleep from the nausea this incident created.

My sponsor was correct about all the inhuman aspects that can evolve in a custody battle such as mine. Cassie tried everything she could to destroy the relationship I had with my little girl. The name-calling and degrading comments were intended to confuse Amanda's feelings for me. The longer I remained out of contact with my daughter the more time this mother had to brainwash her. Whatever the reason was, Cassie couldn't see that her injurious actions were hurting our daughter emotionally and psychologically. Had I not stopped her in court, this mother would have moved up north with my child. By relocating she would have successfully removed me from the life of my youngster, the same way she removed Donny and Brad from the life of their father. Cassie made it obvious that she was using Amanda like a puppet on a string, the pawn on mommy's big chessboard of life.

When parents feud, the little ones are always the victims. How can anyone not remember the dependence they had on their parents? Young and unknowing, innocently they hold on to dad and mom for the love that protects them from harm. To feel safe on daddy's lap or secure in mommy's arms, this is the needed affection that helps a youngster grow up complete and strong. A child wants to feel like he or she belongs, that they're important and their existence means something firstly to their parents. Take a moment to imagine yourself as a little kid, young, without much knowledge, sitting on the couch in the living room hearing your parents launch through the air words of anger, hatred, sarcasm or revenge. Through their little ears, the young heart is filled with confusion and fright. The loud tone of voice causes the child to cringe at the sight of dad and mom. Kids don't deserve to be exposed to this. Parents who don't set the good example by constraining themselves allow their youngsters to witness the atrociousness of grown-ups. Memories of what dad and mom did in their presence are like nightmares that can linger on for the rest of this child's life. When it's time to start a family, the young adult may unintentionally repeat the scenes from his or her childhood that was lacking in love. Harsh words create unseen scars in their young mind that don't go away.

In the morning I called Charlene. When I told her about not being able to talk to my little girl on the phone, she became irritated. Cassie had become progressively worse during the exchanges. Rather than see my daughter continue to be victimized, I made the decision to forfeit the Wednesday visits. Amanda didn't need to keep seeing this acrimony from her mother. My attorney and I agreed that the mother might have some kind of mental problem. If she didn't complete her sessions with the psychiatrist we would have to go back to court and file a motion to compel. This would force her see the doctor. Charlene said that she'd send a letter to Misty informing her of the reason why I chose to cancel my weekday visits.

A few days after the buildings in New York came crashing down; the authorities had all the participants identified. They recognized some of the known terrorists and said that they weren't supposed to be in our country. The pilots were trained in Florida and belonged to a cult that has many followers who live in the United States. Their beliefs are against the faith that started our country. They believe that anyone who doesn't follow their god and partake in their rituals are infidels, and should perish. This cultic activity may be the very poison that's going to infect and destroy our nation. Freedom of religion welcomes countries abroad to bring their absurd practices here to reside. Grandparents and older citizens who know the truth of our country will confirm that this foreign contamination may become our destruction. It's a disgrace when foreigners move here and are treated better than our elderly people are. The faith that brought our forefathers to discover, establish and build the United States of America must always remain pure, never diluted and not forgotten.

According to the news reports, fear of terrorism had the churches nationwide full. If you look back on the history of the United States of America you'll see that we started out as a godly nation. Slowly but surely, this American Heritage is being removed from our public schools. The Christian heart in this country is usually the first to lend a helping hand where disaster strikes. Because many parents have a bible in their home and choose not to read it, the younger children can't know about it. When people read and study the written word of God, they receive an understanding and gain the knowledge that will reconstruct the ways they think or react to anything that faces them. The cleansing power of truth protects them from the trickery of this world. Dad and mom are better able to hand the lesson of morality down to their children. In a family, the older ones with authority who chose to stray from the document written in 1620 that states the reason on which our country's foundation was built help to keep the younger ones uninformed and without direction in their life.

The last weekend before I left for Florida was the time to be with my little girl. Cassie continued to be unsociable and walked the other way soon after I entered the mall. Amanda was happy to see me and wanted to get some beignets from the nearby café. It's funny how she makes a mess with these. At home she wanted to do her computer lessons. Sitting behind her on the beanbag, I watched as she did the activities. "Daddy, Donny bites me on my arm", she told me. "What, why is he doing that", I asked? She went on to say that he's been doing this and that he leaves marks. "Is he playing or does this hurt you", I asked? "It hurts me, he makes me cry", she said. "Have you told mommy", I asked? "Yeah but she says he's only playing", she replied. This guy is nearly 30 years old, he's doing this to our daughter and Cassie allows it. I knew this action was their way of provoking me to violence. If I react, I'm sure the mother would deny that her son did this and make it an issue in court. An event like this would allow her to accuse me of having an anger problem and jeopardize my visitation privileges. We ordered a pizza and watched a video that had some old cartoons on it. Before bed she picked 3 bedtime stories and was fast asleep before I was finished reading them.

In the morning I woke up first, made a cup of coffee and sat on the couch to watch the news until she got up. She came out and sat next to me. "Good morning, sleepyhead, you want some breakfast", I asked her? She had the usual, a bowl of cereal and I set a vitamin out for her. I told her of my new job and that I'll be gone for a short while. At first she was sad about this. She became comforted when I promised her that we'd go to the Aquarium when I came back. Later in the day we went to see Tabby. Afterwards we went by the park to swing. Amanda became hungry so we got us a meal to go and went back to my place. There was a message on my answering machine from Kristy asking if my little girl could go over there and play. "After you eat, you can go play", I told her. Amanda left and came back a short while later with her little pal. My youngster has plenty of toys to play with so her buddy likes to come here. Later that evening Kristy went home. My youngster knows she has to get her bath on Saturday night. I wash her hair and the places she can't reach. Amanda washes her privates or they don't get washed. It has been that way since the beginning. When finished I wrap a towel around her, she goes to her room, dries off and gets dressed. I'll get the brush and blow dry her hair, then we are done. Computer lessons until its time for bed. She picks her bedtime stories and we go lie down. This is part of the routine that we developed.

On Sunday morning we enjoy attending our church on the Manhattan. There are little friends here for my youngster to play with. It was good to see my daughter happy and I felt comfortable with what she was learning. The teachers would give the kids a snack while they taught a lesson from selected scripture in the bible. In the sanctuary I joined the congregation in singing praises and hearing the sermon from our pastor. When the services were over, on our way home we'd talk about what she did and the fun she had. She usually had a paper with the lesson she learned. Our Christian church is the place she loved to go. We'd spend the rest of the day together doing activities until it was time to go meet at the mall. As time went on, Amanda became more reluctant to go back home to Cassie.

On Monday I traveled to Fort Myers Florida to work for NXP. I could see that they were a well-respected company. Dan, the man who hired me was the vice-president. Where I come from, the workers don't get to see the higher ups like this unless you're in trouble. The last time I spoke to a superior was to inform him that I had my third DUI arrest in Portland. Dan told me a little about the project and gathered the paperwork for my exams. It's customary for a company to test all new employees to show that they have the required qualifications for the position they're applying. After I was finished he sent another technician and me to a motel where we could rest up and report for work in the morning. The first day is plant orientation where you're told of the dangerous surroundings and briefed on your duties.

The work here was similar to most x-ray companies. Radiation safety is the first priority. We had enough people to make up two, two-man crews. Our NDT backgrounds varied. The other technician, Dray was from Texas and I was from Louisiana. The techniques we used to do the inspections were different from each other's. The construction company needed each crew to pull a 12 hour shift. This way we would be available for them 24 hours a day. Also there was a third crew working here. They had been on site to finish an ongoing contract with another fabrication company. The main objective from our supervisor was to produce quality work. Considering the experience of us three technicians, we had no problem doing just that. Since this project was going to last for several months, NXP moved Dray and me to live in nearby suites that had kitchens. This helped us conserve our per diem money by cutting down on eating expenses. All the other workers in our three crews lived her locally.

Our job consisted of x-raying boiler tubes in these furnaces that the power company was having built. This involved going into a crawl space that was 12" high with all the equipment we needed to do the inspection. Inside was hazardous with all the dust, rust and hundreds of half-inch bolts that protruded from the surface we crawled on to get to our work areas. My helper sat at the entrance to watch and make sure I didn't get hurt. If there were an accident, he'd be the one to call for help. We had the dayshift and the other technician, and his helper had the nightshift. The third crew would inspect other pipe welds throughout the plant. We remained on standby at the site until a test crew was needed. Most of the time we waited on the construction company to finish their work so we could do ours. On the weekends both crews worked during the day to help the third crew catch up. Our supervisor, Don told me that the estimated time to complete this project would be about six months. This was good news to me because my financial problems would eventually come to an end.

The days turned into weeks. I tried calling Amanda with my cell phone and the machine would always answer. It was uncomfortable to be this far away from home and not know how my little girl was doing. If something bad happened, Cassie had my number but I knew she wouldn't call me. Just being able to talk with my daughter and know that she's okay would help ease my worry. When I have nagging problems under my skin like this, it's tough not say anything. If a person is troubled, sometimes the best therapy is to talk about it. Hosea, the technician from the third crew had a brother who was in a situation like mine. The sister- in-law left with his niece and now they don't get to see the youngster. He told me about some of the terrible events. I was thankful that nothing that extreme happened to me yet.

My co-worker, Link and I became good friends. He and the other helper that was on the nightshift, Clam, grew up together here in Florida. These two were 17 years younger than I was. They had been best pals since they were young. Both lived with their mom and neither had any relationship with their father. They resented authority and didn't like being told what to do. The unrestrained way they behaved showed that they did not take this job too seriously. These were characteristics of when a person has a fatherless childhood. Both of these guys liked to smoke pot and party all night in the lounges. Often they spoke of their late nights out and bragged about the women they hoped to gain sexual favors from. They spent much of their money on strippers at these outings. This explained why Link slept all the time until there was a task for us to do. I begin to talk the same language as they did using words that didn't sound too nice. Talking like this enabled me to fit right in. At one time in my life, I was just like that. They were shocked when I told them that I didn't do drugs or drink anymore. "It's against my faith and I have a little girl I need to set a good example for", I told them.

The more everyone talked, the better we got to know each other. We became familiar with each others backgrounds and this helped us bind together as a team. It began to feel like we were a family. Our focus was to uphold the high reputation of our company by providing good quality test results. When we spoke about past incidents in our lives, my co-workers were surprised to hear that I'm a Christian. They agreed with my beliefs but didn't like to hear the name of God or Jesus. We all had different opinions. Hosea felt that because he once belonged to a gang, he would never be forgiven. Link and I tried to convince him that this was not true. Ike was Hosea's helper and he despised the Catholic Church because of an incident that happened long ago. Amazing is how this topic comes up at work. The job site is no place to talk about what a person believes. In one way or another most all felt that leaders in churches were crooks. Mistakes made by the clergy can cause ones faith to land on shaky ground. A person may then fall away from God and grow to believe that it's useless to have faith in the bible. Rather than learn the truth, it's easier to believe the lie and live in darkness. Regardless of what a man says or does, or an event that occurs, the word of God will never change. It's the choice of an individual whether he or she chooses to believe or not. People who don't know scripture put themselves in danger and live in error. (Matthew 22:29)

Against the wishes of my new employer, I had to make arrangements to go home at the end of the second week in October to be with Amanda. Knowing that Cassie has a drinking problem and having no contact with my daughter by phone troubled me. I already missed a scheduled weekend visit and needed to keep the next so I'd know that my little girl was okay. Dan was concerned that I might not come back to finish the job. He conferred with Rob, the president of the company. Together they made reservations for me to fly and had a rented car waiting for me at the airport in New Orleans. I was thankful for them doing this for Amanda and me. If these personal problems of mine continued to interfere with my work, this would make the sixth job I'd lose. Don was shocked when he heard the warlike experiences I went through to remain in the life of my little girl. He and his ex wife have joint custody of their daughter but he never had the truculence to endure like I did.

Three duplicate messages were left on Cassie's machine informing her that I'd be at the exchange area for my upcoming visit. On Friday I arrived at the mall to find Moe waiting there with Amanda. With a smile, "Daddy", she called and ran over to me. I picked her up and hurried out. We went home and she wanted to play with her toys. I had to make some of the funny voices for her dolls. She'd giggle when I did this. I ordered us a pizza and after we ate, she did her computer lessons until it was time for bed. "Tomorrow we're going to the Aquarium", I told her. Hearing this made her happy. "You're the best daddy in the world, you're my hero", she said. She picked her three bedtime stories for me to read and we got ready for bed. As always, she was asleep before I was finished reading the few she selected.

On Saturday Amanda asked if her two friends that lived here in the apartments could go with us to the Aquarium. Kristy and Millie went with us. “Everyone must stay together” I told them. They really enjoyed themselves and had smiles on their faces the entire time. In awesome wonder the youngsters looked at the water dwelling animals in the glass enclosures. One of the exhibits had a live baby octopus for the kids to see up close and touch. This was a good learning environment for the little ones. Soon after we ate, it was time to leave. We had been here over four hours and tired of walking around. When we got home, the kids went to play. I saw how Amanda was a little too bossy and demanding of her friends. Many times I had to tell her to simmer down and try to be nice. After Kristy and Millie left to go home, I had a talk with my little girl. “Boo, if you aren’t nice to your friends, they’re not gonna want to come over here and play with you, you should always try to be nice to them, that’s why they’re called your friends”, I told her. She understood what I was talking about.

On Sunday morning I called to check in with Tabby and see how everyone was doing. She told me that Mick was very ill. Mary had been bringing him to the hospital for tests and the doctors couldn’t find out what was wrong with him. He had to be medicated because his pain was so intense. It was too early in the morning to call and talk with my brother so I decided to contact him later. I woke Amanda up and made her breakfast. While she ate, we talked a little. I was nervous about the upcoming Halloween holiday and told her not to listen to strangers. “If a man asks if you want to see his puppy or kitty, get away from him and don’t go anywhere by yourself” I said. She looked sad and I asked her why? “I don’t want to go back to my mommy’s house”, she said. Hearing this made me feel terrible. I had to bring her to the mall early so I could be on time to catch my flight back to Florida. On our way to do the trade, “daddy, can I come live with you”, she asked? “Daddy’s doing the best he can boo, right now I can’t do anything”, I said. Her question brought tears to my eyes. “Jesus loves you boo, you can’t live without God in your life and be happy”, I told her. After we turned into the parking lot she asked me to stop and gave me a smooch before we met Cassie.

On the plane I thought about the fun we had at the Aquarium and I was thankful to know that Amanda was okay. Since she was a baby I would always tell her, “Jesus loves you boo”. In her crib I used to say this in her ear while she slept. Carrying her as an infant I’d whisper this to her. As she got older I added the statements my momma told me, "you can't live without God in your life and be happy, and God doesn't sleep". These are facts I wanted her to remember when we weren't able to be together or talk with each other. I had to accept that there'd be no chance of me talking to her on the phone. Apparently my little girl wasn't too happy at her mother's house and all I knew is what she told me. I never did have to ask my daughter a lot of questions. Whether it was Donnie being rude or mean to her, Moe hitting her or Cassie slapping her, Amanda would always tell me when someone did or said anything to hurt her. There was nothing I could do except pray every night for God to protect her.

The news revealed that a war erupted with Afghanistan. The United States joined together with other countries in the battle against terrorism. Many bombs were dropped on specific targets in an attempt to flush these enemies out. Some of them remained safe, hidden in the mountains. The media spoke of these foes, "sleepers", and confirmed that many of them lived here in our country. When their help was needed, they would be called upon to induce damage by means of chemical, biological or conventional warfare. The cause was called the Jihad and their battleground, the United States of America. The combatants were from the al Qaeda and they had people that owned businesses here to fund or support their crusade. They have much hatred and abhor all the people who don't follow the formalities of their cult. Freedom allows these strange practices and absurd religious beliefs to move here and flourish. I've often wondered why followers from this religion aren't seen doing their cultic rituals on television? I've seen Catholic and Christian shows. I don't remember seeing anything about a man called Mohammed. What's the big secret? Some people come here speaking a different language and in kindness, our government helps them learn the native english language of our nation. Why aren't we taught how to speak their language? Most of us don't know what they're saying because we can't understand them. Without knowing what they're talking about, how can we communicate? Only if we pay the price are we given an opportunity to learn the languages of other nations. Maybe one day a television channel will be used just to educate the citizens here so we can speak with our visitors who have now moved here to become residents. Wouldn't that be a nice thing to do for Americans who were born here in the United States?

It was comforting to return to work after my visit. I felt relieved to know that Amanda was alright and this made my job easier. It's hard for a man to work when he has no clue on how his kids are doing. Construction of the project was progressively picking up. The workers seemed to be in a hurry to finish. It was tough to make our helpers behave and do their job when Don was absent. They didn't like being instructed on what to do and there were times that I had to ask them please. These two friends were hard to separate. Clam was always singing songs he considered to be rap while Link referred to this music as pop. When I asked if these songs were about happiness, peace or what, they both laughed. "It's about being a thug, sex and drugs", they replied". I thought about when Amanda is old enough how it will be necessary for me to explain the immoral influence this kind of music can instill. One of Clams favorite songs was by a female who sang about all the places on her body that she desired to be licked. The lyrics she sang were suggestive and revealed that she wasn't too smart either. How could this singer not know that she could get a dog to do all that? Maybe that's why we have a younger generation of males who refer to each other as dogs. When a woman sings a sexually enticing song like this, the world hears how desperate she is.

Clam has a nice girlfriend. He pays all the bills and she keeps his sports car while he's at work so she'll have transportation. She's always late when it's time to pick him up. He made it known to us that their sexual activity was lacking. I've seen this woman only a couple of times and it was easy to see that she dressed to attract males. It appeared to me that she didn't want a man in her life, she wanted men in her life. This big breasted; belly button pierced petite young woman obviously had an appetite too big for one man to fill. The worst mistake a man can make is allowing a woman to control him with her sexuality. Females get aroused knowing that they can dominate a man with sex. She dishonorably copulates to get what she wants and degrades herself in the process. Many females believe this action is a normal way to have their wishes granted. A likely result can be that the man becomes dependent on this woman for the wrong reason. Is a relationship like this grounded in love or centered on lust?

Dray had been telling me of his situation with the mother of their little boy. It sounded so similar to mine. We had Sunday off and I invited him to come over and watch a football game. I bought a 12-

pack and ordered a pizza. We sat and talked while watching the game. He admitted that his ex was making it difficult for him to see his youngster. Since the time when my trouble started with Cassie there had been several men I met in different places that were in the same predicament as mine. In most all the stories I heard, the feelings of the little ones are never considered. When he separates from the woman, mommy will use her children to crush their daddy. After gaining control of his kids, the rancorous woman seeks to get revenge. Automatically mom becomes self-centered and will do whatever she can to make herself feel better. If this means making her children suffer needlessly, then so be it, she don't care. The mother may venture on a rampage where her main goal is to get even, ultimately hurting those who need not be involved. Many women who feel hurt this way will remain persistent in their tactics until they are successful in drowning the man in misery. Eventually, dad finds himself distressed. Dray said he planned to contact an attorney. I could see he was disturbed about all this. It felt like I was looking in a mirror because my dilemma affected me the same way. "Don't worry, it'll get better", I told him. The two beers I drank made me tired so I gave him the remainder of the pack. After he left I climbed into bed and took a nap.

At the end of October I received a call from Pookie. She informed me that Cassie had been seen several mornings driving by my apartment. This made me a bit nervous. As we talked I asked my neighbor how she was doing. She commented about an upcoming court date that had her worried because she didn't have the money to pay her fine. "I might end up in jail, if that happens I don't know what I'm gonna do", she said. There'd be no one there to take care of her daughter because her boyfriend Ted worked during the day. I asked if Ted was going to help her at court and she said he didn't have the money. Kristy is my little girl's friend and I didn't want to see her mother have to be incarcerated like that. I offered to loan her the money so she wouldn't have to be locked up. She accepted and promised to pay me back in the middle of December. I trusted her verbal promise to repay me to be enough. She was very thankful and expressed her gratitude to me for bailing her out of this trouble.

The construction company who contracted us was almost finished their part of the project and two crews were no longer needed. I gave NXP advanced notice and made arrangements to go home in the beginning of November. The time I had been away from home seemed much longer than it actually was. The bad language I used amongst my co-workers would be left here in Florida. It was my hope that Cassie would allow my visits with Amanda to continue. I also wanted to contact my sisters and find out how my brother was doing.

Returning home, I contacted Mick by phone, I remembered how bad he sounded when I called him from Florida. Calling Mary, I wanted to know how he was doing and see if she checked on him lately. "He has fourth stage lung cancer, he's going to die", my sister said. She went on to tell me of all the prescribed medicines he was on for the pain of his disease. I wondered why she told me all this. After hanging up the phone I went to see my brother and found that he wasn't doing too good. In his sedated state, he was still coherent enough to talk with me. He had a rubber glove filled with water that he heated in the microwave and used it as a hot compress. It was distressing to watch him starve for air like this as he fought to fill his lungs with every breath. There was nothing I could do but to stay with him until he felt better. Mick wasn't too happy with the way Mary was treating him. She did all the talking at the hospital and told the doctors what he needed for pain. Of course she'd pick the drugs she liked best. Promising him that things would change, I called Tabby and told her what I found out. It was necessary that she and I take over in the caring of our brother. Now was not the time to talk to Mary, I was too upset. After Mick felt better, I left and went home.

The second weekend of the month was the time to be with my little girl. Walking in I saw that she was still in her school uniform. Cassie was being her usual unsociable self. Amanda ran over to me, I picked her up and we walked out. Once outside where her mother couldn't see us, she gave me a big hug. "I missed you baby girl", I told her. "I missed you too my daddy", she said. After we got in my car, "you have a surprise for me", she asked? Since her mother wouldn't allow us to talk on the phone, my daughter was always on my mind. At home there were some little gifts I picked up in Florida for her. When we arrived at my place she got into some different clothes and looked around to see what I bought for her. A shirt, some pretend jewelry and other little toys were waiting in her bedroom. It didn't take much to make her happy. We played with some of her toys for a while and did some computer lessons until it was time for bed. Before we lay down I saw a large bruise, very dark near the top of her thigh. “Boo what happened to your leg”, I exclaimed! “A boy at school kicked me there”, she said. “Are you sure”, I asked? “Yeah daddy, he kicked me there”, she replied. I was very upset. You would think that $450 every month in tuition would be enough to keep your child safe at school. On Monday I planned to call someone at Top of the Hill Academy and try to find out how an incident like this could have happened.

On Saturday I woke up and was sitting on the couch thinking about what we could do today. Advertisements for the theatre came on and I thought about asking my little girl if that’s where she wanted to go. She woke up and came out to the living room. I made a bowl of cereal and set a vitamin out for her. “What ya wanna do today boo”, I asked her? When I mentioned about the movies she declined the offer. “I’m scared of the theatre”, she said. This had me curious and I wanted to know why she felt this way. There was a movie called “Larry Spotter and the three-headed dog” that made her afraid. She never saw the movie, just scenes from it. I was aware of the misguiding concept this picture portrays. Designed to captivate young minds, this movie leads youngsters to believe that magic is possible and real. Parents are quick to let their kids watch this trash as long as it keeps them satisfied and quiet. The film is found to be frightening and very unbiblical to young viewers. It made me happy to know my little girl wasn’t interested in garbage like that. We decided to go over to City Park and rode the amusement rides until they closed up. In the evening we did our usual activities. She had a bath and did her computer lessons until it was time for bed.

On Sunday we went to our favorite church on the Manhattan. My little girl always has a good time here. When I bring her to the children’s ministry, right away she goes over to her friends and joins in with them. She participates by singing and raising her hands in praise to the Lord. After making sure she’s okay, I walk to the sanctuary to be with the congregation and hear the sermon from my pastor. It’s of great necessity that I attend these services because I’m a sinner. I’m very grateful we have the bible. It serves as evidence that our Father has not left us alone here on earth. This is the core of my faith. I pray for the spirit of understanding and discernment. If God said it, it’s written in his word, I believe that, and this matter is settled. It’s comforting to know that I don’t have to look any further to find the truth. When I have a need for guidance, instruction or correction, I know where to search. (II Timothy 3:16)

After church on our drive home Amanda is full of smiles and happy. We talk about what they did and she shows me on paper the lesson learned. Most of the time the kids are taught about the love of Jesus. This is beautiful and I'm happy that she's learning. I decided to add something new to our activities. I'd start telling a story and at different parts, I'd pause and write the word for her. She would fill in the blanks. There were two dogs that liked to play in the _____; and I'd spell the word grass on the dry-erase board with a marker. Her task was to say the word I spelled. We would continue until there was no more room on the board and then we'd start over. She has a farm with a family and the animals. Of course I have to make up all the voices. I'm the cow, the chicken, the dog, the daddy, the mommy, the little boy and the little girl. Suddenly, my little girl sadly says, "daddy, when I grow up, I'm never gonna keep my kids from seeing their daddy". Her remark confirmed the sorrow she feels as a result of the separation between her and me. Hearing this hurt my heart and my eyes began to fill with tears. "Lets play something else boo", I said. We started doing the activities from the science CD on her computer.

In the evening we met her mommy at the mall and I asked if she knew about the big bruise on Amanda's leg. I tried to get close so I'd hear her when she answered my question. Ignoring me, the mother picked our daughter up and headed the other way. "Get out of my face", Cassie said. "Why do you act so weird", I asked her? "You're weird, you pervert", she hollered. All I did was inquire about my little girl's injury. The way this mother acted was inappropriate. Her spiteful actions and name calling was something I didn't want to be a part of and I refused to chase her for a response. Right away I turned around and left the area.

Early in the morning I called Top of the Hill Academy and told them of the large bruise on my daughter's leg. The lady I spoke with didn't sound too concerned and wasn't aware this incident had occurred. She said they'd look into the matter and assured me that the necessary action would be taken to prevent this from happening again. I asked to have a progress report on how well Amanda was doing in class. I wanted this information in the event that there was something I needed to address with my youngster, such as a behavior or conduct problem. If she was misbehaving, I wanted to know about it. The receptionist asked me to hold the line and she went to check my little girl's file. She came back to the phone and denied me access to the report. "It's the responsibility of the parent who registered the child to provide copies of her progress to the other parent", she told me. They never heard of me or knew that I even existed until my name was found on Amanda's birth certificate. It became evident that Cassie would continue to keep me uninformed about the issues that concerned our daughter.

The next day I agreed to ride with Mary and take Mick to the hospital. After all the usual papers were filled out and the blood work was done, we waited to see the doctor. My brother felt awful and looked like he was in severe pain. In a folder that he carried with him was the pictures of when he won first place in a bodybuilding contest, twenty years ago. It was hard for him to accept that he lost all his weight and had this disease. Two doctors came in and conferred with us. The older of the two verified that his illness was terminal. Mick wanted to know how long did he have left and when was he going to die. No one can provide an answer to a question like this. The older physician began to prescribe some medicine for Mick and Mary walked out to talk with the younger doctor. It was recommended that my brother start chemotherapy to stop the growth of his cancer. He was reluctant to accept the treatment because he didn't like needles and the doses had to be given intravenously. In addition to this he would be given very potent pain relievers. I walked out to go get some water and heard my sister asking the young doctor to prescribe some xanax, nerve pills for our brother. I was aware of how much she liked this drug. On our way home we stopped at a pharmacy to get Mick's prescription for pain. I paid for the medications and we brought my brother to his house. It became clear why he was dissatisfied with the way Mary was handling his affairs.

In the evening Tabby called. She told me that Mick had called her and gave reason why he was so upset with Mary. "She takes him to the doctor and stays with him, but when it's time to get his medicine, she takes him to get it and pays for it, if he gives her half", Tabby told me. So now we knew why Mary was so eager to get involved. She was being his chauffeur so she'd get some of my brother's pain medicine. At this time, our brother was dependent on her because he didn't have a car and wasn't able to drive. From now on Mary's help would not be needed. Tabby denounced my sister's actions and ousted her from taking care of Mick.

This was the straw of my sister's that broke the camel's back. After I accepted that job and traveled to Oregon for work, momma and I kept in touch the inexpensive way, by mail. Her letters were good and I was always glad to get one. A year after I left, things began to get bad for my parents and momma wrote to tell me about it. Jack stole my dad's car. Not having any transportation, my parents were pretty much stranded. Mary claimed that she saw a drug deal outside their apartment. She convinced them to move by her across the river in a complex where she was the manager, and the rent was free. After my folks moved in they ended up paying light bills, phone bills, food bills, etc. For lunchtime Mary would come home and momma would have a meal prepared for her. After she ate, my sister would get up, go back to work, and leave the mess for my mother to clean up. Several nights during the week Mary had boyfriends that would come over. One of them was a married man. Dad and mom always went to bed early. In the morning my mother would see these boyfriends coming out of Mary's room, partially dressed. When Hannah moved back home, my sister's lifestyle didn't change and her daughter saw all these different men. Mary made my folks move out so there would be more room for her daughter. This action caused the living expenses for my parents to triple and they were on a fixed income. She put them in an apartment close to hers and would often invite herself over for dinner. When momma got very sick and was dying of cancer, I traveled home to be with her. Most all of the pain pills she was prescribed had somehow disappeared. No one knew what happened to the medicine. Dad, Mary and Cindy always looked stoned. At this time I had been sober for seven months. In Portland I was taught about dysfunctional families and got to see firsthand how well we fit the description. I clearly remember mom telling me, "when you leave, take what you want and don't come back, you're better off staying up there". This is what I recall at the time my momma died.

At the local market I saw Nat, Pam and their daughter Diana. I said hello to my former neighbors. While Nat and me talked, Pam and their little girl walked away, down to the end of the aisle. "Is your wife upset with me about something", I asked? "No, I don't think so",

Nat replied. He and I chatted a bit more and then went our separate ways to finish shopping.

When I was young and dated Myra, Pam's sister, there wasn't a time I ever met their father. He and their mother divorced when they were young girls and neither had much contact with him. From what I knew about the effects of fatherlessness, some of the symptoms seemed to be present in my friend. It seemed as though her life was somewhat unstable. Pam liked to smoke pot and drink a lot of beer. At home she had four young girls from three different men. The oldest of their children, Jade had her first child. The fact that I left Cassie might have reminded Pam of what her dad did to them, maybe not. She knew of my court battles to stay in Amanda's life because I told her. The only way I wouldn't see my little girl is if I had to work or she was underhandedly taken from me. When I mentioned some of the things I had to contend with in these custody issues with Cassie, "she gives women a bad name", was Pam's response. She didn't like hearing about my faith because her father claimed to believe the same, stating that he was a born again Christian. After his separation from their mother, he didn't make any effort to have a good relationship with her or Myra. A parent who sets this kind of example makes it difficult for his kids to have any faith in what the bible says. Due to his absence, dad can't provide the moral guidance that his children need. (I Timothy 5:8)

Jade was still a teenager, had a baby girl and wasn't married. The father of her child was a young man who was unproductive and non-supporting. She was at the nearby playground with Diana long ago before she got pregnant when I took Amanda there one evening to play. We chatted a bit about the complications I endured in my struggle with Cassie. Through no fault of her own, Jade wasn't able to have a bonding relationship with her biological father and this was something she longed for. She did say that there was some opposition from Pam when a chance to see her dad was discussed. "I wish I could see my dad, what's wrong with Cassie", she asked? "She's trying to eliminate me from Amanda's life like she did with Donny's and Brad's father", I told her. Jade knew how it felt to grow up without a dad. Her empathetic concern for my daughter revealed the pain and emotional distress that she and other fatherless children experience. Many try to fill the void but there'll never be a substitute for daddy's love.

There's a television commercial that is seen many times throughout the day about a young teenager. She comes on and says, "I was on the honor roll and then at 15, I got pregnant, now I have two babies". The commercial continues showing her walking with one while she pushes the other child in a stroller, without the father for these youngsters? It's obvious that this girl made a very irresponsible choice. The advertisement finishes with her saying, "I don't want to live like this, off of other people, I want to be somebody". Here is what can happen when there is no parental education at home. When dad and mom don't provide guidance and correction, teenage girls open themselves up to playful teenage boys who can't be fathers.

As Thanksgiving was approaching I spent all my evenings at Mick's house. Each time I went to see him, he appeared to be getting weaker. He still smoked and drank whisky or beer. When he felt able to do something, he'd get up and move around. At times he was okay and at others he was down and out. One evening while I was there he complained that his hands were hurting him badly. I made a bowl of warm soapy water for him to soak them in. This seemed to make them feel better. The doctors had prescribed oxycoddens and some other strong pain medication for him. All his dope buddies and my cousin, the mischievous one would come over. I remembered some of these people. They all knew I stopped doing drugs and that made them uneasy. When I was there, no one would ask Mick for any of his pills in front of me. My brother didn't want me to stay with him all night. After I left and my car was gone, the dopers came back over. I couldn't stop what was going on over there.

Since I was young, drug and alcohol abuse has always been in our family. For an answer, my faith led me to look at what the bible says about this. Starting with the word sorceries in the book of Revelations (9:21 & 18:23) I used a large concordance that referred me to the word pharmakeia, from which we derive the word pharmacy. It was followed by four more words, which were medication, magic, sorcery and witchcraft. Lets see how all this ties in? Antibiotics used to cure an illness or infection, over the counter pain relievers and cough syrup, any type of treatment that doesn't affect a person's thought or their ability to function might be considered medication. Like magic, alcohol and drugs can be used to make many pains and some emotional discomforts go away temporarily. When a person habitually uses either of these or through continued abuse develops dependence; the inability to stop his or her consumption is also like magic. An honest person won't deny that once they're under the influence from this over indulgence, whether it's drugs or alcohol, their thoughts, behaviors and actions are depraved compared to that of someone who is sober. It's easier for evil to invade one's thinking when he or she is intoxicated. Ideas of immorality will find vacancy in the mind of an inebriated person and become the assistant when it's time for him or her to make a decision. When the toxins take over, unknowingly the user is often susceptible to demonic persuasion. They're more likely to have heinous conversations that bring thoughts of indecency, maliciousness or incite acts of violence. Like the sorcerer, many of their intentions are wicked. Many people who are addicted can not deny their unsuccessful attempts to leave the substances alone. Sometimes when a person has enough alcohol or the right amount of a particular drug, they become very brave or stupid, thinking they can go anywhere and do anything. Ignored is the fact that many users actually become enslaved to this kind of drug abuse. A common trait of the drug abuser is a loss of memory. Objects disappear or get lost, cash is always in a low supply and you mostly bind together with those that have the same habits. When the dope's gone, so are your friends. Alcohol and drugs are like death on the installment plan. Sooner or later, it's bound to pay off. Many don't realize that most all mind-altering drugs have a bewitching attraction that can spellbind a person. What is witchcraft? Is this somewhat like a hex when people continue seeking to ingest, inhale or drink these poisons? (Proverbs 23:29-35)

Mick was still alive but we knew he would soon be gone. All we could do was to stay by his side and watch him painfully suffer. His only alternative was to take the medication and hope that it'd eliminate most of the pain that he felt. Again I noticed his how he kept holding his hands. They were hurting him. I made a bowl of warm soapy water to soak them in. His fingernails had crud underneath so I got some clippers, cleaned them up, cut and filed the ends smooth for him. He was too weak to do anything. After I was finished he sat back to relax in his chair. "Hey Mick, do you believe Jesus is the Son of God, that he died for our sins and rose from the dead", I asked him? In a sedated state, "don't ask me any questions right now", he replied. All I wanted to hear was a confirmation of his faith. Tomorrow, a few days before the holiday we'd be taking him to the hospital to start his chemotherapy treatment.

On the eve of Thanksgiving I was at the exchange area waiting for Cassie to show up. After the required time expired, I made the phone call and left a message on the machine. The mother wasn't going to show up. I brought my judgement papers to the police station and the lieutenant reviewed them. She allowed me to call an officer and make an attempt to go over to Cassie's house to get Amanda. I met with the lawman and showed him my court orders. We drove over to the mother's house and I waited out by the curb while he went up to her door. Moe answered and I saw Cassie come to the door to talk with the officer. Out by the street I heard the loud verbal confrontation from the mother. The lawman came over to me and said, "she's not going to release the child, go back to the station and leave me copy of these judgement papers with the lieutenant, I'm going to stay here and get the information I need for my report". He gave me the number I needed to get a copy of his paperwork for my attorney. I was surprised and thankful that they got involved in this civil matter. It occurred to me that Cassie was going to continue her disregard for what the court ordered. This was the twelfth denial of visitation for me, bringing the total time I lost with Amanda to 160 hours.

There was nothing I could do about this so I went over to Mick's house. He was upset with our cousin, the mischievous one because he was coming over and mooching his pills from him. He was just like Mary, agreeing to be of assistance to my brother in exchange for some of his medicine. It was of no use for me to confront any of these guys. Now was not the time for Mick to see me engage in an argument with anyone. In the past there were times when I'd have people go over to his house to remove the undesirables. No matter where I was, there were friends I had who'd do this dirty work for me. Several times I was out of state, on a job. One time in particular was when this man known as coach, struck Mick while he was asleep. With one phone call, I had the police remove and ban him from the property. Before I was about to leave, a friend whom I grew up with, Roy came over to see my brother. What he saw brought tears to his eyes. "Ya know I love ya", he said to Mick as he sat close by him. Roy got up; shaking his head in disbelief he quietly said, "I didn't know he was this bad". "He's not gonna be with us much longer", I told him. He stayed and talked with us for a good while. Before leaving, he motioned for me to go outside and talk with him. My friend told me of the many times in the late night hours that he had to run people out of this place. Roy confirmed that these dopers were here smoking crack cocaine. Mick had a bout with this drug at one time but I thought he stopped using it. Roy continued to tell me of a documentary he saw on television where some tests were conducted with the use of this substance. Using the lung tissue of a cow as their specimen, the drug was crumbled up and placed on it. A while later when scientist checked on the results of their experiment, they found that this drug had burned holes in the tissue. My friend also told me that crack cocaine sometimes has poisons, like insecticides added to it. It was then that I realized that Mick's continued usage of this drug helped further the irreparable damage to his lungs. It saddened me to know that my brother's condition was his own fault and there was nothing I could do.

In the morning I picked Mick up at his place and took him over to John and Tabby's for Thanksgiving dinner. My sister had converted one of the rooms in her house especially for him. She had been trying to get him to move in and stay with her so he could be looked after and properly taken care of. Just when we were about to eat, two of Mick's dope buddies came over in a green truck. They could see he wasn't feeling good but still tried to get him to join them at their camp on the bayou. Their inconsiderate invitation made me wonder why these guys called themselves his friends? My brother refused because he was too sick, and came back inside. We all sat at the table to have our holiday meal. No one knew that this would be the last time we'd ever see Mick eat anything again. Afterwards, my brother sat in a recliner Tabby put in his room. I sat with him and we listened to his favorite oldie station on the radio and watched a football game. A while later he wanted to go home. Later that night before leaving his place, I wanted to talk with him about Jesus. "Don't ask me any questions", he said. "I'm glad you ate something today, I love ya, boss", I told him. His medicine was making him drowsy. After Mick fell asleep, I sat and looked at this 70-pound man who was once the biggest one in our family. It was hard for me to accept that he was going to die.

At my last weekend of the month I waited at the mall for Cassie to bring Amanda. She arrived late and we did the swap. As usual, nothing was said between the mother and me. "Mommy got me a new video, but she wouldn't let me bring it", my youngster told me. It was a cartoon about a family of pre-historic creatures. These days the media makes a special effort to create shows with dinosaurs and other extinct animals in it. Our kids are bombarded with stories about a group of reptiles that were destroyed in the ice age? They no longer exist so why is there such a need to continuously fill the television screen with this. Skeletal remains and other findings do reveal that they did roam the earth at one time. How do we know that God wasn't too satisfied with this life form and for that reason, buried them in the crust for future use? If anything, little ones should be taught how the liquid from the fossils of these animals give us the product we need to fuel our cars. I didn't object to her watching this because the fictional cartoon characters help to expand her imagination. She told me a little about her class and how much fun it was to be there. Afterwards we ate a pizza and did some lessons on her computer. She liked any activity that seemed to be recreational. We played the quiz game where I'd tell a story and pause at certain words so I can write them on the dry erase board. She became good at pronouncing the word I spelled to complete the sentence. Our routine of doing the same activities became the norm for us. It was important for me to teach Amanda all I could. This way she'd be somewhat prepared for the lessons taught in her school. A lack of knowledge can cause problems for kids these days.

At the end of November after we tended to Mick, Tabby and me were involved in a car accident. A truck for the local cable television company, Pox Cable was speeding on the side shoulder of the road we were on. As we attempted to cross, he struck my car and took the bumper off. Due to the injuries my sister sustained, she had to be taken to the hospital. The sudden stop jolted my vehicle causing her to be slammed into the passenger door. The driver from Pox instantly started to act obnoxious when he saw that Tabby was hurt. My priority was to see that she was taken care of. After the ambulance left I saw the cable man arguing with the officer. He was issued a citation for driving on a part of the road that was not a designated lane. This multi-million dollar company he worked for probably wouldn't have to pay for the damages anyway. Wealthy businesses like this one have enough money to evade justice.

On the second day of December, late at night John called. He told me they were rushing Mick to the hospital. "Meet us in the emergency room, it's bad", he said. I arrived to find my sister crying and being consoled by her husband. Tabby greeted me with a hug, "Mick's gone, he died", she said. "Can I see him", I asked? "They're cleaning him up, they tried to save him", she told me. We talked about Mick's last moments alive. In their kitchen, "Ya know I love you guys", my brother told John and Tabby. Love was a word he never used and when my sister heard him say this, she knew his end was near. Before Mick made it to the recliner, he fell to the ground in their living room, dead. The paramedics came and were unsuccessful in bringing him back to life. A while later we went in to see our brother. On a gurney he lay peacefully still. His motionless state was somewhat of a comfort because we didn't have to watch him suffer and fight to fill his lungs with air anymore. John and Tabby walked out to go meet Mary and her husband. In disbelief, I stood by Mick's side staring at how this disease ate him up to an extent where he looked like a skeleton covered with skin. This was hard for me to accept. "I love ya boss, I'm sorry I didn't do more for you", I said to him. My niece Marie came in and gave me a hug. She appeared to be shocked with all this. "We knew this was coming, at least he's not suffering anymore", she said. Mary walked in crying followed by her husband Trey. "He's gone", Mary sadly asked? In silence, I nodded. The way my two sisters grieved was different from mine. I didn't shed a tear. I couldn't deny being saddened by this traumatic event yet my reaction wasn't like that of my siblings and I didn't know why. There was nothing left for us to do and it was time to go. We agreed to meet at my brother's place in the daytime to discuss funeral arrangements and do whatever cleaning was necessary.

In the morning I met John and Tabby at Mick's house. Walking in I noticed his stove was gone. My sister told me that Cindy sold it. "It didn't belong to her", I said. We found out that the person she sold it to was a crack cocaine dealer. Right away we knew that Cindy used the appliance to feed her drug habit. Together we began to pack up his belongings. While doing this we got a firsthand look at how our brother was living. We all knew about the addiction problems that Mick had. None of us could force him to stop doing the things he did. This was a lifestyle he chose to live. By continually being intoxicated or under the influence of some sort of drug, he seemed to be happy living this way. Trying to find some humor, we talked of how he used beer cans as ornaments on a pine tree branch he called his Christmas tree. I told John how Mick was so happy when I was born because he finally had a brother. Momma let him change my diaper. This made me scream and cry because he accidentally pinned it to my side. Our brother was a good man and was known to many for his helpfulness. Packing up all his stuff was a depressing job for us. Since the start, Social Security refused to assist us in any of the cost for Mick's medical or burial. John and Tabby had to get a loan from the bank to pay for his funeral.

Our family and many of Mick's friends joined together for the services at the funeral parlor. People we hadn't seen for several years came out to pay their respects. There were people he met from the jobs he did as a bartender and some high school buddies. Some of Mick's drug buddies who shared in his habits didn't attend. My brother Jack and sisters Mary and Cindy appeared to be stoned or drunk. I prefer not to be in the company of people, including my siblings when they're in this condition. My aunt, who is a recovering alcoholic told me, "it's bad when your kids are dying, at an early age". Mick was 49 years old. After my niece gave her respects she came over and we chatted about her uncle. "At least he was happy with what he had, if he didn't have something, he did without", Marie said. "Yeah, I know, it looks like we lost him to drugs", I told her. She was reluctant to agree with me but did admit that his chemical abuse was partly to blame for his bad health. We both noticed the intoxicated state of Jack and her two aunts that were here. "You can't help people who do that stuff, they have to wanna help themselves, or wait until they hit rock bottom, then they'll quit", I said.

At the mall I found Moe and Cassie waiting inside with my little girl. Amanda got up and ran to the door when she saw me approaching. "Hey baby girl", I greeted her. "Hi my daddy", she replied. We got in the car and headed to my place. When I told her that her Uncle Mick was gone, she got sad and started to cry. "But I love Uncle Mick", she said. "Baby girl, don't be sad, he's gone to live with the angels", I told her. Knowing this seemed to make her cheer up. Looking at her, I noticed how thin she was. "Boo, have you been eating", I asked? She told me yes and named some of the foods, which were mostly sweets, nothing too nutritional. "Can we get a pizza", she asked? "Okay, tonight you can have one but tomorrow you're going to eat something else", I told her. After we ate she wanted to ride our bikes. A couple of laps around the block and she was tired. Her energy levels seemed unusually low to me. When we returned home she wanted to do some activities from Clifford the big red dog. She got started by herself and without her knowing, I was watching from the living room. I was impressed with how well she was doing. After she completed several of the tasks, I brought her some gummi lifesavers as a treat or reward for her good work. "Your Poppa is so proud of you baby girl, I've been watching you, you're getting so smart", I told her. She was getting sleepy and asked that we go to bed. Picking three bedtime stories for me to read, our night had ended.

In the morning after breakfast Amanda asked if Kristy could come over. "Yeah, but we have to go to church, daddy's getting baptized today", I told her. Informing Pookie of what we were doing today, she allowed her daughter to come with us. They both sat and watched as I was dunked under water, receiving the Holy Spirit. After changing into some dry clothes, we went to the nearby park so they could play. In the evening we all rode our bikes. Afterwards, her little friend went home. I fixed some fishsticks and french fries for my little girl and tried to explain to her the importance of proper nutrition. She understood a little bit of what I was talking about. After her bath we played the quiz game where she pronounces the words I spell on her dry-erase board that fit in to complete the sentence in a story. She grew tired from her long day of play and told me it was time for bed. She got her bedtime stories and brought them to me. As usual, before I was finished reading them she was fast asleep.

When we woke up it was time for breakfast and then off to church we'd go. This is how our Sundays started. After eating, Amanda would get dressed and watch a video until we were ready to leave. "Come on daddy, lets go", she'd call to me. I'd bring her to the youth ministry and then join the congregation for praise and worship. The sermon my pastor would recite always seemed to pertain to something I was going through in my life. Nearly everyone here brings their own bible and follows along with the teachings, which are mostly educational, and never boring. This was different from the Catholic Church that I grew up in. In addition to this, my little girl really enjoys herself when she is here. It made me feel secure to know that Amanda was learning from people who had the same Christian faith as I did.

As our day progressed we did things at my place. Sometimes Amanda would play alone and other times she'd ask me to join her. I'd pretend that I didn't know too much and asked her to teach me. This worked great with her computer lessons. I emphasized the importance of knowing how to spell and we started playing the CD that taught this. The game allowed two players to participate. She's on level 1 and I'm on level 3. Long ago with the flash cards I showed her how all the letters were supposed to sound. I pointed out which letters were the vowels and told her how they were needed when it comes to spelling a word. It surprised me that she remembered all this. When the game started I had to refresh her memory a little. Once she got warmed up it was exciting for her to spell many words by herself. We continued to play until it was time to go meet her mother at the mall. Like always, just before we'd get to the entrance, I stop the car, she gives me her good-bye smooch and I bring her to Cassie.

The holiday was approaching and many in my family still felt the gloom from the loss of our brother. I began to buy gifts for my little girl and set them under the tree. My neighbor was outside one day and we stopped to chat. She told me that I'd have to wait for her to repay the loan she made because at the time, she didn't have the money. "Just let me know when you get it", I said. I trusted when the money she borrowed became available, I'd hear from her. "Kristy's been asking about Amanda, how is she", Pookie asked. "She's fine", I replied. I told her that I'd send my little girl over to play with her daughter on the next weekend visit. Our youngsters had become good friends. As our talk continued, she mentioned how unhappy she was with Ted. "There's no sexual relationship between us, I want to get away from here", Pookie said. This was none of my business and I wondered why she told me this. She knew that New Years was my holiday to be with Amanda and invited us to a friend of hers where they'd be putting on a big firework display. This sounded nice and my little girl would enjoy this event. I asked what time they were getting started and agreed to meet them there.

On the weekend of Christmas I picked Amanda up at the mall. Tina was at the exchange area waiting with my little girl. After we got in my car "you have a surprise for me daddy", she asked? "I have plenty for you boo", I told her. At home I let her open one of her gifts and said she could open the rest of them tomorrow. She asked about her pal so I called to see if Kristy was home. Briefly the youngsters chatted on the phone and my little girl asked if her friend could come over. "Sure boo", I said. Soon there was a knock on my door. With a hug they greeted each other and then played together in her bedroom. Her buddy was two years older and their birthday was on the same date. They were more like sisters than best friends.

On Saturday we spent our time here at my place. We did the usual activities and I asked Amanda how she was doing in school. She had many friends but didn't like the way some of the boys were treating her. There were two in particular and she named them both, telling me what they were doing. "Try to be nice to them boo, and they'll be nice to you", I told her. She wasn't alone. There were two other little girls whom these youngsters were bullying. These kids shouldn't be striking other classmates. I already complained once and the woman told me that she'd to look into this matter. According to my little girl this hasn't happened yet. If this behavior didn't stop, the time would come when I'd have to make a visit to her school.

On Sunday we went to church and returned home. Although our routine seemed like we did the same things all the time, we were never bored. It's important that my youngster knows she belongs and that I'm interested in knowing how she is feeling and what she's thinking. What ever I can do to help her learn must remain my top priority. My work to be a good father is like the lighthouse that guides a ship in the direction it needs to go. All the informational material Amanda has wasn't available to me when I was her age. I have to do all I can to provide for my daughter the opportunities to advance academically. If my dad had taken a better interest in us when we were young and provided the proper guidance, instruction and correction, things may have been different for our family. My father wasn't a good leader. I refuse to be like him.

Outside there is a world of predators that are waiting to devour the minds of our children. The media has invented methods for destroying the moral intellect of our youth. Young kids, who have no concept of fear, get easily impressed or convinced, can become their targets. The lack of parental education can leave these youngsters without a defense, which makes them vulnerable. When children know the outcome of a harmful behavior or a dangerous action, they're less likely to pursue it due to the consequences. Here is the reason all parents need to stay informed and remain involved in the lives of their children. The most horrible feeling that parents can experience is when their son or daughter becomes the addict, the thief, the whore, the homosexual, the drunkard, the murderer, the prisoner, or the victim because dad or mom didn't teach them any better. If they're not warned about these seductions, the world is waiting.

Chapter Nine

CONTENTIONS CONTINUE

At the mall I arrived to get my daughter for our holiday together. The distant sounds of fireworks let us know that the New Years Eve party had started. “Hey boo, how ya doing”, I asked? “I’m fine, are we gonna get some fireworks”, she asked excitedly. “No, a little later we’re gonna go meet Pookie and Kristy, they’ll have some”, I told her. When it was dark we headed over to join our friends. We all met at Betty’s house. There was slight drizzle in the air that stopped soon after we arrived. My neighbor needed to tell me something and we walked outside. “I packed up what I could and left Ted, we’re going to be staying here”, Pookie said. “I’ll call ya when I get that money I owe you, I should be getting it in the mail soon”, she told me. When we went back inside, she introduced me to a friend of hers named Theo. I remember doing a job for this man long ago when I was with SWX. He was in or near his 60s, wealthy and owned a construction company. The affection they had for each other made them appear to be more than just friends. She needed someone stable in her life that could provide security for Kristy and her. When the rain stopped we all went out to start our celebration. Fireworks filled the sky with radiance. Amanda, Kristy and the other kids had fun playing with sparklers. After the light show was over, we all went inside. Us grown-ups chatted while the youngsters pulled out some toys. It was getting late and I told my daughter that we’d be going soon. As we were leaving, Pookie asked me to come see something in the kitchen. “Your little girl said that her mommy wants to change her last name to Dixon”, she told me. “Well, that’s too bad, she can’t do that”, I replied. “I know, I just wanted to tell you that”, she said. I thanked her for giving me this information and we left. Nothing was said about what my neighbor told me when we got home. We each had a bowl of ice cream, watched a cartoon video and went to bed.

In the morning we had breakfast. Afterwards my youngster wanted me to join her for some computer lessons. The weather was nice outside and she asked if we could ride our bikes. We took a few laps around the block and went back home. “Do I have to go back to my mommy’s tonight”, she asked? “Yeah, after while you do”, I said. She wanted to stay with me. When it was close to being time for us to meet her mother at the mall, we sat down and had a talk before we left. “Baby girl, don’t worry about someone changing your last name, that’s not gonna happen, Poppa loves you very much, you’re my little girl and I'll never give up on you", I told her. She was glad to know that she'd be here in three days for a weekend visit.

The previous year gave me 1487 hours to be with my daughter. Ever since that incident at Kids Cottage, the leniency Cassie gave towards my visitation with Amanda had disappeared. It was like everything crashed. My employment caused me to miss two scheduled weekend visits with my little girl and at the present time I had been out of work for nearly two months. This part of the year is when jobs in NDT are hard to find. The local inspection companies didn't have any openings and my reputation for being unreliable remained. The ongoing custody battle that I had been in for nearly three years was still remembered as the personal problem that hampered my availability. This would force me to search for work out of state. If I kept leaving those projects uncompleted, these new employers wouldn't want me either.

On Friday morning as I sat watching the news a surprising phone call came from Kayla. I was happy to hear from her. It had been a long time since we talked. She was currently living across the river and didn't disclose an exact location. We had been chatting for a while when she said that things weren't too good. She told me that she was four months pregnant. The last time we talked she spoke of her choice to be gay. After hearing that she was with child, it was my guess that the homosexual lifestyle was something she didn't prefer. The unplanned role of being a mother was an adjustment she was preparing to make. She said that the father was a good man and they both refused to have an abortion. The regard she had for human life was different from that of her cousin's, Hannah. Kayla's main priority was to take good care of herself and remain healthy so there'd be no complications when it was time to deliver.

News broadcasts continued to talk about the war in Afghanistan that resulted from the attacks on the World Trade Center and the Pentagon. Allied forces were doing everything possible to destroy the Taliban and Al Qaeda, those responsible for these terrorism attacks. Investigations found several businesses around the world to be funding these terrorists. We continued to hear warnings about the "sleepers" who lived here as our neighbors. They were described as people who move here, set up shop, get well connected within their communities and this prevents them from becoming suspects. The media revealed that the hijackers were Moslems and their religious beliefs are much different from that of Americans. Committing suicide, they crashed planes into these buildings and killed thousands, which makes them martyrs in their jihad and sends them to live with their god, Allah. This religion became a topic of discussion for many living here in America. A book called the Koran is the core of their faith, which tells about the revelations that Allah gave the prophet Mohammed. They believe Jesus is a prophet and not the Son of God. Many have sounded the alarm that this is a false religion with followers who suggest that anyone, who doesn't partake in their rituals, should perish or be severely punished. Freedom of religion allows this heresy to propagate across our country. One day in the future, our children may be subdued by this absurd religious practice. It's important for me to remain informed and teach my daughter that the Moslemic view is not part of our American Heritage. According to the document from 1620, this is not the faith or the fundamental belief we used to form the foundation of our country. Would God continue to protect the United States of America if we let Him be replaced with Allah? (I John 4:1-8)

Our country is great. There are so many different nationalities that have made our nation their home. It's no surprise that we are all divergent. Everyone has views that aren't the same. Does that make someone bad? No. Most realize that there is a day and a night. There is a hot and a cold. There is a right way and a wrong way. There is good and there is evil. Many people believe there is a God and a Devil. If we believe this, there's no denial that there's a heaven and a hell. Even an atheist has the knowledge of the Creator and Satan because he has to have something in which he chooses not to believe in. In America we have several religions. When a person finds a few rotten oranges, wouldn't this force him to examine the whole bushel? No one can be too cautious. As for me, I'll adhere to the living Word that I have grown to learn and love. The King James Bible is like a seed. Once I've digested it, a beautiful tree grows and it demands that I live according to its instruction. Its admonition frees me from the wiles of this world and teaches me spiritual morality. Everyone needs air to live. To have the connection with my Heavenly Father, I must have faith. This same faith is like that air I need to live.

In the evening I went to the mall to get my little girl. After we got in the car, Amanda asked to hear her favorite song. I put in the Zoe Girl CD and we drove around so she could listen to her tunes. At home she wanted to watch a cartoon video and eat some pizza. After eating she played in her room. There is a large variety of things for her to do. She pretended to cook for her babies or play with her farm animals. A while later I encouraged her to play the spelling game on her computer. Amanda needed to keep practicing so she'd know how words were spelled. "This is how you'll learn to read", I told her. It was time for bed and she picked her bedtime stories. She asked to read the first one by herself and she didn't need too much help from me. It was rewarding to see her read a book. When I was finished reading the last story, she was still awake. I put in another cartoon video for her to watch until she fell asleep.

On Saturday after breakfast I asked my youngster what she wanted to do today. She didn't feel like going anywhere. Lately she'd enjoy tickling me. She knew that I was ticklish under my arms. As a kid I didn't like this but when she heard me giggle, this made her laugh. It was time for me to put on a show for her with the farm family and animals. I couldn't do this too much because all the different voices made my throat sore. Amanda turned on the computer and put in her art CD. She liked to make different pictures. I was sitting on the couch when she called for me to come see her work. She had made a nice picture for her mother. "That's looks beautiful boo, mommy's gonna like that", I told her. "Daddy can we order a pizza", she asked? "Yeah, I will but you can't eat that all the time, tonight you'll have to eat some yogurt or a banana or something else", I said. Later that night after her bath she ate a banana. We did some more learning activities until it was time for bed. We had to get up early for church.

Sunday started out with services in the morning. The rest of the day we did things at home. This is normally what our time together was like. There was always something for us to do. I started to notice that the computer skills Amanda developed were very good for a five-year-old. She knew how to do her activities better than I did. There were many times when I'd have to ask her how to do something. In the evening we talked a little about how everything was at her mother's house. My little girl told me that her mommy still leaves her with Moe or Donny and that she didn't like that. "Just try to be nice to them and they'll be nice to you", I told her.

To get some exercise, I decided to ride my bicycle and go to the local convenience store. On my way home there was a woman I saw who looked familiar. Driving near I saw it was Lacey. “Hey stranger”, I called. She didn’t recognize me at first until I got closer. She was employed at a nearby animal shelter and was walking home from work. Slowly I rode along side her as we talked. At first we chatted about her job and then she asked how Amanda was doing. I told her that I only get to see my child on the weekends and that things hadn’t changed too much with Cassie and me. Lacey had no harsh feelings towards me and only knew what the mother told her. To my surprise she started to open up and tell me things. She felt sorry for my little girl. There were many times she heard Cassie questioning my youngster about me. “Why you keep asking me that, or stop asking me that”, she’d hear Amanda scream. Sometimes my child would go jump in bed with Lacey so she could get away from her mother. “I couldn’t wait to get away from that place, she drinks too much beer”, the former babysitter said of the mother. She also told me that Cassie was let go from the Cablanka because money was always missing from the cash register while she was at work. By this time we were getting near the apartments where she lived. We said goodbye and I rode away. I was thankful for her telling me all this but didn’t get to ask about why she hit Amanda in the head with her fist.

The next day I went to see about getting some musical CDs from a local record store. I was at an intersection across from the establishment, stopped at a stop sign. I checked to see if it was clear to pass. There was no traffic so I eased out. The sound of a horn was all I heard and a big public service bus hooked on to my car and pulled me out onto the road. The driver halted his vehicle immediately, not far from me. Assessing the damage to my vehicle, I saw that the whole front end had been ripped off and the frame was bent. This couldn’t be fixed. It was bad enough that I was unemployed but now I didn’t have a car to find a job with.

The new week started with me getting a letter from Charlene. I hadn’t been in to see her lately and wondered why she was sending me a bill. I was hoping that this wasn’t some more bad news. I sat down, took a deep breath and opened the envelope. It was a copy of the letter our opposition had sent to the court. Misty filed a notice to withdraw as the opposing counsel from our case. She may not have agreed with Cassie’s actions or this may be a monetary issue. I completed my sessions with Dr. Watson and the mother still had one final meeting before the report could be written. If this weren't done before July, we'd have to start all over again.

Near the end of the week I started working for SWX on Thursday. Dennis had a position available. When I told him that my car was wrecked he offered to send a helper to pick me up at my place. There aren't any x-ray companies that will provide curb service or come get you from your house and provide a ride to work all the time. This inconvenience would affect my ability to be punctual. The new job started tonight and we were assigned to work at a nearby fabrication shop. We arrived at the location and were getting prepared when my cell phone rang. It was my former supervisor Don from NXP. He wanted to know if I'd be interested in coming back to Fort Myers to work at the power plant. I accepted his offer and called Dennis to let him know. My boss wasn't too happy with this news. I felt bad for having to quit and leave after he just hired me back. I told him to keep the money he owed me for working.

On Friday morning I called and asked Charlene to send a letter to Cassie informing her of the job I took in Florida. This way she couldn't make false allegations that I didn't show up at the mall to get my daughter. My weekend visit that started today wouldn't be any fun without transportation. I rented a car and cleaned it up. It looked nice when I was finished. In the evening I went to get Amanda. The mother and I still weren't talking. We went our separate ways after doing the trade. My little girl was excited when she saw the shiny red vehicle. When she heard about my car being in an accident and we may not get it back, this made her sad. "Don't worry, daddy's got a new job and I'll get us another car baby girl", I told her. We went home and did the usual, pizza, cartoons and learning activities until it was time for bed.

It's beneficial for my child that I provide pleasurable memories for her to recall when she's older. To go places and let her see things or do stuff are the occasions I want her to remember. We can spend time here at my place or go out somewhere else. I'll name several activities we can do and she'll pick the one she likes. The options are usually experiences that will teach her. If she doesn't understand something, I can work with her or draw it on the dry erase board until she catches on. I'm not going to be a dad that didn't spend enough time with his child.

We spent our weekend together as we normally do. Amanda didn't want to go anywhere and enjoyed staying here with me. There's never a dull moment and I even let her tickle me. When I look at all the stuff in her room, it's easy to see how God has truly blessed us. After church I told my youngster that I had to go back to work and would be gone for a while. She knew I hadn't been working and that daddy needed money for a new car. I promised to call her. We played some games on her computer and had some left over pizza while watching her favorite cartoons. She continued to do the learning activities on her Clifford the big red dog CD until it was time to meet her mommy at the mall. As we approached the parking lot, I stopped my car. My little girl gave me her goodbye smooch and I drove over to the exchange area.

Before leaving to go out of state I went to get a haircut from Jazzy. She has a part of her house set up for these jobs. As she got started we began to talk about what I've been up to and her family. She informed me that Kyle and she were separated due to his drinking. I've always known Jazzy to be a strong woman but did notice that she was holding back the tears as she told me this news. Her husband's alcoholism became too disruptive for their household. To make their home environment more peaceful, the living arrangements had to change. He had a choice. Leave the booze alone and stay or keep the booze and leave. Kyle moved out and was currently living with her brother. Alcohol is a great remover. It can take money from your wallet, cars from your driveway and here, it displaced a loved one from his family.

Driving home, I thought about my childhood. One of the worst events that happened to me was when my parents split up. My brother and I, along with our two sisters were left to live with momma. Normally, father is the authority figure and is responsible for his kids. With dad being gone, Jack and me didn't have to worry about being disciplined. Living in a home with only one parent allowed us to grow up unrestrained because mom wasn't strict enough. We began hanging around with the wrong crowd. With the help of our sisters, we started smoking pot at an early age. My brother and me may have rebelled against momma because we saw that gender to be weaker. Whatever the reason, many preteens and teens of today who live in single parent homes are reluctant to submit especially when that parent is female. Even after dad and mom reconciled, it was too late. Our parents didn't try hard enough to be good role models.

On Wednesday I flew to Fort Myers. NXP had a rental car waiting for me. I went back to the same motel and checked in. The next day I headed over to the plant for orientation and a drug screen. We had a larger darkroom and our work place had moved to the pipe racks. Most of the welds were 70 to 90 feet up. We could x-ray only when people were gone from our area. Since we were the only inspection company on this project, we were called to provide NDT services for three different construction companies. This made our shifts very long.

The job here was still about the same. We worked at nighttime and even with the sun being gone, it was still hot. Clam and Link hadn't changed their routine. They'd come in, sit down and eat. We knew they liked to smoke pot and both appeared to be stoned when they came into work. Ike started working for one of the construction companies and gave us the list of welds we had to x-ray. It took a while to get prepared for these inspections because of all the data that needed to be on the film for identification purposes. We managed to have just enough time to be ready and start our operations when the workers went on break or took their lunch.

It was tourist season here and plenty people from the northern states drove south for the winter. The rates for my rental car went up to $240 a week and this was too much. I had the insurance payoff from my car and a little money saved in the bank. If I bought a used car, I'd just be buying someone else's troubles. A big down payment would enable me to have lower monthly notes. I went to the vice president and asked him for a loan. Dan gave me the amount that I needed and my quest to find another Neptune Essel II began.

At work I talked with Don and Hosea about buying a vehicle. I never was too good when it came to understanding finance charges. As they were talking, Clam joined in. My supervisor was very smart with numbers. He was quick to pull out the calculator and prove that he was correct. Hosea invited me to come by his house on the weekend for a barbecue and we could talk more about it. They all agreed with me that the rental car was too expensive. I planned on going by the nearest dealership tomorrow and start looking for the vehicle I wanted.

There were two places that sold Neptunes. One was here in the city and the other in Naples. At Fort Myers a pudgy salesman with a loud mouth greeted me. He picked the car he wanted me to buy. I didn't appreciate that or the way he beat on the vehicle. "It's too soon to make a decision, I need more time", I told him. Down to Naples I drove. I had hoped the people down here were nicer. Cody, the salesman was more informative and friendlier. I looked at the car I wanted and filled out a credit application. They'd run it through and call me in the morning.

That night at work I told Hosea what happened. "Is it what you want, do you like it", he asked? I told him that I was satisfied. Don and Clam started to ask me a lot of questions about the price. I couldn't remember everything and their reactions made me a little nervous. Hosea told me that if the dealership called in the morning, he wanted to go to car lot with me.

In the morning I got the call. Leaving the rental at the motel, I rode with my co-worker, his wife Sheena and their two boys. We arrived at the Neptune dealership in Naples to find my car all cleaned up and on the showroom floor. Cody had all the paperwork ready. Hosea and his wife looked at the car and complemented me on my selection. Sheena did some accounting work at one time and noticed how the contract was missing some things the salesman told me about. He took the paperwork to Harry, the sales manager. They called me in the office and Sheena followed. Cody walked out. They lowered the percentage rate by 3 points and gave me a zero deductible on my warranty. These adjustments made the new car cheaper than my other one. "You have a pen", I asked? On the first of February, I bought another Neptune Essel II.

On Saturday I met Hosea at his house for a celebration barbecue. We talked about my new purchase and our work at the plant. He had two little boys that seemed to be battling for our attention. After everyone ate, we sat down to watch television. The channel never changed from the children's network. This was a method they used to occupy the minds of their kids. I noticed how these youngsters didn't want to heed what their mother would tell them. She often had to raise her voice to make them behave. Several times my friends used obscene language. "You talk like that in front of your kids", I asked Hosea? "I'd rather them hear it from me", he replied. I didn't like to talk like that especially when there are little ones present. It was useless for me to voice my opinion because these are not my children. I asked them to bring out some of their toys. Dean, the older of the two was 4-years old and Zac, was 3. He understood me and came out with some colorful items while his younger brother watched. I asked him to pick out the toys that were the color I named. He did real well. We did this for a while as Hosea and Sheena looked on. It was easy to see that their sons were mostly longing for attention.

In the evening I called to speak with Amanda. Much to my surprise, Cassie let her answer the phone. "Hello", she answered. "Hi boo, it's daddy", I said "Hi my daddy", she exclaimed! "How you doing", I asked her? "My mommy said you gave up your weekends with me", she responded sadly. "That's not true, you know daddy wrecked his car, I'm working so I can get us another one, I'll be home as soon as I can", I told her. I quickly changed the subject and we talked for a short while. I could hear her mother's voice in the background and knew that our chat was being monitored. Just to know that my daughter was okay and to tell her that I love and miss her was the reason for my call. The roaming charges on my cell phone are too much for me. This high fee is why I would only try to reach my little girl once or twice a week.

A major worry for me was not knowing what Amanda is allowed to do while she's at her mother's house. With Mardi Gras approaching, there was no way I could be sure that my little girl wouldn't be caught up in this spirit of idolatry. Millions of people don't have a clue how this annual celebration began or what it actually represents. This holiday ascends from the tribal rituals of fertility in ancient Rome that welcomed the arrival of spring. Most parades are named after false gods and pagan deities. Bacchus, the god of wine and revelry is associated with the Bacchanalia festival. Pandora, is considered the first woman created, not Eve. Babylon is not a god but is known for its wickedness and represents everything that is false in religion. Drunkenness, revelry, licentiousness and indecency characterize all of the celebrations in one way or another. All the excitement blinds the parade goers from the dark demonic forces that drive the carnival. In some churches people are criticized for raising their hands in praise to the Lord but at a parade, worthless plastic necklaces, trinkets or aluminum doubloons gets all the followers to shout and raise their hands in worship to the crews of Baal. Donny and Brad have not seen their dad in over twenty years and love the Mardi Gras. If Cassie's sons want to pay homage to this sinful party, that's their choice. I'm Amanda's father and feel that if she doesn't know about this caravan passing through the city, she won't want to go. To participate in this annual event brings spiritual defilement to everyone who profess that they love God. There is a religion that don't discourage its congregation from attending but tells them to be careful at the celebration. When it's over, go to church and they'll smear ashes on your forehead so you can start your forty days of abstinence. Sorry, I like to eat meats on Fridays. (I Timothy 4:1-4)

Work went on as usual. The construction company gave us a limited amount of time to do our work. Radiation Safety Requirements is a big part of our job. We arrived at the area early to set up barricades and get prepared for the inspections. Hosea wanted to get another person because our production was low. A former employee, Darren wanted to come back to work at NPX if a position became available. Everyone called him the dinosaur because he was nearly 7 feet tall and huge like a linebacker from the national football league. His only hang up was that he had a bad temper problem resulting from a bitter relationship with a former girlfriend.

Hosea is our lead man and he's responsible for all the operations. He became increasingly dissatisfied with the performance of Clam and Link. Both became sluggish when it was time to get started. These two guys were unusually forgetful. All x-ray exposures have to be timed and the inaccuracy when doing this causes the film to be unacceptable. When a technician has to do his work all over because the helper can't pay attention to his watch, it's irritating. It angered Hosea when Clam admitted to smoking pot everyday on his way to work. Knowing this, our lead man asked Dan to rehire Darren. In the middle of February the dinosaur arrived. He had no problem carrying any of the equipment and didn't have to be told what to do. Hosea and I saw how he was able to do the work of two men and his assistance made our operations easier.

As time went on, the list Ike gave us was getting bigger. It felt like we were playing a game of catch up. When the workers took a break or went to lunch, this didn't give us enough time to finish the nightly assignment. We did the best we could for our clients. Radiography is actually a test on the qualification of welders. When the welds are defective, the welder has to grind the bad area out and re-weld it. This is how repairs are made. The same spot is x-rayed again to make sure that all the defects have been removed. In the morning the clients would look at the film with Hosea. They weren't too happy with the welders making plenty of bad welds.

We came in one night to find our list was small. There wasn't much for us to do but we still had to remain on site at the plant. Hosea talked about a new game he bought called grand theft auto and had it in his truck. All he needed was a television and they could play the game. We were finished work at lunchtime and bored. Dinosaur lived close to the plant and offered to go home and get his television. Everyone except me was familiar with this game. Watching from a afar, I was thoroughly stunned with this game. The thief, or criminal is armed with all kinds of weapons that'll shoot helicopters out of the sky, blow up cars and cut people in half. Roaming through the city, killing anyone and everyone, he steals cars. When the police approach, with one shot their head is decapitated and the blood gushes out all over the place. The gore, death and violent destruction in this game were unbelievable. It troubled me to know that this kind of material and others like it was available to teens. If parents knew the dangers of games like these, I'm positive dad and mom wouldn't allow their teenagers to play with them.

Near the end of the month, the two helpers came in drunk after being out all night. Clam slept while Link and me went to do a job. More work came in after lunch and Hosea wanted to go do it. He took Darren and Link with him while Clam continued to sleep. It wasn't too long before they all returned with our lead man being very angry. As they were getting started, Link got sick and vomited on Hosea. Because these guys showed up for work inebriated, both were sent home indefinitely? Dinosaur had no problem replacing these two drunkards.

In March we finally began to catch up. We had developed a routine that enabled us to get more work done. Sometimes we'd have every weld inspected on the list Ike gave us. Darren was a big help to Hosea and me. I saw the temper problem everyone spoke about. His present girlfriend was too demanding of him and he didn't like that. When I mentioned about being in a custody battle, the Dinosaur knew just what I was going through. As a youngster he had to deal with that when his parents divorced. He stayed in Maine with his mom and his dad moved here to Florida. "My mom used to beat the *_* out of me when I was a little kid", he told me. He was angry with his father for spending his college tuition. His dad took the money and used it to buy a diamond ring for his younger fiancée. "Are you going through a divorce", he asked? "Nope, never been married because I haven't met my wife yet", I replied. He looked surprised when I told him where I'd find her. "Momma told me if I wanted to meet a good woman that she'd be in church and that's true", I said. When Darren wasn't working with NXP, he was a barback at a local nightclub. I told him how my faith saved me. He seemed to be disinterested in talking about God. Church was a place he didn't attend or like to talk about. The good news I've learned about came from reading scripture and the different pastors from all the ministries I belong to. To Christians, the Word of God strengthens their faith and it's the most valuable gift. It's like precious pearls to a jeweler. It's not easy for me to try and explain to someone this good news I've found when in doing so, promotes discomfort or disagreements. (Matthew 7:6)

The situation Darren found himself in was very similar to mine. He wasn't sure if he loved this woman but the sex was great. This was how my relationship with Cassie started. Blinded by lust, I was attached to a woman who became the mother of my child. One difference was that Dinosaur's girlfriend also loved females. At the local shopping center here in Florida there were times I saw how young women were seen to be overly friendly with each other in public. Prevalent amongst many of the college age females of today is the desire to follow the ongoing trend of bisexuality and homosexuality. Television is very successful in portraying that many women prefer this degenerate lifestyle. As they cleave to each other, this helps deter them from ever wanting to be married. A woman like this doesn't want a man when she can buy the part of him she likes to use. Dinosaur told me that this kind of behavior is on display at some of the local nightclubs. "You ought to see the way they rub and kiss on each other", Darren told me. His stories revealed that many of these females enjoy their choice to degrade themselves.

Work was slowing down. There wasn't that many welds left for us to x-ray. At the middle of the month our clients informed us that there'd be about two weeks of work left and the job was finished. This notice made me happy. With all the inspections for this project almost done, a third person on our crew wouldn't be needed. I requested to leave at the end of this month so I could be home for Easter. One night while talking about little girl, I told Hosea that it was time for her to learn the Lords prayer. "That's a good idea", he said. If he could release one of us, he'd allow me to return home. I had already missed four scheduled weekends of parenting time with my youngster. Her mother's vengeful tactics made me nervous. The last time I spoke to Amanda, Cassie was trying hard to brainwash her, saying that I gave up my weekends with her. This spiteful mother continued to tell my child emotionally hurtful things.

The project was almost complete and I got permission to leave. This dismissal is what I was hoping for. I'd be home in time to celebrate the holiday with Amanda. As the job was coming to a close I got prepared for my long travel. Hosea told me that there'd be additional work to expand part of this power plant at the end of the year. He urged me to try and make myself available. "I'll come back when the work begins", I told him. I arrived home on Wednesday and got ready for the Easter weekend with my daughter. Two messages were left on Cassie's answering machine so she'd know that I'd be waiting at the exchange area.

According to my calendar, this last weekend that included the holiday was mine to be with my little girl. On Friday evening I went by the mall to get my youngster. I had been gone for nine weeks and when I saw her, she appeared to have grown. Happily, Amanda ran over to me. I took her by the hand and we walked to my new car. The shiny vehicle excited her and she was happy to get in. "You have a surprise for me", she asked? "I sure do, they're at home but you have to find them", I told her. New CDs, toys and shirts were waiting for her at my place. We did our usual activities. At night before bed I told her about the new prayer that I wanted to teach her. With eyes wide open, she watched me as I prayed, "Our Father who art in Heaven". After finishing I told her that she'd be saying it tomorrow night. "Okay daddy", she said.

On Saturday we went to City Park and rode the amusement rides. My little girl wanted one of her friends to go with us. We stopped over at my nephew's place and picked up his daughter Karen. The kids had a fun time. Afterwards we went home for pizza and the youngsters played for a while. In the evening we made a short visit when we brought Karen back. Later that night when Amanda was doing some activities on her computer, she told me how Donny is slapping her and making her cry. "Are you doing anything to make him angry with you", I asked? "No, I'm not doing anything", she replied. As I thought about him doing this to her, it was clear that Cassie was trying to provoke me to anger, violence or both. It was sickening how this mother let her oldest son, a man hit on our 6-year-old daughter. I couldn't figure our why Cassie allowed this to go on. "Boo, all I can say is try to be nice to him and stay away from him, daddy's going to see what he can do about this", I said. To make her happy I did a show with the farm family. Of course I have to make all these funny sounds. She enjoys it when I do this. At bedtime she repeated the Lords prayer after me. From start to finish, she did real well.

On Easter Sunday I woke up with a sore throat and was sick. It may have been from doing all the funny voices last night with the farm animals. Amanda didn't feel good either. I told her these shows were too much and that I was going to build her a puppet theatre. While eating breakfast we watched cartoons. In the afternoon we both felt a little better and played the quiz game on her dry erase board. "Hey boo, do you ever hear the phone ring about the same time everyday, mostly in the evenings", I asked? "Yeah", she replied. "Do you know who it is" I inquired? "You", she responded. When Amanda has the phone in her hand and goes to answer it, "don't you even think about it", Cassie threatens. My daughter told me her mother wouldn't let her speak with me when I call. We spent the rest of the day talking about today's holiday and the importance of it. My little girl knows that Jesus died for our sins and he rose from the dead. He ascended into heaven, he's alive and doing well, living with God. In the evening my youngster didn't want to go home. Again she asked to come live with me. "I wish I could stay with you and see my mommy on the weekends", she told me. At the mall I noticed that Cassie brought Donny with her. After we did the trade, I figured out what this mom was up to. She knows my little girl means the world to me. She allows her son to smack Amanda knowing that she'll tell her daddy. This mother was hoping that when I saw Donny, a fistfight would ensue. Then she could walk right into the police station, file a complaint and I'd go to jail.

On Monday morning, April fools day I went to see Charlene. I was very upset about being denied my telephone privileges. Donny is slapping my daughter and Cassie brings him to the exchanges. My attorney wasn't happy with what she heard. We both agreed it was time for another court appearance. I also asked to resume my weekday visits. "I can arrange that", she said. Since Cassie no longer had an attorney, Charlene would send a letter notifying her of this reinstatement of my Wednesday visitation. My attorney wrote down a bunch of notes, I made a payment to start the proceedings and she'd get back to me with a court date.

At about noon I went to a local appliance store to get a refrigerator box and make the theatre for Amanda. It turned into a very big job. With lots of construction paper, paint, cardboard and glue, I made a showcase. It had a fan inside, a sound system and lighting, and curtains that were controlled from the inside. I bought stuffed animals to do shows with. This was a surprise my little girl was going to love. I finished eight days later, just before my first Wednesday visit.

Arriving at the mall I saw my little girl sitting inside. The mother wouldn't walk her out to meet me so I had to park and go in. I walked over and handed Cassie the monthly support. It had been a long time since I was able to get close enough and hand it to her myself. Usually she runs away. After we got in the car, "I have a surprise for you", I told Amanda. "What is it", she asked? "You have to wait until we get home", I said. When we walked in she immediately ran over to the colorful box. "What is it daddy", she asked? Her question made me laugh. "I'll show ya", I said. Turning it on, I climbed in and did a show for her. She laughed and giggled when I did this. We had a good time. A while later we stopped to take a break. She was hungry and asked me to order a pizza. "Okay, but when you come over this weekend you're gonna eat something else, you can't have pizza all the time", I told her. "Okay daddy", she said.

When our weekend started, my daughter was thrilled about putting on a show. She liked all the stuffed animals. Afterwards we did some spelling activities on her computer. There's an art CD she has and wanted to make a picture for her mommy. "If you need any help, call me", I told her. It's important to help her do this. I'm not like Cassie. It doesn't bother me when my little girl talks about her mother. I'm certain that Amanda recognizes the difference between the two households of her parents. Over there she can't talk about me and here she can mention her mother or whomever. I try to keep our routines more structured and carefully monitor what she watches on television. When my youngster wants to do something, she'll usually come ask me. Most of the time she wants me to join her. At bedtime she picks her books, we'll say our prayers together and then lay down. She likes the funny voices I use when reading her stories.

Saturday morning I woke up to the rain tapping on my window. I knew we'd be spending the day at home. I sat on the couch and watched television until my little one got up. She came out and sat next to me. "Morning boo, what ya want for breakfast", I asked her? After eating, she'll usually find something to do. She forgot about the new CDs that I bought home from Florida. One of them teaches about math and she hadn't used it yet. "Why don't we play this one boo, you need to learn how numbers are used so you'll be able to count money and tell time", I told her. Later that night my little girl sounded congested. Cassie smokes three packs of cigarettes a day. Donny and Brad are also smokers. If that house isn't ventilated, my little girl is there all day breathing in their second hand smoke. "Let me put some vapor rub on ya boo", I asked? As I was applying the ointment, I saw some slight bruising. The same two boys at school had kicked her in the back and chest. These injuries were hurting her. "Don't worry, I'm gonna take care of this", I told her. Now it was time for me to visit the principal. They needed to take some kind of action that would make these bullies leave Amanda alone.

After church on Sunday we talked about what she learned in her class. My little girl would bring her bible with her and all the kids were given a snack. From scripture, the teachers taught the children different things about God and Jesus. On my own I was looking for a way to help my daughter learn more about the stories in the bible. When we got home she did the activities from her Reader Rabbit math CD. Using mathematics, she started the construction of a boat. This game took a long time and helped her learn basic arithmetic. She got tired of playing so we took a break and had some ice cream. We watched cartoons until it was time to go meet her mother at the mall. Like always, before we left Amanda had to change back into the clothes she came over in. As I turned into parking lot, I stopped my car. She gave me her good bye smooch and we drove over to the exchange area where Cassie was waiting.

Monday morning I typed a letter addressed to Charlene. I wrote about my discontent with the way these kids were mistreating my youngster and implied that I had pictures of all these injuries. I threatened to take legal action if the bullying from these boys didn't stop. I continued the note with these statements: "These incidents of abuse to Amanda make me wonder if the teachers know that if the problems with these little boys aren't corrected now, when they're older they may find it acceptable to overpower girls as a means to get what they want". "What does it take before the parents of unrestrained children are notified"? "This is a very dangerous situation that has obviously been overlooked by the school and the teachers". "When unruly bullies start inflicting bodily harm on my daughter and the teachers allow this sort of behavior, that is when I, as her father will take the necessary legal action that is needed to stop this abuse abruptly". I got dressed in a nice suit and headed over to the school. I walked in the gym and saw two big women sitting in the corner, laughing and joking. Over on the other end was a large group of kids by themselves, unsupervised. With no one watching them, this is how little ones get hurt. This is what $450 a month gets you at Top of the Hill Academy. I went to the office and waited to see the principal. She came out and we walked into her office. I told her what happened to Amanda and asked that something be done about these two boys. Handing her the letter, "My attorney said that I needed to come over and give you this", I said. Her eyes widened as she read the whole page. "We just had a meeting on discipline, I will look into this right away and take care of everything", she told me. With a handshake, our meeting was over. Before leaving I took a walk around the school. Women dominated this facility. At an early age, some kids decide that they don't want to be controlled by a woman. Was it possible that these boys, although they were young, have already chosen to rebel against females or were these two youngsters re-enacting the wrestling stunts they learn from television on the girls?

When Amanda came over for the next weekday visit I asked how everything was at school? She told me that those two boys had been separated from her and the other little girls she plays with. The bullies didn't bother any of the other classmates or my little girl anymore. The letter I wrote had served its purpose. When I asked how everything was at home she told me that Moe had moved to Tennessee. We continued to build the boat with her the math CD. When she got many of the answers correct, a boat part was given and added to the construction. She got hungry so I ordered us a pizza. While eating we watched cartoons and soon it was time for us to go meet Cassie at the mall. Our time was short and we did our trade in the usual way.

The last weekend of the month I planned to add more to our routine. Amanda had grown to know much about God. Now was the time to continue telling her words of truth so she would remember them when we were apart. After I picked my youngster up, we had some beignets at the local café in the mall. At home she played with her toys, did some learning activities and then she got hungry. While waiting for the pizza to arrive I saw how well she was doing with her computer lessons. "Your poppa's so proud of you baby girl", I told her. As we were eating, the perfect opportunity came for me to start talking about God. My little girl saw an incident at school where a little boy hit another kid and the teacher didn't see it. "Hey boo let me tell you something, when someone, like that little boy does something bad and no one saw him do it and he thinks he got away with it, he's wrong; God don't sleep and He saw what that little boy did", I told her. My child knows that our Heavenly Father is omnipotent and has His angels to watch over us. A while later we had a bowl of ice cream and it was time for bed. She picked her stories and brought them to me. Before we lay down, Amanda really enjoyed saying the Lords prayer for both of us. She was fast asleep before I could finish reading her favorites.

The next day I decided to do something we hadn't done in a long time. Amanda woke up and had a bowl of cereal for breakfast. After she ate I gave her a vitamin and told her, "we're going to City Park in a little while". Her eyes lit up with excitement. Today it would be my little girl and me. None of her friends were invited because it's easier to have her undivided attention when there's no distractions. The roller coaster is Amanda's favorite. Spending the afternoon riding it 20 or 30 times lets me know that I'm not as young as I used to be. "Come on daddy", she'd call to me. At home I continued inculcating her with different phrases that I felt she needed to remember. Long ago I started doing this and made her repeat them back to me. Through repetition, many of these sayings were still firmly fixed in her memory. She had no problem recalling all that I taught her. The most important one that my momma always told me is "You can't live without God in your life and be happy". I'd start it and she'd finish it. "If you don't have something nice to say about someone", I said. "Then don't say anything at all" she'd finish. "If you want people to be nice to you", I'd start. "You have to be nice to them" she'd finish. With everything going on in our country I told her repeatedly not to talk with strangers, particularly grown-ups she didn't know. "They'll offer you candy, want to show you an animal they have or be real nice so they can get close enough to grab you", I told her. Never go outside by yourself. Always make sure that mommy is close by. At home we did our usual activities until it got late. She picked her stories and said our prayers. I wanted her to know that she could pray anytime she wants to. "God doesn't sleep and He's everywhere", I told her.

After church we went home to do something around the house. For a while she played by herself and then wanted me to join her in the spelling game. As we were playing, my little girl sadly told me how Donny calls her names and makes her cry. Amanda is very softhearted and name-calling was something that quickly hurts her feelings. The mother permits her grown up sons to taunt our daughter. When I was young, momma always told us that sticks and stones may break our bones but names will never hurt us. My youngster already knew this saying so I taught her how to make it work. "Lets take a rest, poppa wants to show you what you can do about this", I told her. She knows what a ceiling fan is and when it's on high, the wind blows real hard. I thoroughly explained to her what a table fan is and how it works in the same way. "When someone calls you a name, what you do is keep what their face looks like in your mind and go your own way", I urged. "Afterwards, all you have to do is think about this table fan when it's on high and imagine them spitting into it", I told her. "It'll be funny when the picture in your mind shows them doing this and you may laugh about it" I finished. "Do not tell that person or anyone else what you're doing because it can make him or her angry", I warned. If someone tries to be mean and they see that their attempts aren't working, the confusion from this usually causes them to stop. This was my way of turning an insult into laughter. Amanda found humor in my explanation of this. Not all the seeds I plant die; only the ones I forget to water. "No matter what happens, always try to be nice to him", I told her. (Proverbs 25:21-22)

On my first weekend in May, I forfeited my parenting time with Amanda at the request of her mother. My daughter wanted to attend a school function and be with her classmates. This was okay and I didn't mind. My youngster had some little girls she liked to play with and being with them made her happy. Cassie promised to make up for my lost time. I knew she wouldn't make up for anything. Sunday was

Mother's day and our little girl was supposed to be with her mom. This is part of the judgement and Amanda would be with me on Father's day.

The following weekday visit arrived and I picked up Amanda at the mall. We were getting in my car when, "daddy, those boys are showing their underwear", she told me. I looked over and saw two young males wearing their pants down at the bottom of their butts, exposing the boxer shorts they had on. As we drove home I told her that it wasn't their fault for the way they dressed. "Their daddy and mommy never taught them how to put on a pair of pants the right way", I said. To let kids dress down this way as a form of expression allows them to grow up and become delinquents. The media shows musicians dressing like this and they encourage their followers to dress the same so all of them will look uneducated. It's ludicrous for a kid to wear his pants below his butt. A friend of mine who is a teenager told me about the belief these young males have. They want everyone to know that they are thugs from the ghetto and angry at society. Many are addicted to drugs and alcohol. They have no respect for the safety and wellbeing of others and demand to be heard. By force they will try to take whatever they want, not caring about who they hurt in the process. Most of them are impoverished and live in a single parent home supported by welfare. They don't have a good relationship with their dad, or know where he is. Here is a prime example of the effects from fatherlessness in the home.

The next weekday visit surprised me when I was able to get close enough and hand Cassie the monthly support again. We still weren't talking and like the last time, she just said thanks. It was my hope that for the sake of our child we could act more social towards each other. At home my little girl had fun doing her activities. Her lessons were becoming easier. I always did my best to teach her whatever I could. Many times she talked of how she wished her mommy and me would get back together. "Baby girl, it's not your fault that we aren't together", I told her. My youngster understood why I couldn't be with her mother. (II Corinthians 6:14-18)

In the morning I checked my mail and found a letter from Charlene. It was a notice telling me that we'd be back in court for the sixth time. Our date was set in the beginning of June. My attorney and I were seeking to force the completion of the evaluation with Dr. Watson. More than two years ago at our second court appearance this examination was ordered. We needed this to move forward with our proceedings. I wasn't sure if the mother had been notified about our scheduled hearing. Once she received the subpoena, friendliness is one trait she wouldn't have. For Amanda's benefit, I would be polite to Cassie no matter what she said to me.

Cassie called me on Monday and asked if I'd give her the support for June. She told me it was needed for Amanda's graduation at the end of the week. I had to check with my lawyer first and said I'd call her back. Charlene told me to make sure I keep a record of the payment. I called Cassie and asked her if I could attend the ceremony? She responded by saying that of the four tickets sent to her, she kept one and returned the others and she didn't have a ticket to give me. I agreed to give her the support check on Wednesday when we met at the mall to do the exchange. After we hung up I called the school. The lady said that all the tickets were sold out and she suggested I speak to Bel, the coordinator of the ceremony. Bel told me that if I came early and asked for her, she'd see to it that I got in to watch my little girl graduate.

On Friday I went to the school early and was able to get a seat in the second row. Cassie and Tina arrived just before everything got underway. I wondered how Brad's girlfriend was able to get a ticket. Cassie must have lied about keeping one ticket for her and returning the other three. After the ceremony was over I planned on taking our little one to get some pizza. We could go out or have it delivered to my place. Cassie had already made other plans. While the kids were playing, I reminded the mother that it was my weekend and that we'd be going when Amanda was ready to leave. Mommy blew a fuse when I told her this. When she heard my intentions of keeping our scheduled weekend, she became very anti social. I didn't have to be told that her mother didn't want me here at this function. As the celebration was ending my daughter introduced me to one of her classmates. He was having a birthday party on Sunday and we were invited to attend. I told Amanda that we'd go after church was over.

After breakfast on Saturday we tried to complete construction of the boat on her math CD. She was getting good at solving the mathematical problems. Although she got many of the activities correct, the boat still wasn't finished. We decided to work on it later. "Daddy, I want to play with Kristy", she told me. "I been trying to see if she could come over but her mommy always says she's doing something", I said. Ever since I told Pookie about what Frank said, after they moved she never let her daughter come over and play with Amanda. My little girl wanted to put in the art CD so she could make another picture for her mommy. We spent our evening in the usual way. Computer lessons, the quiz game, she plays with her toys, we watch videos and eat some pizza. The pepperoni, cheese, bread and sauce in the pizza that she likes contains four food groups. Slowly I'd work with her on eating different kinds of food.

Sunday started out in the usual way. Sometimes my little girl doesn't want to get up. I carry her to the living room and lay her on the couch. Shortly afterwards she's awake and then I fix her breakfast. When she's finished, all I have to do is tell her to get ready for church or else we'll be late. Then she'll go put on the outfit she wants to wear. After church we played the quiz game until it was time for the birthday party. Her friend lived nearby and we walked over to his house. Many of her classmates were there and we stayed until the evening. The parents of her little school buddy owned businesses right up the street. They invited me to stop by their shops one day during the week so our kids could play. We went home and Amanda changed into the clothes she came over in because it was time to meet her mother at the mall. As we headed to the exchange area, "I'm glad you had fun today boo", I told her. Pulling in the lot, I stopped my car. She gave me her goodbye smooch and I drove over to the entrance.

My sister Cindy was in town for a doctor's visit. The severe pains in her side needed to be diagnosed and she made several trips to the hospital. This is how Mick's illness started. She was at Tabby's house and asked me to bring Amanda over because she never met my little girl. On the last Wednesday visit of this month, I picked up my youngster at the mall. Cassie walked her over to my car. As I opened the passenger door, the mother turned and walked away. My daughter had lipstick and make-up on again. My plan was to take her over so she could meet Cindy and I knew this war paint on her face wasn't going to be appreciated by Tabby. We walked in and I introduced Amanda to the aunt she never met. When my sister saw her face, she called me to the other room. "Uh, what's she doing with make-up and lipstick on", Tabby asked? "Cassie's letting her do that", I told her. We walked back into the kitchen where Cindy and my youngster were having a good time talking. In a firm tone of voice, "who's putting lipstick and make-up on you", my sister asked? "My mommy lets me do it", she responded. "You're to young to have that junk on your face, it looks ugly because it hides your beauty", Tabby told Amanda. At first her statement made my youngster sad. It hurt her feelings. After she removed the make-up and lipstick, "there's the little girl I know and love", my sister said. Tabby's big hug made Amanda happy. She didn't want to put on makeup anymore.

On the last day in May I went to a Christian book store to look for a CD that had learning activities from the bible. They didn't have any. On my way out, some videos I saw caught my attention. I'm not one to just buy anything especially when it concerns Amanda. Looking at the package, I read the contents. "Thank you Jesus", I said quietly. Superbook bible video was the name. There were four volumes and each one had two tapes. Each tape had three stories. This is what I needed for my daughter. I bought them all. Now I had 8 tapes with 24 stories from the bible for my youngster to watch. At home I set them by the television so they'd be seen when Amanda walked in. I watched one and was very impressed with what I saw. The stories were biblically accurate enough for children. The characters referred to the bible as "Superbook".

On the first day of June I started my week with Amanda. Her mother didn't show up. When I called, my little girl answered and said her mommy wouldn't bring her to the mall. I told my daughter that I'd wait there anyway. Cassie had Donny bring my youngster to meet me. The court ordered that neither of her sons were to be present during the exchanges. It didn't matter what was written or what the judge said; this mother was going to do whatever she wanted to.

We started our Sunday in the usual manner. First breakfast, then church. After the services we came home, changed and rode the amusement rides at City Park. We returned to my place and had plenty of things to do. My youngster enjoyed watching the new Superbook videos I bought for her. In the evening we went bike riding. Early in the morning on Monday, Cassie called. Amanda gave her a call back and I heard them talking about her kitty cat. We went swimming for a long time. I made sure she had plenty of sunscreen on. The pool monitor, Mr. Black and me would always discuss scripture while we sat watching the kids. In the evening my little girl wanted to call her mommy. While they were talking, my youngster got real sad. "Daddy, can I go home and see my kitty", she asked? I didn't have to be like the mother and allowed her to go but she had to be back in 3 hours. We did the exchanges at the local carwash. When Amanda came home we ate; she watched the new videos and played her spelling game.

On Tuesday it was time for us to be in court. My little girl went to visit her aunt Tabby and I headed over to meet my attorney at her office. Charlene wasn't there and no one knew where she was. I called a few days earlier and she told me what time to be there. She never did show up so I walked over to the courthouse. Getting off of the elevator I saw her coming out of the judges chamber. We both looked around for Cassie and she wasn't here. My lawyer gave me a signed copy of the previous judgement that ordered us to have the evaluation with Dr. Watson. I was finished but the mother still had one more session to complete. Until the doctor's report was sent to us, it'd be a waste of time and money to go to court. Cassie ignored the judge's order.

In the evening I told Amanda that she needed to clean her room. "No", she said. "Well you better pick up what you want to keep and I'll throw the rest away", I told her. I wasn't going to discard anything and was trying to make her stop acting smart aleck. She was doing her lessons and asked me to join her in the spelling game. She became frustrated when she couldn't get some of the words correct. In anger she suddenly stomped on my thigh and this hurt. "That's it, we're not playing anymore", I said. Getting up, I took the disc out and turned off her computer. Her action had me upset and it was time for some discipline. In my opinion, our hands are to be used for loving and caressing. I don't believe in spanking my child with them. A parent who continues to whack his or her youngster with their hand may find the little one recoiling when it's time for a hug. I have a magazine rolled up that sits next to my microwave. This was the second time I had to spank Amanda. The first was when she deliberately lied to me. I walked in and the sight of the magazine made her start crying. A time out wasn't going to do it this time and she knew what was about to happen. Before doing anything, I told her why this action was necessary. "You're not going to tell me no or kick me anymore", I said. Twice I swatted her bottom and she wailed. The force wasn't hard. "You broke my heart", she cried. My little girl got her feelings hurt. I went out and sat on the couch to watch some television. It wasn't long until Amanda came out and apologized for what she did. She asked me to do the spelling game with her. We played until it was time for bed. She picked out her stories and said our prayers. Before we went to sleep, "baby girl, poppa loves you and I didn't like having to spank you but when I say something, you need to listen to me", I told her. "Okay daddy", she said.

Wednesday started with a trip to the zoo. We had a wonderful time. My little girl loves all the animals. Amanda and me went swimming when we returned home. Mr. Black came out to see how everyone was doing. He and I sat talking about scripture as the kids swam. At home we ate and watched her Superbook videos. Later that night while my youngster was getting her bath, "daddy what's suicide", she inquired? Shocked by her question, "Where did you hear that word", I asked? She heard her mommy and Donny talking about it. "I'll tell you what it means in a minute", I said. After drying her hair she sat down with me so I could teach her the word she had asked me about. With the dictionary I showed her how suicide means to kill oneself on purpose. "We all live on God's timetable, He says when we are to be born and when we are to die", I said. "To interfere with this in anyway is like telling God that we don't need Him and taking the life He gave us and throwing it back in His face", I told her. "Doing this will send you to hell, Christians don't kill themselves, they love God and they know He has a plan for their life", I assured. People who take their own life will one day have to answer for that. She picked her books and said our prayers. Before I was finished reading, she was sound asleep.

The next day we were at the pool again. Amanda was doing very well with her swimming. At one end it was 7 foot deep and that's where she stayed most of the time. My hard work in teaching her to swim had paid off. I never let her run around because that's how kids slip and get hurt. In the evening she wanted to call her mommy. The phone conversation was about the kitty again and my little girl wanted to go see her pet. I didn't object to this and allowed her to go for 3 hours. We met her mother at the local carwash again. She returned and spent the rest of the night playing in her room until it was time for bed. On Friday it was about the same. We were back at the pool and spent our day here at home. In the evening she continued building the boat with her Reader Rabbit math CD. She became very interested in the bible stories on her new Superbook videos. At bedtime we followed our same routine. The next day we were back at the pool. Later in the day Amanda wanted to eat some beignets so we drove over to the local café. Afterwards we strolled through the mall and then returned home. I had been telling my little girl that sooner or later she'd be sleeping in her own bed. She wanted to start tonight. To make her feel safe I put my television and VCR in her room. She said our prayers; I read her stories and put a cassette in for her to watch. This was the first time she slept in her own bed. Our Sunday started out the same way. After breakfast we went to church. As always, she had a good time. We came home and went swimming. Amanda was excited to be going to her mommy's this evening because she missed her kitty cat. We spent the rest of the day doing some activities on her computer. When it was time, we did the exchange in the usual manner.

On my weekday visit Amanda brought her kitty with her. We went to the local department store and bought some catnip for the pet. When she put in her math CD, I remained close by to help her. Even though my little girl was 6, she still didn't have a good understanding when it came to numbers. I knew if we continued to practice, she'd catch on. She became hungry and wanted the usual, pizza. As we sat eating, "hey boo, are there times when you're at home with nothing to do and wish you could come see daddy", I asked. "Yeah", she replied. "Do you ever ask mommy if you can", I inquired? "I don't do that no more, my mommy gets real mad, I'm afraid she'll slap me again", she told me. "Okay boo", I said. Hearing her say this made sick to my stomach. I picked up my plate and went to the kitchen. In silence I thought about what my little girl revealed. It was time for us to do the exchange. In the parking lot I stopped my car and said "Your daddy loves you very much and I'll never give up on you boo". When I looked at her, she was puckered up for our goodbye smooch. I brought her to the entrance of the mall where we saw her mother waiting. "I love ya boo", I said as she walked away.

The next day I found a letter from my lawyer in the mailbox. I was curious as to why she would be sending me a notice. At home I opened the envelope and saw it was a bill for $430. This news was disturbing. The last time we met at her office I paid her $1000. Twelve denials of visitation, I never get to chat with Amanda on the telephone, the mother refuses to complete her sessions with Dr. Watson or show up in court and I have to pay more money. I couldn't say anything about this debt to Charlene. She's a specialist and I needed to keep her on my side. Cassie was making a mockery of the court and my attorney. Gathering up my receipts from all these legal proceedings and adding them up came to a total of $12,050. This was the initiation expense to my ongoing custody battle. A large portion of my earnings was used to battle with Cassie for a chance to be in my daughter's life. I didn't hesitate to count my blessings. At least I got to see Amanda. The defective family court system is known for stripping many fathers of this privilege.

On Friday I called Cassie to tell her that I'd be at the mall tomorrow on Saturday, the day before the Father's Day holiday to pick Amanda up. There was no answer so I left a message. Driving by her house I saw the white convertible, Brad's car and Tina's car parked out front. This mother just didn't want to answer her phone. A for sale sign stood out by the sidewalk. My former neighbor Doris was outside her house. She's the mother of my friend Charles. She saw me and I motioned for her to come near so we could talk. Long ago she gave me some valuable advice on my situation. "Just go and build a good relationship with your little girl, don't worry, Cassie's gonna go broke because her sons always have their hand out, wanting money", Doris told me. Her intuition was precise. I asked if she saw my daughter. "Yeah, she's fine, I saw her a little while ago, you see that house is up for sale huh, I told you that would happen", she said. She also confirmed that Donny and Brad were staying there and that they all drink a lot of beer. We both agreed that this habit of theirs wasn't good for Amanda. It was worrisome to know that my child had to live with these alcoholics. I admitted to Doris that all she told me had come to pass and thanked her for the many ways she and Charles helped me.

According to the judgement from December 1999, it states that specific holiday visitations shall be from 6pm the day preceding the holiday until 6pm on the day of the holiday and that this visitation shall supercede all regularly scheduled ones. At the appointed time I waited at the exchange area. The mother didn't show up. When my waiting time expired, I called and got her answering machine. She wouldn't answer the phone so I left two messages. I talked with the police and then went back home. On the one day of the year when the father role is celebrated, Cassie refuses to show up and denies me visitation for the thirteenth time.

The wrongful actions of Cassie didn't prevent me from going to church on Sunday. Now was a time I needed to be with the congregation. When I got home there were two messages from Amanda on my cell phone. She said that her mommy was bringing her to the mall at noon and wanted to know if I'd be there to pick her up. It was almost 1pm when I got home. I called my daughter to tell her I'd be waiting. We met at the exchange area. "I'll pick her up at this time tomorrow", her mother told me. "Yeah, okay", I replied. After her mom left, my little girl and me walked into the police station to file a report. We didn't have to stay too long. The officer remembered me from yesterday when he told how they couldn't get involved in civil matters. He had no problem doing the paperwork because Cassie's actions made him upset too.

We went home to enjoy Fathers Day. Amanda was sorry that she didn't get me anything. "Yes you did", I told her. I bought a card to her and said, "this is my gift from you, all you have to do is sign it". "Thanks my daddy", she said. We tried to complete the boat on her math CD again. This task was unusually long but it was fun. In the evening we had some pizza and watched a Superbook video. When it was time for bed my little girl wanted to sleep in her own bed. "I'm a big girl", she said. I set up the television and VCR for her. She said our prayers and I read her stories. "Just call if you need me to come back", I told her. "Okay daddy", she said. I went in my room to do some calculations before I lay down. Cassie's neglect to follow orders and be on time caused Amanda to miss church. She was 19 hours late in bringing my little girl to the exchange area. Adding this to the previous, my total time lost was now 179 hours.

My daughter got up the next morning and told me she had a good dream. "You had a new new car that was red, white and blue", she said. We only had a few hours to be with each other so I suggested we either play a game or watch a video. She got her favorite Superbook video. During the exchanges, Cassie always looks friendly to Amanda. I knew my little girl was somewhat afraid of her mommy and decided to ask a little about how things were at home. As we sat on the couch I asked, "hey boo, your mommy looks happy to see you when we meet at the mall, is she still being mean to you"? "She's acting that way, at home she's mean to me", she said. We watched the video and I didn't ask her anything else. When it was time she got dressed in the clothes she came over in and we went to the mall.

Advertisements on the television warned that a former talk show host was going to be airing a show to inform youngsters that same sex parenting is normal and acceptable. Her freedom to express these views was supported by the Anti-Christian Litigation Unit. In an attempt to reach a large number of kids, she selected a children's station to broadcast this deceitfulness. The network, whose audience is mostly young kids, allowed the big celebrity to go public with her lesbian lifestyle and affirm that homosexuals can be moral parents too. If this woman wants to be gay, that's her choice. Why should our children have to know about this abnormal behavior? How does this work? Who's the man and who's the woman? What differentiates the genders? It must be confusing when a child sees two dads or two moms showing unnatural affection for each other. As kids get older they get smarter and when it's realized that what their parents are doing is wrong, they may not honor a dad or mom who perform these acts that are against the laws of nature. Because our society is increasingly accepting homosexuality as being normal, we have our youth growing up to believe that being gay is a healthy alternative lifestyle.

It wasn't easy to find NDT work. My reputation for being unreliable made it hard for me to find a job at the local inspection companies. In addition to this was the fact that our nation's economy was bad. A new department store called Palstop opened and was hiring. A grocery section was added and this attracted lots of people. My friends said that profits from retail sales of this store were the highest in our country. My many trips to this store allowed me to befriend one of the cashiers who worked here. I thought about applying for a job and asked my friend about her wages. "Does this place make a lot of money", I asked her. "Before lunch I made $11,000", she told me. The lady at the register next to her said she pulled in $24,000 before lunch. I was stunned at these amounts. "How much are you getting paid, if you don't mind me asking", I inquired? "I get $6.50 an hour", she replied. "Me too", the other lady said. Both agreed that this was not the best place to work but they needed the money. The "stop at Palstop where everyone's your Pal" motto forces them to wear a "can I assist you" sign on their back. Both these ladies told me how they're on their feet all day, except for lunch and if they work over 40 hours a week, they get in trouble. "You gotta be kidding me", I exclaimed. After leaving I thought about what they said. These ladies had no reason to lie. The owners of Palstop were greedy money pigs. This big nationwide chain is extremely wealthy, selfish and unfair to their employees. I don't have to be a Harvey Scholar to know the reason why our economy's so bad is because no one has enough money to spend. In cities where the cost of living is high, the starting wages ought to be $9.95 an hour with overtime hours also. I think that might give younger people an incentive to find a job and work. Wouldn't higher wages give someone more of the money that's needed to restore this economy of ours that's hurting?

As I continued looking for a job, a miracle happened. The next day I received a phone call from the vice president of NXP. Dan had a 10-day job here in Louisiana starting in one week. An airplane factory called Northern Grumbler in River Charles needed inspection on an aircraft and he wanted to know if I was interested. "Yeah, I want the job", I told him. We talked a little bit about what was going on with me. "You getting to see your daughter", he asked? "Yeah, only when it's scheduled by the judgement", I said. When I told of how Cassie didn't show up for court and that she almost denied me visitation on Fathers Day, Dan was amazed that she wasn't put in jail. "How does she get away with doing this", he asked? "It's the faulty family court system, she's the mother and I can't afford my attorney to go to court with", I told him.

Just before my weekday visit was to begin, Cassie called and asked me to meet them at the carwash. I talked with Amanda and she asked, "Can my kitty come over"? "Sure boo", I said. We went to the local store to buy some food for her pet. At home we played her spelling game. She wanted me to put on a puppet show while we waited for our pizza. As we were eating I put in one of her Superbook videos. Her favorites were David and Goliath, Jonah and the whale, and Moses. Our time together on this visit goes by quickly. Even if Amanda wanted to stay here, we both knew what the answer would be if we asked Cassie. The way this mother scared her little girl from asking to spend more time with me, her father, was inhuman.

At noon on Friday I saw Cassie at the grocery with Amanda. My youngster asked if she could stay home this weekend. Mommy was going to take her to a water park. Because of my job with NXP, this would be the last time I'd get to see my little girl until I came back. I told her no and said that we had too many things to do. Using the tone of voice so her mother could hear me I said, "I'll be picking you up at the mall this evening". This mother knew it was my weekend but made plans with our daughter anyway. Cassie continued to do anything she could to disrupt my relationship with Amanda. Her mother ignored the fact that she's my child too.

In the evening when we met at the exchange area, my little girl had forgotten about what happened earlier today at the store. The pool was still open and she wanted to go for a swim. Afterwards we played the quiz game and I ordered us a pizza. Amanda usually selected the cartoons she wanted to watch and lately she picked her Superbook videos. Her interest in these stories from the bible was growing. I assured her that all they told about could be found in the Word of God. I was thankful that she was learning this and saying our prayers by herself.

Saturday morning after breakfast I told my little girl that we were going to the zoo today. It was hot and I knew that we wouldn't stay there too long. The high temperatures and humidity were conditions both of us didn't like too much. Cassie loved to bake her skin in the sun but Amanda and me were just the opposite. We preferred the air-conditioning. We stayed at the zoo for a few hours and then came home to swim. This was a good way for us to cool off. A while later we played the quiz game. She did activities with her art CD. "Here daddy, I made you this", she said handing me a picture. "This is beautiful baby girl, let me see, where should I put it", I questioned? With a piece of tape, I hung it in my room. All around our place, on the walls in my room and hers, and held on my refrigerator with magnets is her artwork. These remind me of my little angel and they show us how creative she can be. After her bath we both had a bowl of ice cream. Our night ended with prayers and bedtime stories.

In the morning we prepared for church. On our way home after the services I asked my little girl what she wanted to do today. She didn't answer. "Want me to see if Diana can go to City Park", I asked? With excitement, "yeah, thanks daddy", she replied. I called Pam and she said that her daughter could come with us. We got ourselves ready and headed across the river to the park. It's better when my little girl has a friend to go with us. That way I don't have to get on all these rides that can make my back sore. In the evening we came home and the girls played. When it was time to go, Amanda switched into the clothes she came over in. We dropped Diana off at her house and headed to the mall to meet Cassie. At the exchange area I saw her mother was very intoxicated. She's driving drunk again with our daughter in the car.

It was close to bedtime for me when the phone rang. My caller ID showed it was Cassie. It scared me to think why she'd be calling so late. Our conversation began with her telling me that I could have domiciliary custody of Amanda. "Isn't that what you want, isn't that why you keep taking me to court", she asked? This mother sounded inebriated. I tried explaining to her that all I wanted was to have more time with my little girl. "If you're serious, I'll call Charlene in the morning and she'll get all the paperwork ready", I told her. It was my hope that Cassie was being honest in her decision to do this. "Do you have Amanda registered in school yet", I asked? "Yeah, she's registered", her mother replied. "Where do you have her registered at" I inquired? "Don't worry, she's registered, why do you want to know", she asked? "Because she's my daughter too and I want to know", I answered. "Well you should treat her like your daughter and not your concubine", Cassie snarled. "What are you talking about", I exclaimed? Her remark riled me. Now I knew this mother was drunk. Had I kept talking, questions about why our little girl was left in the care of Moe and that abusive babysitter would have come out. To prevent Amanda from getting hurt or in trouble, I didn't ask her mother anything about the environment at that place. The best part of this conversation was when she hung up on me.

On Monday I called Top of the Hill Academy to find out if Amanda was registered there. The first grade classes were full and her name wasn't on their list. I was hoping to find a private school for my little girl to attend. The teachers at the public schools here don't take too much of an interest in the children. Many of them are just there to collect a check. Not far from where I lived was Perrytown Academy and they had four openings left. The woman I spoke with urged me to come by and fill out the paperwork to reserve a spot for Amanda. I had to pay the required, non-refundable $350 registration fee. Doing as she told me, I got in my car and drove over. Walking in, I introduced myself to an obese woman. "Hi, I'm Rhonda, I talked to you on the phone", she said. I brought copies of Amanda's birth certificate and her shot records so the school would have them on file. As I filled out the paperwork, this large lady had to go to the back for some reason. She had a tough time just getting out of her chair. I'm thankful that I never had a weight problem. It'd be impossible to do my job. I couldn't do the climbing or carry the equipment with all those extra pounds. My work combined with a theory I have helps me stay fit. If my tires are full, I'm not going to keep pumping in air until they blow up. This illustration works great when I substitute my stomach for the tires and food for the air. Rhonda came back in and sat down. "Ah, that felt better", she said. It was my guess that she had to go to the bathroom. The application for enrollment was filled out and I went back home.

The job with NXP in River Charles started on my last weekday visit of this month. I phoned Cassie the day before to inform her that I'd be out of town and my visits would resume when I returned. Of course she didn't answer so I left a message on her answering machine. While I was packing she called me. This chat started with her reneging on the offer she made the other night about giving me domiciliary custody. "I'll never let you have my daughter, I just said that because I was angry", she told me. Sounded to me like she was drunk again. She insisted that I forfeit this job and keep my visitation tomorrow because there was something she needed to do. I offered to make arrangements for her neighbor Jasmine to baby sit. She was enraged with that idea. Due to the tone of her voice, I refused to continue our conversation. She was insistent on arguing with me. At this time I had been out of work for 3 months. If I did what she ordered me to do and gave up this assignment, I'd lose my apartment, my car, and everything I have.

The job commenced in the usual way. Orientation, scope of the project and everyone is told what their duties will be. We worked in a large hangar that had 4 aircraft in it. On the first day we set up our equipment and Don helped us get familiar with the test methods we'd be using. The engineers selected the various locations on the plane they wanted us to inspect. They knew all the areas that were under the most stress. On the second day we started our inspections. A representative from Northern, Tim reviewed all the film to make sure it had what they needed to see. After he finished looking at our x-rays, it went to the inspectors for final acceptance.

A local television station began broadcasting a court issue that was circulating all across our nation. An atheist was seeking to remove God from the pledge of allegiance. It was frightening to see that by twisting the laws around in the constitution, how one man could erase Him from the minds and hearts of our children. This unbeliever wasn't there in 1789 when our founding fathers wrote these laws. For him to attack the schools where young children with undeveloped minds attend sounds like he's doing the work of Satan. This man's action planted a seed in the unbelieving minds of many further causing them to think that we don't need God. This is what happens when we reject the conservative judges and swear in the liberal ones. The reporter went on to talk of how our country was coping with the terrorist attacks. A replay of when members of congress were on some steps singing "God bless America", was shown. They boldly ask for blessings but refuse to change their ways. As I watched some of those responsible for allowing the worst sins in our country to persist, sing this song, in my mind, the words had changed to "God have mercy on America". For killing millions of our babies before You have the chance to breath the breathe of life in them, for expelling You from the schools of our children and the parents who hide You from the hearts of their young, "God have mercy on America". It's easy to see what happens when we let the wicked politicians govern our country? (Proverbs 29:2)

Work went on as usual. Dray and me were on the dayshift and Hosea and Darren were on the nightshift. I never inspected an airplane before and began to make plenty of mistakes. Don would tell me not to worry about it. He knew I was trying. It was humiliating to have over 20 years experience and not be able to turn in acceptable film. The wing of an airplane has many configurations inside that interfere with the direct passage of x-rays. The needed accuracy in this test method was time consuming. If you're measurement is off by a half-inch, the shot won't come out and you have to do it all over again. This project was a learning experience.

The 12-hour shift we worked wasn't leaving much time to do anything else. It was unusual to have Dan on this job with us. Normally the vice president stays in the office. I found out that he and Don had much confidence in my work performance but it wasn't them I had to satisfy, it was the representative from Northern. We were making progress in completing many of the inspections and the inspectors appreciated this. The engineers divided the aircraft into sections. After we x-rayed one portion, Don, Dan and Tim would discuss where we were to go next. I liked talking with Tim because he was the assistant pastor of a small church and he knew a lot about the Word of God. On Independence Day I tried to call Amanda. Just like always, I got the machine. Since this job began I called everyday and

Cassie wouldn't let my little girl answer the phone so we could talk. I was thankful that this job would only last 10 days.

On the eighth day my supervisor asked me to pick up the pace a bit because we were falling behind on our schedule. This was not our fault. Don told Dray and me how the night shift was having numerous problems resulting in their film being unsatisfactory. My co-worker knew the nightshift would have trouble. This turned out to be a long day. When we finished, there wasn't too much left to do. Tim was happy with our work and it looked like the project was going to be completed on time. The film processor, Wally invited all us workers to a party at the pool. In the evening we gathered for a celebration. We had a barbecue and some beer. I didn't want to drink because I know how the booze affects me. Rather than offend my friends, I had a few with them. After everyone ate, we sat and talked for a good while. It wasn't too long before I got tired and decided to call it a night. "I'll see yall in the morning", I told them.

On Saturday we arrived to find that there was plenty left to do. We had to be finished today. Our company depended on us to complete all the inspections. By this time I had developed a way to target the areas I needed to x-ray. The end of our shift was near when Don came out to ask Dray and me if we'd stay late to meet the deadline. We ended up working18 hours. I was surprised when my supervisor came out to talk with me, saying, "you did a great job, Tim said your film was the best that he's ever seen". X-ray companies where I used to work usually didn't compliment me. Here at NXP, if you did a good job, they recognized you for it. That bit of appreciation will go a long way. I liked working with Don because he's smart and gives good advice. I value my friendship with Dan because he didn't know me too well, but still loaned me the money to buy my car. When times were rough for me, it was Hosea, Dray and Darren who said that Cassie was a real witch and I didn't deserve what she was doing to me.

The next day everything was packed up and ready to move out. Everyone helped to clean our work area. The trash had to be picked up and the equipment stored for transport. Don and Wally had major disagreements about how to tow the trailer. Their argument was amusing to all of us. After finishing, we all went back to the motel. I was at the pool when Darren came out to get some sun. "Where's Hosea", I asked. "Sheena made him leave, they're already on their way home to Houston", he told me. A short while later Dray came out and joined us. They began to tell me the trouble Hosea has with Sheena. She doesn't want to work or stay at home and watch their two boys. He put his name on the dotted line and sunk himself deep in debt with those vehicles they drive. Hosea doesn't like to discipline his kids because he wants them to like him. Sheena has no control over the boys. She threatens that if Hosea don't do as she says, then she'll divorce him and leave with his children. "Ya know, I remember hearing her say that she'd get a divorce", I said. All of us felt bad for Hosea and the trap that he was in. Here was another example of how a woman will use the children to crush and drain a man for all he has. I haven't heard stories where dad uses the kids to hurt mom, but I'm sure they exist.

In the middle of the month my week with Amanda began. We did our exchange at the local carwash. When I picked up my youngster, Cassie told me that her house was sold and Amanda was registered at a school across the river. She wouldn't tell me where. The mother urged me to withdraw her enrollment at Perrytown Academy. I did as her mommy suggested and drove over to inform the school of this change. It was my hope that Rhonda would understand and give me back the registration fee I paid. By telling them now, they'd have a month to fill the vacancy. "No, we can't, it said on the paper you signed that it's non-refundable", she told me. "Well, my daughter won't be going here so I'll have to cancel the check", I said. As we were leaving, "I didn't like this school anyway", Amanda told me. The large lady intimidated my little girl. I expected to get a summons from the Justice of the Peace to appear in small claims court for canceling my payment. That $350 was enough to buy Rhonda groceries for a week.

In the evening Amanda asked if her friend Diana could come swimming with us. I called Pam and asked for permission. When we drove over to pick up her buddy, my little girl was afraid to get out of the car because she didn't want her mommy next door to see her. After the kids were finished and the pool closed, we walked down to the nearby playground. The many mosquitoes were very thirsty. These bugs didn't bother the kids too much but they were eating me alive. Before bringing her pal back home we made plans for tomorrow. Our evening ended with the usual activities. My little girl made some more pictures for me to hang on my wall. I love it when she brings something to me. "Here my daddy, I made this for you", she says. As I look at her, I see my eyes looking back at me. Remembering this helps me when I'm far from home. When it was time for bed, Amanda picked her stories, said our prayers and we lay down.

About noon the next day we all went to the aquarium. This air-conditioned environment lets us stay out of the exhausting heat and humidity down here in the south. Amanda had been here before and acted like a tour guide for Diana. Both were amazed at the water dwelling creatures. In the gift shop we saw these little battery operated fans that lit up when you turned them on. They made a good souvenir so we each had to have one. Cassie called so I gave my cell phone to Amanda so they could talk. This place has plenty of exhibits to look at and mostly what we do is walk around until we're tired. We had been here for a long time when the girls asked if they could go home for a swim. Mr. Black and me had our usual scripture discussion while the youngsters played in the pool. At home I suggested that my little girl call her mom. Her mother didn't answer. The time came for us to bring her little friend home. Amanda wasn't happy about this. I told her Diana could come back tomorrow. When we returned it was time for her bath. Afterwards we did a few lessons; she picked her books, said our prayers and we lay down.

My youngster decided she wanted to stay home today. She gave Diana my phone number and told her to call when she was ready to come back over. Her buddy never did call. We went to the mall for some beignets. Afterwards we walked to a nearby toy store. I saw a small stereo with a microphone called a kareoke system. This would be good for our puppet theatre. When we got home I installed the unit and made sure it worked. The next day we took turns doing some puppet shows. We had fun. A decoration of mine that sits on a table in my living room is a tic tac toe game that came from Mick's place. My youngster sees it all the time and asked me what it was. The thought of playing never crossed my mind. I told her about it and showed her how to play. We sat down and played for a long while until it got late and time for bed.

On Saturday we decided to go swimming. Amanda didn't want to put on any sunscreen. "If you don't wear any of this, we can't go to the pool", I told her. She met a little girl named Ann and invited her to come over and play. I knew this child's mother. These two made her room look like a hurricane hit it. In the evening when it was time for her pal to go home, I told them they needed to clean up that room. They both worked together picking up all the toys and when they finished, I went in to see how well they did. Everything was straightened out and looked good enough to me. When Amanda has a job or small task like this to do, I look for progress in her work, not perfection. As a reward, I gave them both a treat. On Sunday we went to church and spent our day at home. She made another picture for me to hang on the wall. If we weren't doing computer lessons, a puppet show, eating pizza or watching a video, we were busy doing something else. In the evening we rode our bikes. I always tried my best to create warm and cheerful memories for her. She enjoyed everything we did. Monday was about the same but on Tuesday we were in her room and Amanda told how Clifford still smelled clean. "Daddy did a good job cleaning him up huh boo"? That's when she told me, "Daddy, I put the hair gel on him". We talked a little about this. The truth of the matter was Cassie knew what our little one was doing to the toy and did nothing to stop her. "That's okay boo, he's clean now", I told her. I wasn't upset at all. It was still early in the day so I decided to take her to the zoo. Afterwards we went swimming and spent our evening in the usual way. The next day she wanted to go home early because she missed her kitty cat. We called Cassie and met her at the carwash.

On Monday I received an unexpected call from my little girl. Her mother was in the shower and she wanted to chat for a bit. "If my mommy comes out I'll have to hang up real fast, okay daddy", she warned. I was happy to hear from my daughter but I didn't want her to get in any trouble. There was no way of knowing what Cassie would do to Amanda if she were caught on the phone talking with me. I remembered my conversation with the babysitter about the way this mother treated our child. "We better get off the phone boo, I'll see you soon, okay", I asked? "Okay daddy", she replied. "I love you", I told her. "I love you too", she responded.

My youngster wanted to go swimming so I picked her up early on Wednesday. Her mom sent her over with a small purse that had her swimsuit in it. Amanda came out wearing a bikini. "That's not gonna work, go back into your room and put on one of the bathing suits that poppa bought for you", I demanded. "Why, my mommy lets me wear this at home", she asked? "Well I'm not your mommy and if you want to go swimming, you need to go change", I told her. Reluctantly, she went to her room and came out in a one piece. "That's good boo, your skin will be better protected", I said. At the pool I talked with Mr. Black about what happened at my place. He agreed with my decision to make Amanda change suits. "If you don't preserve her now, when she gets older she'll think it's okay to wear string bikinis and skimpy outfits", he said. "Her mother sunbathes in the backyard in a bikini and she wore scanty dresses when she went to work", I told him. "Then that's who she's learning from", said Mr. Black. My little one got out the pool and was ready to go. She was hungry after her swim and asked me to order a pizza. We sat down to eat and watch a Superbook video. Shortly afterwards we had to meet her mother. After getting dressed in the clothes she came over in, we drove to the mall.

My decision to make Amanda change her swimwear ran through my mind. Had I given in, when she's older the consequences from my absence of having a backbone may have become more visible. Out in the public eye you'll see females today who dress like they've escaped from Cleavage County or were born on Buttock Bayou. There isn't a worldly woman alive that tells the retailer, "I'd like to buy an outfit I can wear so no one will look or stare at me". Some women want to be noticed even if it means giving up their dignity by wearing something that'll reveal as much of their flesh that the law will allow. These females love to wear anything that will expose every curve, nook and cranny on their body. What a turn on for her when she can attract the eyes of several men just by walking in a room. Having big boobs is a plus because she thinks they'll give her the power needed to subdue him. Inside, her heart's wicked. Sometimes her looks are all she has. Worldly females are lewdly intelligent, cunning and know exactly what they're doing when it comes to alluring men sexually. It's vitally important to keep in mind that beauty is only skin deep. If a woman really loves her man, she won't put herself on display for men to gloat at. What I have to accept is that there's no guarantee that my little girl won't be like this. If I give up on her and don't teach what God expects; chances are great that she'll be pulled into a society that teaches sexual promiscuity is the only way to have one's desires fulfilled. I can't wrestle against these powers when I'm not able to recognize them. (Ephesians 6:12)

The month of August started with a weekend for us. We came home and went directly to the pool. I was hoping to see the monitor but he didn't come out. When my youngster had enough of swimming, it was time to go. At home we continued doing construction on the boat with her math CD. She was close to being finished. "Daddy, I'm hungry, can we order a pizza", she asked? "Okay boo but later on you will eat something else", I told her. We ate and watched one of her cartoon videos. She was tired from her swim and asked to go to bed. Picking her books, I said our prayers and started reading. After I read one book, she was asleep.

Saturday was our day to be homebodies. Amanda didn't want to go anywhere. We played plenty games of tic tac toe. When we started, I won some of the games but in the end, she won most of them. In the evening she wanted to ride her bike so we went down by the playground. She likes to play down here. At home I put on a puppet show for her. After her bath she picked a Storybook video and we had some ice cream. She was learning much from the bible stories. It's important that I help her stay interested in the Word and teach all I can. Outside there are many bands of musicians seeking to poison the minds of our children. I refuse to unleash my little girl into a world where the contents of some music or its suggestive lyrics are used to destroy every moral fiber of our kids.

Our Sunday started with breakfast and church. Yesterday we didn't work on the boat and I urged her to put the CD in. We only had about 5 pieces left to get and it would be complete. I stayed with her until she got warmed up and knew what she was doing. I was fixing me some coffee when Amanda screamed, "daddy come see". Dropping my spoon, I ran in her room. On the water I saw the rabbit and the lion sailing in the boat. She accomplished her task and built the boat. "Good girl, I'm so proud of you", I told her. My little girl was very happy. I gave her two treats for her hard work. There were some CDs that she didn't play anymore and I asked if she wanted to bring them to her mommy's house? "No, I want to keep them here, at my mom's I have games, here I have learning stuff", she told me. "Does your mom teach you anything" I inquired? "Yeah sometimes, but you're a better teacher, you teach me real good", Amanda told me. I'm thorough when it comes to showing my little girl something. When she said that I was better than her mother was, this remark revealed how different Cassie and me are towards the education of our daughter. I never pass up an opportunity to teach Amanda something that will further her learning capacity. Her mother relied on entertainment and games.

On the Tuesday before my second weekday visit, Cassie called to say that the sale on her house didn't go through. "Can you get her back in Perrytown", she asked? It was too late; I had already cancelled the enrollment fee. Here is where the lack of communication hurts a couple when it comes to the welfare of their child. Our little girl would have to attend the school that was around the corner from her mother's house. I wasn't too happy about her getting a public education but this facility was close, convenient and free. Whatever the teachers didn't teach my youngster, at my place I would try to educate her with all the CDs she has. It was my job to help her learn about God and Jesus because it's against the law in our country for public schools to teach this.

On the morning of my weekend I met with Charlene. Our judgements from all the previous appearances were lacking. I felt there was too much secrecy on Cassie's behalf. If possible, I wanted to have full joint custody. This would entitle me to be more informed about the issues concerning my daughter. My attorney told me that the evaluation would become an obstacle because it wasn't completed. She wrote down some notes and asked me to call her later next week. In the evening we met at the carwash. We went home and spent our time playing tic tac toe, eating pizza while watching bible videos and doing puppet shows. When it got late, my little girl picked her stories, said our prayers, we lay down and she was fast asleep.

Saturday was spent doing activities around the house. In the evening we walked around the apartment complex to get some fresh air. "Do you want to go swimming boo", I asked? "No, that's okay", she answered. We spoke with Mr. Black for a while and headed back to my place. After many games of tic tac toe, it was time for pizza and a video. She wanted to play her math CD again and had trouble getting some of the answers correct. After you build a boat, the game continues onto the next level, which is much harder. I reset the controls and that made it easier for her. We had a bowl of ice cream and watched a video she hadn't seen in a long time. Soon it was time for her bath. After drying her hair, my little girl asked for some water. She liked the water out the Brita pitcher. It's filters out the deadly sediments that can get trapped inside my body. "I like the way this water taste", she told me. "Hey boo does mommy still have the filter on her faucet at home in the kitchen", I asked? "No, she don't, I don't like the way her water taste", she answered. I asked if she wanted me to get her a pitcher like mine. She wanted one but was afraid her mommy wouldn't let her use it. Right away I remembered the rusted pipes I saw in that house when I installed the flex hose and valves after Cassie and me moved in. It worried me to know that my little girl was drinking rusty water out the faucets where she lived.

In the morning we prepared for church. We returned home to do some activities and hang around the house. I was out of milk so we took a ride to the grocery. After gathering all that I needed, we headed to the front. While we waited in line, I looked at the magazines. Tabloids are great. They can either build a person up or tear a person down. Making a trip to the grocery store lets me see latest propaganda distributed. While at the check out counter, I had a look at the latest news. The young misguided prancer was caught where she wasn't supposed to be and her lesbian lifestyle was exposed. The big celebrity's pregnant lesbian girlfriend has moved away, leaving the large woman heartbroken. A famous Latino diva was divorced after being married for one year. I remember this singer saying her love don't cost anything. If she marries only to get divorced a year later, her love isn't worth anything either. In the lower left hand corner was a story about the woman who lived in a big white house. Some people say she was known as the first lesbian with a husband that serviced the female interns. I remembered her spouse denying that he dishonored their wedding vows on national television. While waiting to pay for my items, I decided to read this article. Rumor has it that if she gets the popular vote; she'll be the leader of a great nation. Then she can give all the girlfriends in her party a job and turn her white house back into a cathouse. We can look forward to same sex marriages being legal. Since homosexuals can't produce children, she'll make it easier for lesbians and gay men to get their own child to destroy. Because homosexuals are handicapped in the child conception process, she'll give them privileges superior to those of heterosexual couples. Teenagers won't need to have parental consent to have an abortion. The meaning of Civil Liberties means to act as one likes without hindrance. If elected, the first lesbian will be given the chance to prepare a stage for massive ungodliness thereby paving the way for moral destruction and damnation of our children, teenagers and young adults. How long will God protect a country that kills their babies, allows homosexuality to flourish, and has people who live in complete disregard of the commands He gave us? Catastrophic events might be His warnings to change our ways?

In the evening my little girl wanted to go home early so she could see her kitty. "Let me tell you something, I don't get to see you too often and now that you're here, you want to go home, after you do some lessons, we'll call your mommy", I told her. I wanted her to do activities on her math, science and reading CDs. "I think you can to this, wanna know why", I challenged? "Why daddy", she asked? "Because you're smart", I told her. This sounded like a fair deal to her but it was a method of distraction to me. If she'd get interested in her lessons, she'd forget about going home early. Time went by quickly. Completing the activities on the three subjects, she put her CDs away, shut off her computer and we left to meet her mother at the carwash.

On the day before our weekday together, Amanda called to tell me that the dog next door killed her kitty. "Aw boo, daddy's sorry to hear that, you okay", I asked? "Yeah, I'm okay," she said. She told me that she already got another kitty cat and just wanted to call and tell me what that dog did to her other one. She didn't want to stay on the phone. In the background I heard her mother saying something. I told her that we'd see each other tomorrow.

Before our weekday visit, I called Pam to ask if Diana could come over and go swimming with Amanda. She wasn't there and Jade answered. We talked for a little bit and she told me about taking my little girl to get another cat. I asked how her daughter was and if she had been able to see her father lately. "Yeah, but I don't go see him anymore", she said. She went on to say that her dad would come pick her up and they'd go by his friend's house. While there, he'd drink continuously. Watching him get drunk was about the extent of their visit. Long ago she told me of her wish to have a good relationship with her dad and now she saw firsthand what kind of man he was. Instead of being sober, he chose to drink. This was a huge letdown for her. Pam was trying to save Jade from seeing what kind of a person her father was. The alcohol abuse that she witnesses may cause her to become a drinker, in an attempt to ease the pain. In my younger days I saw my folks getting smashed lots of times. In my older years, I thought it was acceptable to do this. I chose friends that were getting high and drinking. Looking back I can see how I followed in the footsteps of my parents and became an addict and an alcoholic.

In the evening at the carwash I picked up Amanda and Diana. We went home and directly to the pool. I sat with Mr. Black and talked about scripture and we discussed the remarkable job that President Bush was doing in our country. “The democratic liberals are very mad, they want him out of office”, my friend told me. “Why is that”, I asked? “Because he’s a Christian and the liberals hate Christians”, said Mr. Black. This made sense to me. Democrats strongly support civil liberties in a media that’s damaging and destroying the minds and hearts of many people, both young and old. We chatted a little more until the girls were ready to get out. “Can we order a pizza”, my youngster asked? We said goodbye to the monitor and went home so I could get them something to eat. After eating they played with toys. My little girl was getting upset with what her pal said to her. We talked about what they were saying. Diana repeated the hateful things that she learned from her sister Jasmine. I asked her to stop acting mean and said they should be nice to each other. Shortly after this we went to meet Cassie at the carwash.

My next weekday visit arrived and we met at the carwash. “Hi my daddy”, Amanda said. “Hi boo, how ya doing”, I asked? She brought her new kitty with her this time. It was a brown striped cat, different from the black one she had. We went home and right away she asked for some pizza. I ordered one for us and we sat down to eat. We watched a bible video and talked. After we were finished eating she wanted to play tic tac toe. “You like this game huh boo”, I asked her? “Yeah, it’s fun”, she answered. She wanted to do a puppet show first and then I had to do one. After this we did a few short lessons on her computer and then it was time to go. At the corner by the stop sign, I’d stop my car, she’d give me a goodbye smooch and then I’d turn to go meet Cassie at the carwash. “I love ya boo” I’d tell her before turning to walk away.

On the weekend my little girl called to ask if I’d pick her up at the carwash and could Diana come over so they could to swimming? “Sure boo”, I told her. The girls came over and we all went to the pool. At sundown her little buddy wasn’t ready to go home so she called her mom. Pam gave permission for her to spend the night. The kids had fun playing with the toys and eating pizza. It was getting late and I told them to straighten up that room a little bit because they’d be going to bed soon. "Yall need to get some sleep because we're going to City Park tomorrow", I said. I set my television and VCR in her room for them and they climbed in bed.

The cloudiness on Saturday had cleared up in the afternoon and we headed across the river. It was good that Diana came with us because that meant I didn't have to get on any of the rides. All the kids who have come here with Amanda love this park. The youngsters used up a lot of energy going from ride to ride. Not long after we rode the train around the park they wanted to leave. With all the heat, it was time for a swim. At home they ate pizza and watched videos. Later it was time to take Diana over to her house. When we came back, Amanda had a bath and asked me to do some spelling activities with her. As we played the game, "daddy, my mommy wants me to be a catholic", she said. "That's okay, when you get older daddy will show you why he doesn't want to go to that church anymore", I told her. Cassie knows how I feel about Catholicism and obviously told our daughter this hoping to annoy me. Early in our relationship her mother told me how she hated the catholic religion and claimed that several members of this church looked on while Donny and Brad's father beat her. The bystanders didn't intervene. I have nothing against those who follow the religion of my youth. There are many good people with high morals who are catholic. I'm not comfortable with their formalities and the repetitious practices. Because Christianity teaches the truth that sets me free, I choose to be a Christian.

In my youth us kids were obedient to our parents. We may have disagreed with much but still followed their instruction. I value most of the things my parents taught me. In my early thirties I began listening to a Christian radio station over 400 miles away. That impelled me to take a closer look at the religion I was brought up in. I discovered many contradictions. My research resulted in making a life changing decision. I made a thorough search in the Word of God and wasn't able to find the word purgatory. I don't remember anyone bringing his or her bible to church but my dad always brought his checkbook. As children, our folks insisted we give reverence to the priest and call him father. (Matthew 23:9) Growing up, momma would often encourage us to say the rosary. (Matthew 6:7) Before we could have communion we had to go to confession. This is when I entered a telephone booth type structure to confess my sins to the priest in the window. After telling him all that I did, for absolution he would administer his penance for me to say. The seriousness of my sin determined the length of my penance. If I wasn't too bad, he only gave me a few prayers to say. If I was very bad, I had plenty to say. I now look at this to be like putting a price on sin. I don't believe in paying homage to images that resemble the servants of God because that seems like statue worship to me. There's no way I can say that I am without sin. (Romans 3:23) There's only One to whom I confess my sins. (I John 1:7-10) The bible reveals who has the power to forgive sins. (Luke 5:24) Momma worshipped the pope. I've seen leaders of the world kiss the pontiff's hand. Some people may consider him to be God's representative here on earth. There's only one mediator between God and man. (I Timothy 2:5) It's important for me to know how I must worship God. (John 4:24) Because I know what the word once means, I can't believe in reincarnation. (Hebrews 9:27) I firmly believe that hell does exist and is hot with flames. (Luke 16:19-31) I need to know how I am to receive the Kingdom of God. (Luke 18:16-17) I am a grown man but to God, I am a little child. This is why I refer to myself as one of his children. At the time Revelations was written, I believe "that great city" is Rome. (Revelation 17:18) Catholicism is too liberal and here are just some of the reasons I choose to separate myself from this organized religion.

It's very difficult being a Christian. To many we are an outcast. While the world screams tolerance, we preach intolerance of false religions, homosexuality, abortion and all the other sins that erase the morality from our country. God fearing Christians, who are steadfast in their faith, are very much aware that when his or her time on earth is over, they will have to answer for the way they lived their life here. Mindful of the consequences for living in unrighteousness causes us to live an upright lifestyle. In faith we plant ourselves in the undefiled truth from the Word of God. To Christians, our textbook of life is called the bible. We attach ourselves to this text and rely on it for instruction, guidance and correction. In addition to this it teaches us how to live, love and grow. Our pastors aren't held to celibacy. We don't worry about our leaders molesting the children of the congregation. Knowing that we are despised by many, I decided to find out why. For Christians, most marriages don't end up in divorce court. Kids grow up to honor their parents. Most teenagers remain pure, dislike boisterous music and are less likely to run away from home. People learn how they should treat each other respectfully. Chemical addictions, abortion and homosexuality can't exist. Prophecies have come to pass. There's so much that the Word of God teaches. Many of those who oppose Christianity claim that a man wrote the bible. Why would a man write a book to condemn himself with? (II Timothy 3:14-17 & II Peter 1:20-21)

Sunday started with church for us. At home Amanda turned on her computer and put the art CD in so she could make a picture for her mommy. I did a puppet show for her while we waited for our pizza. In the evening she wanted to ride her bike and asked me to take the training wheels off. "Are you sure", I asked? "Yeah my daddy, I'm sure", she said. Doing as she requested, I was surprised to see that she could ride without them. "That's great baby girl, you're doing good", I told her. My little girl was growing up. We rode around until she got tired. After we came home she asked, "daddy, am I going home tonight"? "No, tomorrow is our holiday, and you go home in the evening", I said. She missed her kitty cat and wanted to go see her pet. I decided to let her go but she had to come back in a few hours. She called later to say that her tummy was hurting and asked to stay at her mommy's. I told her no. At night after we said our prayers Amanda told how her mother made her call and say she was sick. Cassie wanted her to stay over there.

On Monday we spent our holiday at home. Amanda had some lessons to do and I set them out for her. Math, science and reading were the subjects. "You can do this too, I think you can because you're smart", I told her. Afterwards she could go home early to see her kitty. She never did ask to go home. She had fun dancing to Zoe Girl. I'm glad she likes Christian music. These songs are powerful weapons in exposing the evils within a person. I've always known this to happen and saw it in Florida. If I had Christian music on, no one liked to hear songs about Jesus and they often changed the station or turned it down. Both Clam and Link would say, "I can't listen to that". Most secular music of today promotes rebellion, disobedience and irreverence. A very successful way to destroy a society is through its mind with barbaric music. I hear some of the music from my youth but I prefer listening to Christian music. (Matthew 12:30)

Parents, regardless of what they choose to do must realize that when they use a courtroom to settle personal issues, their children, in one way or another always end up getting hurt. To use kids in a tug of war between daddy and mommy creates irreparable emotional, psychological or spiritual damage. Whether it's monetary matters or custody reasons, with a determination to win, dad and mom fail to realize their youngsters have hearts too. Most of the time their little feelings are never considered. When everything is said and done, the judge will make the final decision. The parents are held to the judgement like a ball and chain. The young children grow up confused and end up feeling responsible. These engraved memories will haunt them forever. Jesus himself told what would be better for those who offend the little ones. (Matthew 18:3-6)

It has been a year since terrorists murdered thousands of people in New York. Our churches are no longer full. My life, like the lives of many is forever changed. Most people recognize the false religions that have invaded our country. The murderers were identified as Moslems and their belief is identical to that of Islam. The King James Version of the bible does not say that Allah or Mohammed even existed. In 1620, breaking the chains of tyranny, people known as the separatists boarded a ship and set off for a distant land in search of freedom. These 102 passengers were known as pilgrims, and today we celebrate a holiday in their honor called Thanksgiving. Due to the behavior of an unruly bunch onboard the boat, they saw the need for some sort of government. To ensure that the mutinous talk amongst a group of the voyagers would not progress, the men decided and agreed to compose a historical document called the "Mayflower Compact". In this writing you will see fundamentals for the formation of America and the true reason for their voyage. In the name of God, by the grace of God, for the glory of God, and advancement of the Christian faith was their cause. Because the word "faith" is used here, could that mean, like the separatist, Christians separate themselves from all the organized religions? Not too many young adults, teenagers or preteens have read this transcript or know that it exists. The liberals are doing all they can to erase the American Heritage from the hearts and minds of people here in the United States of America. Even if I wasn't aware of this old document, the bible tells me that long ago, who it was that were called Christians. (Acts 11:26)

My story ends here on 9/11. My custody war has stretched over 42 months. I worked only 72 days this year. I've never been late on my child support; all my insurance and bills thus far are paid, and I've never been out of food. We go wherever and my little girl has fun when she's with me. I don't regret my time with Cassie because without that, we wouldn't have Amanda. In the beginning of our separation, I suffered torment for my sinful disobedience. Since that night I surrendered all to God, my burden is light. He taught me the importance of forgiveness, gave me the gift of discernment, and faith in Him helps me to disperse bitterness from my heart. My longsuffering has paid off. A seventh court appearance may not do us any good. If the judge takes our child away from us, there's nothing I can do. Many of my friends and co-workers comment about the wrongs done to me. With a smile I tell them how I possess the prize that many wish they had, "I have the love and honor of my child". There's no doubt about whom fought this battle for me. He popped open the shackle to set Amanda and me free. (John 8:36)

Acknowledgements

To my Heavenly Father, my Creator, my God, thank you for loving me at times when I didn't feel worthy. Thank you for what you've given me, Thank you for what you've taken away; but most of all, Thank you for the gifts you've left me. (Romans 8:14-16)

To Jesus Christ, my savior, son of the living God, Thank you for the price you paid for me, a sinner. I am forever thankful for the Truth you have given us thereby confirming that we have not been left alone here on earth. You are with us, even until the end. (Matthew 28:18-20)

The Holy Ghost, the Spirit, the Comforter, Thank you for drawing me close to God through His son. The gentle voice that said, "don't say that, say this; don't do that, do this; don't go there, go here", was you. Thank you for your guidance and correction. (John 14:26)

BOOKS:

The King James Version of the Bible (not the New International Version)

Strong's Exhaustive Concordance of the Bible

Webster's New World Dictionary

MINISTRIES:

Reel to Reel Ministry – Brentwood, Tennessee (for videos: Hard Truth & Hells Bells)

Grace to You Ministry – Panorama City, California (helping Parents with God's plan for parenting)

Mercy Ministries of America – Nashville, Tennessee (true Grace and Mercy for troubled women)

Touching Hands Ministries – Meridian Mississippi (teaching the Truth through Evangelism)

Focus on the Family – Colorado Springs, Colorado (helping Families grow in the Word of God)

In Touch Ministries – Atlanta, Georgia (educating Believers in God's Word)

Joyce Meyer Ministries – Fenton, Missouri (affirmation of the Truth in the Word of God)

White Dove Fellowship – Harvey, Louisiana (proving that Freedom is in the Spirit of God)

For Faith and Family – Nashville, Tennessee (informing families with the truth from God's Word)

THE CHRISTIAN ARTISTS THAT HELP FEED PEOPLE SPIRITUALLY WITH MUSIC

Point of Grace (their first album), Fred Hammond (spirit of David), Rebecca St. James (her first album)

Carman (the Standard), Zoe Girl (their first album) Bob Carlisle (shades of grace) DC Talk (intermission)

Steven Curtis Chapman (signs of life), Twila Paris (beyond a dream), Anointed (under the influence)

Newsboys (not ashamed), Aaron Jeoffrey (self titled), Jars of Clay (the eleventh hour) Ginny Owens,

Michael W. Smith, Crystal Lewis, Jennifer Knapp, Clay Crosse, Nicole Nordeman, Sandi Patty, Sierra,

Jon Gibson, Out of the Grey, Burlap to Cashmere, Third Day, and all who sing praises to the Lord.

SPECIAL THANKS TO:

My family and friends, specifically my sister and her husband for supporting and standing by me when times were tough. Had it not been for you, my time to see Amanda may not have been. Thank you. To my attorney Charlene, for showing me what a specialist can do. To the many friends who gave me valuable advice which helped point me in the right direction. To the employers who terminated me due to my custody battle, I'm sorry but my child will always be first. To all those who offended me, that just made me stronger.

Note From the Author

Please be informed that the views in this book may be offensive to some however, they do not pertain to the virtuous, obedient, faithful people who live their life following the Truth that comes from the Word of God.

CPSIA information can be obtained
at www.ICGtesting.com
Printed in the USA
LVHW100039280323
742726LV00005B/142

9 781952 302428